How to Catch Feelings for Jesus

How to Catch Feelings for Jesus

A Step-by-Step Guide to Loving Jesus

Andrew Christopher Uttaro

RESOURCE *Publications* · Eugene, Oregon

HOW TO CATCH FEELINGS FOR JESUS
A Step-by-Step Guide to Loving Jesus

Copyright © 2022 Andrew Christopher Uttaro. All rights reserved. Except for brief quotations in critical publications or reviews, no part of this book may be reproduced in any manner without prior written permission from the publisher. Write: Permissions, Wipf and Stock Publishers, 199 W. 8th Ave., Suite 3, Eugene, OR 97401.

Resource Publications
An Imprint of Wipf and Stock Publishers
199 W. 8th Ave., Suite 3
Eugene, OR 97401

www.wipfandstock.com

PAPERBACK ISBN: 978-1-6667-3859-9
HARDCOVER ISBN: 978-1-6667-9949-1
EBOOK ISBN: 978-1-6667-9950-7

11/04/22

Scripture quotations are from the New American Bible, rev. ed., copyright @ 2010, 1991, 1986, 1970 Confraternity of Christian Doctrine, Inc., Washington, DC. All rights reserved.

The Christ of the Breadlines, by Fritz Eichenberg (1950), is copyright © 2022 Estate of Fritz Eichenberg / licensed by VAGA at Artists Rights Society (ARS), NY. Used by permission.

To all those who formed me in love and patience: family, friends, and those blessed acquaintances along the way.

God meant for things to be so much easier than we have made them.
—DOROTHY DAY

Contents

Images, Charts, and Illustrations | ix
Introduction | xi

1. Second Man | 1
    Why Jesus? | 3
    What Is Second Man? | 7
    God and Others | 11
    Trying Something Better | 17

2. New Life | 21
    The Cycle of New Life | 23
    The Map of New Life | 26
    Holiness and Happiness Are the Same Thing | 31
    Hearing God | 38
    The Soul and the Infinite within | 46

3. Gratefulness Is the Key to Happiness; Justice Is the Key to Progress | 53
    Healing and Religion's Cultural Embeddedness | 54
    A Call to All People | 63
    Consent and the Divine Yes | 69
    Let's Talk about This Faith Thing | 76
    Justice Is the Key to Progress | 86
    Transformative beyond Informative | 99

4. Jesus Christ Is the Reason | 108
    Knowing Jesus | 110
    Jesus as Objective Meaning | 116
    Jesus as Existential Destiny | 123
    Jesus as the Goal of Our Efforts | 130
    Jesus as the Mystical Body of the Church | 137

5. So That His Will May Be My Will | 147
    Dreams of Theosis and Jesus's Call to Mental Health | 148
    Witness by Reciprocity | 154
    Gardeners of the Mind and Soul | 158
    Discernment: Suggestion, Not Imposition | 167

6. Co-workers with Christ | 177
    God Works through Everyday Things Too | 179
    Our Time and Place | 184
    A Brief History of Christianity in the World | 189
    History as the Epicenter of God's Grace | 199
    Possessiveness and the Crisis of Christianity Today | 205
    What Is a Universal Church? | 213
    How to Build an Actually Universal Church | 219
    A Mercy-First Church for an Ideology-First World | 228

Epilogue | 237
Bibliography | 243
Index | 245

Images, Charts, and Illustrations

Figure 1: Relational Response Axis | 14

Figure 2: *The Christ of the Breadlines*, by Fritz Eichenberg (1950) | 16

Figure 3: Cycle of New Life Chart | 26

Figure 4: Map of New Life Chart | 30

Figure 5: Process of Healing Chart | 55

Figure 6: *The Virgin Mary*, by Circle of Domenico Corvi (1721–1803) | 74

Figure 7: Fate of the Apostles Chart | 81

Figure 8: *Figure of Christ*, by Heinrich Hofmann (1884) | 125

Figure 9: Apse of St. Clement Basilica, Rome | 139

Introduction

I WAS NEVER ONE for self-help books. Theoretically, I'm the target demographic. I'm an open-minded, spiritual dude with some serious social awkwardness. My mom once got me a book teaching preteens social mores. I threw that one under my bed. I'm generally a few bad days in a row away from an existential crisis. That said, I'm also . . . like not, though . . . I like to think I have it together . . . but I'm also not trying to brag. Perhaps that's why I'm writing a ham-fisted disclaimer. This isn't a self-help book on the basic level that Jesus is another being to whom, no matter how predisposed we may be to him, we will always have resistance in our hearts. That said, I really do think Jesus is the most helpful person in my own life.

Forgive me, and I cannot emphasize this enough: I really don't think I know better than you. I am not trying to be a teacher here. In fact, what this book is about should be uniquely personal for each individual reader. You should read it with your own personality and life experience populating the examples and reference points. To the degree I am providing my own examples, they're just that: examples to clarify the direction of a thought. I'm no oracle of Jesus, no matter how many Jesus facts I may flex in the pages of this book.

There is a popular saying among youth ministers and religious teachers the Christian world over: "A relationship with Jesus is caught, not taught." You gotta love a good religion-themed rhyme. Some would extend the idea to religiosity in general, depending on how meta they want to get about this stuff. "Caught, not taught" is one of those religious truisms you could apply to most every kind of religious belief anywhere. But those who work in religious circles say it because we've screwed it up so badly for . . . a couple generations now, at least? Okay, I can speak only for us American Catholics, to some degree. We have definitely screwed it up, even as our Church was actively trying to fix it. Trust me, I'll get to *all* that.

The reason I provided you with that notable quotable, "Caught, not taught," is because it's the undergirding principle of the whole premise of this little book. Most people aren't taught how to be religious by some masterful teacher on a windswept hilltop. Sure, there is a not small contingent of religious folk who would tell you that's how they became lifelong Christians. They read some beautiful poetry, or they read a great theologian, and boom: Jesus found. God bless those folks. I always required quite a bit more nurture than a couple lines of striking proverbial wisdom. This book is firstly for those of us who struggle to see ourselves as religious people or even particularly spiritual people. I do include myself in that group in spite of, well . . . writing a book about knowing Jesus. We are the awkward, oh so awkward, many who generally know no faith in Jesus . . . just because . . . well, there is a lot there to talk about.

Let me make this clear: this is about a relationship. The greatest innovation of the Protestant Reformation was that it looked to make God and loving God an accessible life goal again for us commoners. The born-again movement of the last century or so has gone a little over the top in that respect, but the core thing there helps us get back to our roots. That idea: that Christian faith is about a relationship with God is the key to being sincerely Christian in the modern world. But that dynamic, too, the dynamic of relationship before religion, is also a bit overwrought in many Christian circles these days. You might have a road map already in mind of how you think this is going to go, based upon past experience of this or that rendition of what a relationship with Jesus looks like.

I think if you really give my book a chance, you might discover a few things in a new light. Perhaps the really intractable things you've avoided in the past won't be so overwhelming anymore. Perhaps you're picking up this book as someone already in the deep end of Christian faith. There's a lot for you here too: the truth is, our conversion to Christ isn't a once-in-a-lifetime event, it's an ongoing development. Either way, you've got to catch the thirst first. The thirst, to continue the usage of the slang of my adolescence, is exactly what you think it is: a desire. You have to catch a thirst for Jesus if you're going to have a relationship and all that comes from that. Real religious devotion is the meeting of two wills. And it really is like any other relationship with another being, sometimes more than you might realize.

Let's zoom in even more: maybe you could see yourself having a more intimate relationship with Jesus, but it's a bit uncomfortable to think about. Maybe you were never the type to throw your hands in the air and sing praise music. Maybe the whole idea of being publicly vulnerable, as Christian practice often encourages us to do, activates your anxiety. It's too cringy. This is the millennial religious struggle, if you will: the trappings of religious faith are intimidating . . . well, that, and the image problem Christianity has right now with hypocritical, fundamentalist partisans on one hand and a massive sex abuse crisis on the other. Oh, do we have a lot to discuss! This book is a remedy for the difficulty of the millennial religious struggle, if I execute it properly. Bear with me here, I'm trying. I'm counting on you to fill in the personal gaps and make it relevant in your own life if I can make the big points accessible enough.

Also, this is something of an intimate venture for me. This book is built around the framework of my own relationship with Jesus. I call it "God's Canon in My Life." Yes, I have big geek energy throwing around the word *canon*, but it's also about vulnerability. Any narcissism or vain belief I'm some kind of spiritual knower in writing this is washed away by letting you into this very personal phraseology. That, and I'm sharing some stories here that are known to me and only a few others in order to paint a bigger picture that may speak to you in a new way.

These are just the words I picked to define core truths of a relationship with Jesus that, at the end of the day, should really be in your own words. A relationship with Jesus is always personal. If it's not, it really is just empty religion performed for the sake of cultural or political partisanship. Religion for show is just toxic. That is an unhealthiness I pray deep down that you and I both avoid. I'm just someone trying to be vulnerable enough to help others do the same long enough to catch feelings for Jesus. And if we get to that point, we can then begin to build a relationship with Jesus that is worth having in our lives. Jesus always loves us more than we hate ourselves.

The usage of "catch feelings" in the title is very intentional. It implies an accidentalness immediately preceded by "how to," which implies we're doing something on purpose . . . accidentally. Take the feelings part of it with a grain of salt: this is deeper than feelings; I just needed a snappy, candid title. If you read this book—if you've read this far at all, frankly—you might be interested in the "how to," but I hope you also understand the "catch feelings" part. That "caught, not taught" truism is something woefully underappreciated in how we approach religion these days. I'll be the first to admit many forms of religion attract the conformist, moralizer type. The religion of Jesus is no exception to this. As much as you might have just groaned "no duh," the question then arises: how can we catch feelings for a person when half the crowd who claims to know him would rather bounce a book off your skull? Set aside the irony that you are literally reading my book right now and trust me: encountering the true Jesus is the goal here. He is the one for whom we're focused on catching feelings.

Finally, I do hope I'm somewhat brief through this book. The longer I go on, the more esoteric I get, so I apologize for those parts in advance. I will go on tangents a lot, but hopefully, they will be relevant. I was always one of those kids who enjoyed making lists and building ordered systems. I played the popular PC game *SimCity* a lot as a child, to the point my older sister begged me to come outside and play. I should've known I'd be religiously inclined then. For me, the real spiritual exercise was letting go of the ordered thinking long enough to do things as unorganized as playing outside with other children. When I did go outside with my sister and play, I was better for it. That's really the inspiration of this book: letting go of the ways we hold ourselves back from a sincere relationship with Jesus and making an effort to catch feelings in a way that belongs to us—a reciprocal relationship we're better for having in our lives and want to keep around.

Shoot, that was a really good ending to the introduction, but one more thing: please read this book from start to finish the first time through. There are parts of the latter chapters that don't really hit right unless you have the context of the earlier chapters. This personal "canon" I'm sharing with you is a ladder: you climb it. I guess that may go without saying, but here I am saying it. Can you tell I really just want you to get the most out of this book? Alright, how about I don't ruin this before we even get started. Let's get down to the meat and potatoes here.

CHAPTER ONE

Second Man

LET'S ASK THE QUESTION. *The question.* Yeah, the primary question that goes before any search for a higher meaning: why? Why bother looking for some religious truth or spiritual reality in the first place? The answer to that question is ultimately personal. The only really generalizable answer to that question I think I could provide is that we're predisposed as human beings to look for the divine. That's true whether or not we invented it all just because we want the divine to exist. That's true with or without religion. Our earliest ancestors drew divine beings on the walls of the caves. There is evidence of religious devotion as far back as there is evidence of human settlement. There's been some kind of divine thirst in us from the start of our existence.

In our modern world, we have a lot of reasons to just call bullshit on the whole idea of anything existing beyond the quantifiable reality. I'd venture to guess most people aren't so naïve as to think only empirically provable truths are worth one's time in life, but that thought is always nagging under the surface. Even devoted professional skeptics researching every different scientific pursuit would tell you we can't look at the whole universe so narrowly. There are things about life that don't really line up with questions the scientific method is designed to solve. There just seems to be too much to our lived experience to think it could all ultimately be reduced to neurons firing in a really smart ape's noggin.

Maybe we are looking for meaning in places where there isn't any, but until we know there is no higher meaning for sure, why rule out the possibility? That would also be an unprovable, unquantifiable conclusion. How do we convince ourselves there is no higher meaning or associated higher being? Philosophically speaking, it's impossible to ever know if there is anything beyond our understanding because then it wouldn't be beyond our understanding. Whoa . . . *blinks confusedly* . . . let's reel it back in. To that first why-question, why bother looking for some higher meaning at all, we might answer: because it seems like there might be something greater out there, and the most popular way of knowing of our time—the scientific method—by definition will never even approach such an answer. Why not look for it, if our hearts and minds naturally inquire so much about it? If one form of knowing won't find you the answer, look elsewhere with another way to know things. Scientific skepticism is a great way to pursue knowledge, but it rarely tells you the answer to questions like who a good life partner might be, why is there something instead of nothing, or why should we not resurrect dinosaurs? In that, it's obvious to say a different kind of inquiry might be necessary.

The common redirect of those who would stand against the idea of any divine being(s) is to ask how, not why. This seems like a nice logical turn at first: *how* is always a more straightforward question logically and is less dialectically challenging. From evolutionary biology to theoretical physics, we have many answers to how-questions. When we get annoyed at religious figures for calling this or that thing a miracle, it's this modern sensibility that the question has to start with the *how*: it's not a miracle because *x*, *y*, and *z* natural phenomenon. All those things might be entirely correct, but why does that make the whole thing less miraculous? Approaching the divine involves a broader view of the meaningfulness of things.

Aspiring to know the divine, a relationship with God, is not a how-question; it's a why-question. We can answer the how of gravity in a satisfactory way: elements with mass attract objects of smaller mass organizing into planets, stars, and so on. But the why is not even something that same kind of questioning can answer. Why does that work that way? That might seem like a nonsensical question to ask at all, but this is the nature of how we relate to God. We find our way into pondering the divine once we realize nothing is nonsense if it's real. Why-questions that force us to accept our definitions of what is "real" are often painfully limited these days. We find God intellectually in the why-questions. Once you've got a working relationship with God, then you'll find answers to how-questions within your own life, but that's a later chapter's problem.

Why Jesus?

For the purposes of this book, the question is really: why Jesus? For those of us who live in places that are bathed in the Christian religion going back generations, following Jesus, loving Jesus, and the whole aura around him in general kinda seems like a small step above being really into Elvis. Yeah, this guy did some pretty great stuff, and I won't fault you for thinking he's a pretty great guy to emulate—but I don't want to dress up in that wig or that shiny, gold suit. To continue the Elvis metaphor, the fan club is a bit whacky at times, and in more than a couple cases, they're straight up toxic and abusive. This Jesus guy is worth knowing of in an academic sense, but perhaps the more involved act of catching feelings for him and doing something about it is a bit more than I want. All told, that's a fair conclusion if Jesus was just a great celebrity like Elvis. With Jesus, his mythos, and the religion that's formed around his gospel, it's hard to blame you for walking the other way, given how some of his fans have brought his name into quite a bit of scandal—for centuries upon millennia.

There is a certain barrier at entry to knowing Jesus in a personal way that is often condescending, awkward, or both. We already bonded over social awkwardness in the introduction, but you may be more annoyed with the condescending apologist just waiting for the moment to correct your nascent knowledge with some fine detail that doesn't mean anything to the laymen. I know that world more closely than I care to admit; and I could hear those folks critiquing the last paragraph with the old "Jesus necessarily prompts a decision" point as I wrote it. That is, Jesus claimed to be the Son of God, so if he's not, he can't just be a nice philosopher; he'd be a horrific madman. The condescending apologist lacks emotional intelligence, and that's a discussion for a later chapter. As we ask why-Jesus here, we're not asking a purely philosophical question: we're asking a question that predates the theologians, apologists, and religion itself, for that matter. This is a question explicit in fundamental things about the human experience.

The shorthand for those fundamental things I'm trying to get at is Second Man. Those are my words (and many others'—I realize it's not an original combination of words) for something even bigger than the religion that claims to follow Jesus. This is the entry point to believing in Jesus for anyone anywhere, whether or not they even have access to the Christian faith: recognizing the underlying spirituality every person with a desire to simply be a good person already has. As St. Edith Stein once said: "Whoever seeks the truth is seeking God, whether they know it or not."[1] In other words, if you just want to be a good person in life, you're already standing at the door to Jesus's place. It's remarkably that simple, but let's explore this a bit.

Think of Second Man as synonymous with being self-giving, selfless, merciful, or just a person of good will, in the phraseology of the Bible. I have met plenty of nonreligious people who are of good will, so to speak. Let's dispense with the idea you have to be religious to be a good person. I think that's old-world thinking. I think it's a harmful idea, to be blunt. I really believe the vast majority of people, like 99% plus, are good people, in that they want to be good in the personal sense. They don't want to hurt others, they don't want to be a mess (though sometimes we all are), and they do want to do the right thing, even if their vision for it isn't necessarily correct. Yes, we're selfish beings also by way of our most basic survival instincts. We are animals in the strict sense, just making it by day to day. But once we're a single step outside that evolutionary, utilitarian churn, it becomes clear to even our primordial, monkey-brain conscience, that doing good in life begins with being selfless and giving to one another in all kinds of social bonds. The genesis of Second Man, the dawn of common good, is prehistoric.

Yes, religion in its earliest forms doesn't exactly look selfless. Offering sacrifices to appease the rains or promote fertility and good health are forms of early religious practices that don't necessarily point down the way of a God of mercy. But even in the earliest forms of religion, there was a thirst for goodness, a thirst for righteousness and virtue, that has never left us since. It may be helpful to look at stages of religious development through human history—from the prehistoric appeasing of the spirits of fortune and fertility to more modern religions, which are just different rituals and codes for selflessness.

Most all modern spiritualities could be summarized as purposeful self-improvement in order to be . . . a good person. Of course, there are distinct myths and dogmas, but the practical core is often very similar before you get to the storytelling of it all. I'm not trying to say all religion is the same; I mean to say the instinctual basis for modern religion is. The theological understanding of how the divine reaches out to us and how we are to reach out to . . . *it* is really the stuff of religion. But the Second Man instinct predates organized religion. It speaks to us on that visceral

---

1. Edith Stein, as quoted in John Paul II, "For the Canonization," §5.

human level. When it comes to the aforementioned why-questions, Second Man is the answer, both socially and personally.

Those why-questions we all seem to ask are informed by this curious shared pursuit of religious truth across all human history; and that basic idea that we ought to give to one another becomes something of a universal answer as it grows into more realized beliefs. If you prefer the spiritual-not-religious dichotomy, this is the spirituality before the religiosity. Sure, social cooperation and collective fraternity certainly have survival benefits. I always appreciate the nomadic criticism that religion is a tool of civilization for conformity, but I can't go down all the rabbit holes in chapter 1. Bear with me.

Second Man is the universal, pre-religious spiritual truth. At that, you might ask: but why does that spirit of giving and cooperation uniting all of us need to amount to religion? And why do we as humans, in light of our history . . . uh . . . generally struggle with it? To be blunt: this instinct doesn't lead to religion for increasingly more people. The Second Man instinct delivers us to Jesus's door, not over the threshold. For that, we must envision the other side of the equation: how we conceive of the divine reaching out to us.

But that movement implies another question: what makes this vision of things, that divine beings interact with humanity, credible? To answer that, we have to go deeper into our own conceptions of how belief systems are credible.

This can be the most accessible and also the least appealing step on the way. There is a certain inherent incredulity from the outside looking in on Christian faith—and, really, religion in general. It can feel safer to not take on the baggage of religious belief, but that hesitancy to take that next step is often informed not by the very numerous examples of failed cooperation and bad religion so much as the misconception that believing in someone like Jesus makes one childish, for lack of a better term. If one isn't already faithful to a fundamentally myth-driven dogma, then those who are will generally seem somewhat silly and naïve. I love the religion of the Flying Spaghetti Monster meme because it points out that apparent foolishness in religious belief: who would believe ridiculous myths of supernatural beings?

The core relational principle of most religion is a principle I'd argue the vast majority of nonreligious people also practice if they even remotely consider themselves to be good people, as we laid out earlier. We can all be superstitious (which isn't synonymous with religious, by the way); we all have illogical practices we do for comfort, community, or self-improvement. Astrology is a popular such practice that has survived all changes in society and transcends the borders between religion, superstition, and loose spiritual practice. Belief in a higher power or some spiritual truth seems crazy on first glance, but why reduce it to absurdity? Is it not just everyday people trying to find the words for the intangible matter of goodness? Let's demystify spirituality and religious belief in general.

First off: the word *myth* in the study of religion does not mean myths like Bigfoot or the Loch Ness Monster. It's not some unproven thing that is almost certainly literally untrue by the most basic scientific inquiry. The usage of myth in religious studies is more like an unproven thing that doesn't need to be literally true and that, actually, a lot of people really believe in, whether or not it can be proven (in fact, oftentimes we're talking about things that could never be proven). In other words, miracles are extras for belief, not their primary target. Myth in the religious context is narrative or ethical design coalescing around things that are true in myriad different kinds of ways. These things are not empirically true, as far as any human person could ever determine.

One might call this faith, but this is more accurately called devotion, which is more like a by-product of faith. We're devoted to spiritualized lived experiences that often contribute to a broader mythos. That lived experience part is what separates religion from both the nefarious badlands of conspiracy theory as well as the mere creativity of fiction. It's almost obvious to say, but it's worth repeating for clarity here: science and religion are not diametrically opposed things. One seeks to prove things literally, while the other doesn't really concern itself with proving much of anything *literally*—just teaching parables, pillars of good living, and the more existential reasons to help those around you. If science and religion were food groups, religion would be fruits, and science would be your various grains. They are both part of a balanced diet but are not really similar tastewise. Both groups could be on your plate at the same time, depending on what your meal is.

We'll talk more about that faith-and-reason false rivalry in later chapters. Good religion and Good science actually inform each other in certain ways, but let's return to the core premise here: selflessness. Let's drill down on this supposedly universal idea of Second Man I've put in front of you. What am I talking about here?

What Is Second Man?

Second Man (generalized selflessness, if you will) is the common truth that links together everyone who thinks seriously about the human experience. Being generous and kind to one another is just an expectation for good people, however often it is disregarded. Living in organized society requires us to be reasonably self-giving, or there would be no social contract holding us all together. We don't fly off into fisticuffs at the smallest disrespect because we have a shared social contract that says you don't do that. We have to accommodate each other to some degree. In a free society, you have whatever reason you want for respecting the social contract. Whether we do so primarily through religion or by any other way, it's still that core principle called selflessness that holds us all together—that primordial spirituality.

Selflessness is a virtue beyond mere interpersonal relationships too. We dissociate even within ourselves when we can't think bigger than our immediate struggles. A self-giving heart is certainly important in scientific pursuits because you have to take your own vanity and preconceived notions out of the picture to be effective in proving or disproving a hypothesis. Few things are more intellectually selfless than publishing a piece of research you did and sending it off to be raked over in the peer-review process by scores of other researchers. Yet when religious folks are overt about their self-giving, assuming they're sincere and not doing it for show, it seems tacky on some level. Selflessness being the core principle of religious practice shouldn't be seen as naïve by outsiders; it should be seen as the core standard of human civilization, whether you're interested in a specific mythos or not.

Let me rein in the grandiose here. This is a personal philosophy I'm talking about, after all. Second Man are the words for this first article of God's Canon in My Life because they're just a perfectly simple way to summarize this concept of self-gift. The phrase Second Man is used in different religious and pseudo-spiritual circles all the time. I like this band called Switchfoot—specifically, I loved their music at a certain time in my life. Yeah, heap on the ridicule: religious guy likes a corny Christian music band. I know. Switchfoot put out this album in 2003 called *The Beautiful Letdown*. In my humble opinion, it is the single best contemporary Christian music album ever written, and it's not really close (I think gospel music is a different category, so don't kill me). A lot of their music at the time did a great job encapsulating the disruptive change of growing up, while simultaneously describing the best-case scenario of coming of age: discovering selflessness. It was exactly what I needed when I needed it at that point in my teenage years.

I was going into my senior year in high school, with a lot of doubt about what came next for me. This wasn't just what career I'd pursue; this was my struggle with what my philosophy in life would be. I'd been casually religious for years at that point, but now I was nearing a pretty significant decision-point in life. I begged God to give me some clarity here. When I say I was begging God, I mean yelling fights with tears and anger. That simple set of two words, Second Man, broke me free of the paralyzing fear that a wrong move going forward would lead to failure and a chain reaction of mistakes. Religious realizations often arise in these moments: a new meaning is thrust upon something we previously thought to be a tired platitude. God can give us clarity however he might, including what we thought was mundane. God gave me clarity, alright. He kept it really simple for me to understand. In retrospect, it's like I didn't even know God before then. God isn't our accuser, waiting to judge us; Jesus came to save and affirm, to bring divine mercy.

I am a diction-obsessed dork, but I would not consider myself a detail-oriented worker at all. I need clear directions to do any task effectively, and if I'm going to be creative, it's truly from within (yeah, I can be a little insufferable). After I heard those words, it stirred a bit of a spiritual self-discovery in my life. I would discover the same fundamental revelation—selflessness as a rule for life—as others had discovered it and would find some referring to it as "Third Man." The premise of that is simple: I am second to God and others, priority-wise, so that makes me third; but I always heaped God and others together, making myself Second Man. Now, if you thought that was pedantic, let me really drive you crazy: Third Man came to represent such a level of spiritual vanity to me that I simply merged it with the term from literature *third person*. Obviously, to write in the third person is to refer to yourself as if another person. Example: "Andrew really thinks he's not losing readers right now, getting this deep into the minutia of phraseology." The reason I tell you this is because there is a distinct risk of overdoing this as well.

Sometimes our selflessness can ruin our own self-worth and therefore harm our relationship with others and Jesus, almost as if our giving selves are a different person than our self-caring selves, a kind of mental dysmorphia, if you will. That's unhealthy, and it's often what I hear people say when they wonder what the endgame of loving Jesus is. I know what the New

Testament says in terms of "dying to oneself" and the language around humility. I'm comfortable saying that not Jesus nor any of his apostles want you to lose your mind en route to selflessness in Christian holiness. You matter in all this giving of yourself. That's worth a more elaborate sidebar...

Jesus cares about your mental health. Don't think he wants you to refuse all help that doesn't bear his name. That's silly. The self-image dysmorphia where we lose ourselves in giving is not an end in itself. It points us in the direction of the deeper meaning of selflessness in reciprocation. Being second to God and others also comes with the risk of becoming empty performance whenever we become detached from our own needs—our spiritual needs, mental needs, and just the need to feel reciprocated love and appreciation. Reciprocated love, and in an even deeper sense, love initiated without expecting reciprocation (simply out of goodwill for the other), is an interpersonal virtuous cycle that even agnostic and Nonreligious people are in pursuit of. It's the stuff of truly healthy, life-giving relationships. That's what Second Man strives for.

We're selfless for an important purpose beyond mere self-improvement: we give for the sake of others, not ourselves. We give to others for the other's sake. Jesus can be our reward and engine of that selflessness. It's a participation in God's very nature insomuch as it is honest love. Jesus is the ultimate guide to the healthy way to self-give without expecting anything in return. It's one of those annoying mysteries of faith in Jesus, that we are most healthy, we are most ourselves, when we are giving, not consuming. We'll come back to that. For now, remember it's very important that you take care of yourself. Sidebar over.

Let's zoom out to broader groups of people beyond the individual. Even among self-identifying nonreligious people, there is a spirituality around selflessness developing into church-like community groups. Sunday Assembly is a growing nonreligious movement that focuses on the uplifting elements of traditional worship gatherings. Some practitioners refer to it as "celebrating life." Humans yearn for connection first and meaning second. As we've already touched on briefly, one reason religion exists at all is because groups of people decided to give meaning to the rules of the social contract that seemed arbitrary otherwise. Yes, religion also frequently became a tool for oppression and genocide (trust me, we'll come back around to that), but the underlying idea is as fundamental as any other mode of human thinking. It's organic. It's community and meaning, organized around giving selflessly to one another. No matter where in space and time you live, people often organize around some virtuous core belief about themselves or the universe.

Jesus really nailed a nice framework for selflessness as a way of living. Nailed, oops—no pun intended there. What we've been going over so far is all preface to who he actually is canonically. There are two ways of trying to understand Jesus: a christological starting point and an anthropological starting point. A really basic way to look at Christian thought is who Jesus is in the context of human experience before we even get into creeds and whatnot (anthropological starting point). Nowadays, I think we yearn for something that speaks to lived experience more than anything else. That's what we've been talking about with primordial spirituality and all that jazz. In this anthropological starting point, Jesus comes in as an archetype of that widespread, preexisting belief system.

Jesus is the ultimate paradigm for self-giving. That's not to say others haven't done a good job with the same framework either. Karl Rahner, the titan of twentieth-century theology who built up much of the theological underpinning of the Second Vatican Council (big Catholic event in the 1960s), spoke of all religions as meditations on the divine that is, in fact, remote from nobody. All religions, through very different ways and means, contemplate divinity in some way—whether that be divine harmony, divine peace, divine love, or all of the above. That is the religious instinct, the yearning for the divine, that is in some way evident to all.

By asserting that Second Man, the self-giving that runs throughout Jesus's gospel, is a universal human experience, I'm not trying to triumphantly proclaim a Christian superiority. I'm trying to let you in on why my brain was so thoroughly blown by this concept. To use a biblical citation: "And he marked out their appointed times in history and the boundaries of their lands. God did this so that they would seek him and perhaps reach out for him and find him, though he is not far from any one of us" (Acts 17:26–27). Indeed God, inasmuch as he is the divine substance of selfless, self-giving love (Second Man), exists to all people of faith and, really, anyone of good will, across all times and places (that's also why I believe in baptizing space aliens when we meet them, but that's another book). Without sounding too "it's all the same": Jesus was God's most successful attempt to reach out to us (christological starting point). This is a book about Jesus, after all. That's really the fundamental premise of the message of this Jesus for whom we're trying to catch feelings: self-giving love.

God and Others

We have passed the first biblical citation checkpoint! Don't worry, I am not going to lay those on too thick in the early going here, same with those Catholic references. My hope is for this book to be accessible to everyone, including those with some religious trauma induced by those fervently rattling off bible verses. God, in spite of all the evil done in his name, is a present human experience described in different words. That nagging divine intuition that everyone seems to have. It's profound in large part because it's universal but so very intimate to every human being, no matter where they exist in time and space. Jesus is the intersection of this very universal spiritual reality and the very personal yearning for what transcends our brief spans of time alive—our natural religiosity, if you will. Jesus represents the divine becoming human. Jesus represents the divine available for all, made accessible in vulnerable human flesh, the incarnation.. This is, in essence, why I believe the religion of Jesus Christ. Hopefully, that's also part of the reason you picked up this book and have read this far.

This universal sense of God in self-giving that I claim Jesus most fully represents is relevant to you not as a force subverting your own autonomy. Yes, giving of self is to some extent dying to oneself for the other; but this is a process that builds us up much more than it breaks us down. This is where believing in a religious idea decisively exits the realm of apparent silliness into the dynamic of why we do what we do with our lives. The key here is the holy element of consent. I use that word in the overarching sense: consent is the two-way road where both parties engage together as fully respected separate souls. If God is love, then he is also consent. This clarifies a lot of the right and wrong at play in religion.

We are held and cherished by the divine love of God permeating all existence but can enter into this explicit relationship only once we say yes. We naturally feel abandoned by the divine not because God is absent from us but because we have to consent to the relationship in a definitive way. Jesus comes into our lives in a powerful way, no matter how universal I try to make it sound, only if we say yes to him. We are made in the likeness and splendor of God, the *Imago Dei*, and therefore are all inextricably rooted in God; but, unlike trees, whose roots hold them in the ground, we are given the choice of how we will grow.

God allows the choice of access to himself as evidence of respect for the divine nature of free will within us. Jesus's words often come across as commands, but the calling there isn't into a spiritual slavery for fear of damnation; it's a call to open your mind to this broader interconnectivity of everything. And this is hard even after we say yes because the universe is a chaotic place, as the melee of entropy and free will affects it. We can't control it, and we can't control God as condition to our yes either. For any of this to make sense, we have to embrace things broader than our control. We yearn to control all of our lived experience, though we know it isn't that simple. God won't be something we control that way if we really experience him, though he will respect our autonomy. This is why loving Jesus requires we don't demand empirical knowledge of all things. It's impossible to contain God, so you need to be more open-minded than that. If you think you've got God painted into a corner, you don't have him at all. It is, like any worthwhile relationship, a dance between two consenting wills.

It bears repeating because we all seek to control too much: if "capturing" God is a prerequisite to a relationship with Jesus, you'll never get there. I hate to put up any barriers, but that one is over my head. But if you're willing to say yes and open your mind and soul, Jesus will come on in.

Jesus isn't calling us to submit to a new set of moral propositions as much as he is calling us out of the narrow space of our egos, our own "small soul" (*pusilla anima*), into the giant space of the "great soul" (*magna anima*), a transformation from constant self-regard into self-giving. This is how Second Man, though it makes us second, elevates us somewhere we couldn't go otherwise. We have to venture beyond ourselves to be more fully what we could be. Jesus is our guide to the fullness of what we can be in him—our christomorphic destiny, in big theological words.

Recap: Self-gift is a natural spiritual experience, more widespread than any single religion or philosophy. It's simple, but it's absolutely immense. It calls us outside ourselves, beyond incidental gifts given to others. When you are truly selfless, you give of yourself not just from the excess you have to spare but the truest gift of yourself, simply for the good of the other. It's a drive that underlies all spirituality, even the nonreligious kinds. It is what elevates our lives and the beliefs we hold beyond mere creative rambling. Now, let's get out of my rambling back into some practical examples.

The person most responsible for me as a spiritual person, outside of my family, is a woman named Dawn. She was the youth minister at my church when I was growing up. I would say for my childhood parish, she was the most influential layperson, but she herself would tell you she's too humble for such praise. She was, in her work but also in the example of how she herself lived her life, the antidote to the negative forces that make a young person first disbelieve in God and then in themselves. She would, as she always does, point to Jesus. She had such a huge impact on the liturgical and sacramental life of the parish that some of our fellow parishioners called her Pastor Dawn. A lot of churches have these laypeople who play huge roles in parish life. Dawn is one of those special people who gave so much life to the spiritual seeds within young people when I happened to be coming up through my formative teen years.

Dawn lived her role in the church. She ran retreats and service camps like a professional and allowed space for teens to discover their own spirituality while also very much being a Catholic youth minister. I would simply not be the person I am today without her. The whole "caught, not taught" thing was certainly something I first heard through her. In the later years of my high school participation in youth ministry, I became a student leader on retreats. Dawn encouraged me to do so not just because I was a frequent attendee but as a way to overcome some serious social awkwardness I had, which made other things difficult. She nurtured me through the obstacles of my own spirituality and was the first one to really show me how to share it with others. Nothing is more difficult than being vulnerable with others, and when it comes to spirituality, there is a real strength required to share your insights. I really would compare it to the fear of social chastisement that public speakers and stand-up comedians face—except I rarely was able to be particularly funny.

The grace of encounter will be a recurring theme in this book. Dawn was leading a youth ministry program in a fairly small town with a rather homogenous population. In other words: not a lot of different kinds of people and lifestyles. A large part of what she was doing was not just connecting young people to their faith and helping them reconcile with it but also teaching us the grace of encounter. She was teaching us what it really meant to encounter someone as our faith taught us they were: fellow children of God. After I graduated from high school, I would still come back to help out sometimes. I would even succeed her as Youth minister at our parish for a couple years, but we'll come back to that later. I could go on and on about Dawn's impact on me, but I wouldn't want to embarrass her with too much praise. You'll see her impact in other places as God's Canon in My Life develops.

As remarkable as people who are so selfless, so profoundly second-oriented, may seem, these role models in our lives are so extraordinary partly because they've found some kind of balance within two big parts of life. I'm a visual learner, so this is a really good explainer for folks like me: the relational response axis. You might have seen something like this before. People who have in some way "mastered" selflessness, if such a thing is possible, have really just come to an understanding, sustainable collection of relationships along the vertical and horizontal axis seen below. The vertical relationships primarily refer to God and how we are doing with him. I also like to think of any sufficiently heady relationship on this axis as well: your relationship with your own mental health, your relationship with lost relatives, and your relationship with your own strengths and weaknesses. The horizontal relationships are others. These are all the people in your life, ranging from an intimate partner all the way out to rare acquaintances and strangers. We respond to God and others according to how we're doing on both the vertical and horizontal axes.

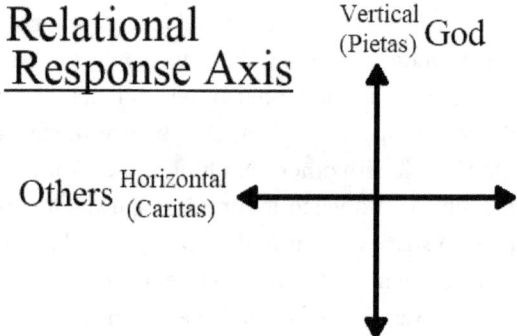

Figure 1: Relational Response Axis

Maybe it seems like vertically relating to God and our inner selves would be the harder axis here, but I really believe the kind of encounter that is required of our horizontal relationships is much harder to cultivate. You're always stuck in a room with yourself. Figuring out that relationship is every individual person's life work. Having healthy, reciprocal relationships with others is something else entirely. In order to truly encounter another, we have to decenter ourselves and our own preoccupations. Oftentimes, our most transcendent, memorable life events involve us opening up to a broader understanding of some relationship along one of these axes. When it comes to others, these epiphanies are almost always calls to some real, concrete actions.

I did several service trips to Philadelphia when I was in college. I have a fondness for that city in large part because it was the site of many religious experiences for me. It became something of a holy city for me. Those familiar with the general ethos of Philadelphia might get a kick out of calling it a "holy city." But that's the next insightful metaphor of Second Man here: just like a holy city doesn't really need to appear holy to anyone to in fact be holy, so too does our gift of self not need to be self-evidently holy, nor does it need to erase who we are.

What you're doing may not necessarily seem like holy work, but most things done out of love are holy. In loving someone sincerely, out of your heart of hearts, you are holy, whether or not you feel like you deserve a fancy hat for it. That is assuming we avoid the mental dysmorphia selflessness can bring on, as I mentioned earlier. Holy life is something your specific personality is built for, even if you think you're a terrible wrongdoer. Oftentimes it is the wrongdoers, the sinners, who do some of God's grandest works. We are unique through our giving, not in spite of it. Just like our sincerest creative ideas are original from within, so too our most powerful gifts of self are from our most genuine, most real selves.

This first step is awfully empty and discouraging if it isn't something you really believe in with your own brain and heart. Sure, we all need a me-day every now and again, but as a general rule, being second can do you quite some good in life, if you don't lose your mind trying. Being second is a personal conviction that you discover for yourself when you realize you want the world to be better for your having been in it. It's an eclipse of the personal and existential that only you can decide to embrace and find the strength within you to live out every day—just like that endeavor into being a teen leader took some encouraging and building up of strength from within for me.

One Philadelphia soup kitchen broke into my heart with a wordless image. The crosshatched image of a Depression-era breadline is seared into my psyche: the black-and-white picture of the hungry people with a haloed figure in the middle representing Jesus. It's called *The Christ of the Breadlines*. The artist, Fritz Eichenberg, did a considerable number of illustrations, but this one takes the cake, in my book. Indeed, that haunting message from Jesus—"Whatever you did for one of the least of these brothers and sisters of mine, you did for me" (Matt 25:40)—drives at the conscience of anyone with a selfless instinct.

Being second isn't about being afraid that the next guy in line could be God in disguise, in a deeply unnerving edition of *Undercover Boss*; it's about treating everyone with the dignity that builds us all up. Apart from the halo, nothing is particularly distinctive about Jesus; he's just another hungry member of the masses waiting for his chance at sustenance. Even the halo almost melts away into the background. Being second is about encountering another person as another person. The dignity of human life can get lost in our made-up divisions of class, race, nationality, and gender. Second Man calls us to brush all that aside and encounter one another as people—as human beings made in the image of God himself among us.

Figure 2: *The Christ of the Breadlines*, by Fritz Eichenberg (1950)

That's a religious message, sure, but it's also just a human message. If we can't see and empathize with each other's cold, vulnerable humanity, we won't find peace and meaning in life. My favorite anonymous piece of folk wisdom is "Gratefulness is the key to happiness." As the table of contents tells you, that will have a whole chapter unto itself. For now, it is insightful to contemplate empathy as a core value of any worthwhile human society. Where it is lacking, humanity itself is missing. Gratefulness is the engine of empathy. Every little thing we attain in this life is something to be treasured, especially the people around us. The people around us, particularly the family we find ourselves in, are our only real treasures in life. Grateful people rarely ignore the helpless because they recognize how life is best with love in it. Grateful people rarely fail to love God and others.

Yes, of course, being second to others in the group sense can end up hurting us, without that precious reciprocity we talked about earlier. Sometimes, even our families betray us. Sometimes, those we strive to help can disappoint us. But this is a good time to zero in on our most subtle, latent views of others. Like most responsible parents, mine taught me to respect other people—that is, unless they give you a really good reason not to. How we treat our fellow people is everything. We treat others poorly out of a certain vanity. We tend to be narcissistic creatures by habit. We are the heroes of our own stories. Mentally speaking, we tend to view others only as accessories to our own existence. That's deeply rooted in human nature, and it's also pretty terrible. It's something to be unlearned, if you will.

Trying Something Better

In the study of psychology, we can think of this through the lens of the three facets of Freudian identity: id, ego, and superego. In brief, the id is your most basic survival instincts and human inclinations. The superego is the many layers of morality, social mores, and our own projections upon the world around us as aspirational or reactionary constructs. The ego is the mediator who makes the decisions as the arbiter of your willpower. When Jesus comes onto the scene, announcing his ministry to us, he is calling us to open our minds to the divine reality that is beyond the natural state obsessed with mere survival. To the superego: stop moralizing yourself into anxiety about a fundamentally flawed world. You have to let go of mere constructs of the world and hold on to people. To the id: orient yourself toward the healthily ordered goodness of how God created those myriad desires. Moderation, of course, but gratefulness moreover. To the ego: come out of the state of fear; Jesus is safety, as the completion of God reaching out to us. Jesus's most basic starting message to us is to move from the primordial fear of the human condition that divides us and closes us off in egotism to invent all kinds of chauvinism, and enter into a radical trust between human beings. From the small raft of ego to the great ship of Jesus Christ.

Second Man is, in some ways, a rejection of the darker side of human nature. Forgive a sports analogy here; after just bringing up Philadelphia, I feel it's appropriate. Mascots are meant to be playful symbols of a team's identity. They're custom designed to be lampooned, and even fans of the team generally endorse them only because it's their guy. Now, if the mascot isn't your guy, you might be inclined to boo him, sneer, and even become hostile at his presence. Philadelphia Eagles (American football) fans are regarded with universal scorn because there was one instance in the late 1960s where they threw snowballs at perhaps the only universally loved mascot: Santa Claus. Yeah, they threw snowballs at Santa Claus.

To express hostility to such a mascot is hard to defend—although I'm told he had it coming. In this whacky example, you might be able to see how we are shaken out of selfishness into a higher state of mind. As soon as one of those snowballs connects, anyone with a conscience and a selfless bone in their body immediately realizes this went too far. "Wait, why am I assaulting this guy for wearing a Santa costume?" There's a whole discussion to be had about groupthink here, but let's consider the individual for a moment: harming a mascot, a mere symbol of something, draws out how insane humanity can be.

We are defensive to the bone, programmed by survival to do so, and to consider others at all is the very first spark of the divine. Second Man is born where dignity is visible. Now, of course, there is a massive gulf between not throwing snowballs at another person dressed like a universal symbol of childlike joy and truly living a selfless life. But the beginning of it is right there. It's made accessible to us, even in our most absurd moments.

Make no mistake: being second to others is work. The more of yourself you put on the line being second, the more it represents a deep expression of your sincerest love. I'll come right out and say, I don't think marriage, or any long-term committed relationship, really works unless there is a level of giving oneself sacrificially. There is risk there, sure. But few of life's greatest adventures require no risk, and hopefully, if you're marrying someone, you've established some of that sweet, sweet reciprocity with them. That reciprocity is what gives you the confidence to think you can work out anything with a life partner. Second Man itself, I suppose, is something of a risk: the risk of no reciprocity, the risk of no sincere encounter with someone else similarly selfless. As we move into the later chapters of this book, we'll talk more and more about the specifics of Jesus and faith in him, but for now, let's stay zoomed out. We asked some why-questions to start. Let's go back to the why-Jesus question we started this chapter with.

You don't even need to assign his name to it if you're not ready for that step. It's not even just religious: any functioning adult with a sense of human decency can wrap their mind around the value of selflessness before it even becomes a religious thing. That's hard to find only when love of oneself smothers this universal truth in one's heart. Giving of oneself is a pillar of good human life, and giving of oneself without any certainty of repayment is the divine possibility for human life. The ignition to catching feelings for Jesus is that simple: self-gift. It's everywhere in this simple possibility that we might love in a way that is somewhat reckless. It's a leap of faith, but it's either a trampoline or a pool at the bottom. Maybe you've gotten really wet in past hops and only caught a couple glorious bounces back toward the heavens, but once you've jumped enough times, you don't worry anymore: you just enjoy it like you're flying.

Jesus will show you how to take that jump if you let him. And he invites us to take the jump in so many different ways, but some invitations may make sense only to you personally. Jesus's invitation may be in the illustration of the soup kitchen, or song lyrics at the right time, or the care of a mentor who opens your mind in ways that change your viewpoint and confidence. This first step on the ladder is something you've probably encountered before. Now that you have the invitation from Jesus, will you be vulnerable with him long enough to catch feelings? Will you consent to having him in your life in a way that is healthy and helpful? You don't need to answer now; we still have a lot of ground to cover.

I'm going to try to wrap up every chapter in this book with a prayer. Prayer is also one of those things that religious people do that can seem naïve and inaccessible. In reality, prayer is just thinking with another. It's just a vulnerable conversation with someone you trust is mature enough for that. The conversation friends have reminiscing about their shared memories is prayer. The "what are we" conversation a new couple has is a prayer. The conversation a couple has about having kids is a prayer. The conversation a family has about the death of a loved one is a prayer. The conversation a repentant addict has with a counselor is a prayer. The hoping fervently, even verbally, for that promotion or next accomplishment is a prayer. That's all prayer—we just don't often call it that. Religious people just tend to formalize it in rote prayers with repetitive design. I'm not the overly formal type with most things, but I also appreciate a prayer I don't need to construct on the spot either.

I keep a journal, which, as I've grown into an adult, has essentially morphed into a prayer book. I took to writing rote prayers on retreats and youth groups as a teenager. I didn't really start thinking I was writing prayers as much as I was writing down what I wanted to say to God in the clearest terms possible. It was always tinged with the frustrations of my relationships with others too. That Switchfoot album I mentioned earlier hit me like a prayer. It was a way I could express to God where I thought our relationship was to go at that particular junction in my life. It was, in a way, God telling me about his part of that. My faith was never blind, it was always a relationship; and good prayer tends to give conversation to a relationship.

I will concede this prayer is a little dense for the first chapter of this book. In a way though, it's both about this chapter and all the chapters yet to come. It may also be nice for you to not have to do any heavy lifting prayerwise right off the bat. It's called "Second Man for." What am I Second Man for? It's rooted in that service camp in 2011 I've been alluding to this whole chapter. I was at the intersection of a big life decision and just a prevailing wind in my life toward the unknown. This prayer has lines I wrote then, but most of it came together in later years. Some prayers we make up on the spot, some come together like patchwork tapestries of a relationship developing in our lives patiently over years.

One last little nugget about prayer: when we say "amen" at the end, we're essentially saying "so be it" or "may it be done." We're sort of saying: "I will do it." Food for thought as you struggle to finish a prayer.

I am Second.
Second to God and others:
Second to God so that my will may be his will;
because dissonance between our wills is the only true suffering in life.
God is my greatest love and highest priority, in sincerity and gratefulness.
I am Second.
Second to God and others:
Second to others so that all may know you, Lord,
because the fullness of human life is life in Christ.
I am Second.
Second to God and others:
Second to God and others because Jesus has claimed me with his blood,
and you have captured my heart in this life;
showing my soul that human yearning finds satisfaction only in you.
Amen.

CHAPTER TWO

New Life

WHILE THE IDEA OF being selfless may not be the most surprising first step on this journey, it's absolutely essential for the later rungs of this ladder. The second rung of my spiritual canon is a bit more nebulous: New Life. What does that even mean? To be very honest, it's the one to which I come back the most to ponder. Initially, it was just my understanding of the idea that things are different after that first yes to Jesus. The actual conversion comes next. Christianity has, over the centuries, turned into thousands of varieties of conversion. The diversity of Christian beliefs in the world today shows you just how varied the interpretations of conversion are. How to pick one with any "objectivity," if such a thing is possible with religion at all, is something that comes with a lot of thought, trial, and error.

The degree to which you are "living a new life" because of your faith is admittedly a weird barometer. The conversion of your life to something new after sincerely encountering Jesus is simultaneously unavoidable in route to a sustainable relationship with Jesus and easily misunderstood. But stick to Jesus here, and you'll find the way, if you can forgive that corniness for now. He really will show you the way, once you know how to listen.

In a very basic way, New Life in Christ is just caring about Jesus enough to consciously have him as part of your life. Let's build on what we've already gone through first: selflessness. Second Man scratches the surface of a real relationship with Jesus, while New Life is the transforming of our hearts for his presence in our lives. If Second Man is what gets you to the door, this is passing through the threshold. It's going from being what can be just a passively good person to something more specific. I am aware of the jump that exists between simply being second to others as a sufficiently good rule of life and seeking a personal transformation with Jesus. If you need to think of it as mere close friendship for now, that's a great foundation to build on. Friendship with God is the purpose of religion, reputedly according to St. Thomas Aquinas. Welcome Jesus into your life just like welcoming any new friend. Don't feel awkward about a getting-to-know-you phase. That's how all friendships begin.

The degree to which Jesus is a difficult addition to our lives depends on the sincerity of the friendship. Jesus actually wants to be a part of our lives, and that does require making space, just like any other relationship. We'll talk a lot about all kinds of misconceptions and other issues that make this difficult in the next chapter, but for now, consider this new relationship on a purely practical level: you have to get to know the person you're welcoming in. You have to know them for who they really are, not just how they're spoken of by others.

One of the core tenets of the mindfulness movement in recent years has been a concept called "getting behind the waterfall." This is one way of talking about a certain emotional self-awareness. If you don't allow yourself to haphazardly go over every waterfall of feelings and impulses, you pull back behind the waterfall to look at what you're doing—you introspect. You have probably done this at least superficially at some point in your life. Perhaps you do it more than you'd like. Emotions and impulses can have spiritual power, showing us where we are in need as a person, but to be mindful of them at all is a step toward self-control. To be Second Man, to be selfless, requires a self-control rooted in knowing yourself well enough to be conscious of why you feel this way and what lies behind it motivationally. Part of New Life in Christ is a self-acceptance brought on by self-control and self-understanding.

There are folks who don't want to be kind-spirited at all, and oftentimes that's not really a choice as much as it's a deep-rooted fear of making choices or being known, known by others, or even by ourselves in a deeper way, for fear of what the implications of that might be. We have to be mature enough within ourselves to take on things that challenge us. Life becomes static and degrades back into mere survival when we don't look to the next choice to be made.

The Cycle of New Life

A relationship with Jesus is a choice, and we have to be honest with ourselves long enough to contemplate it beyond the theoretical—to the personal level. This is where New Life begins: a self-awareness that allows us to introspect. After all, new things don't tend to last in your life unless you give them some thought first. But this is not introspection for its own sake—rather, a self-reflection that lends itself to understanding why more complex, self-giving relationships are enlightening and empowering.

Why might I want Jesus in my life? Why do you welcome anyone into your life? Hopefully, new friendships come into your life when you see a way for both you and the other to have a positive impact on each other. Sometimes, it is precisely in the shortcomings to that standard where we see the potential: we recognize needs and the will to grow, which is always helped by another soul coming along on the journey (avoiding toxic codependency, of course). That's where interpersonal openness is born. That openness is the catalyst of Second Man, but it's also the motion of a deeper relationship. This is how our hearts open to all kinds of love. When we're sincerely open to another being occupying a space in our heart. That's where the space for Jesus Christ opens up, and we start to go deeper than just being selfless towards others. Corny though that may sound, it is a state of mind too: it's a choice to welcome. When we are moved to be merciful to one another in this state of mind, Jesus begins his work in us.

After the crucifixion and death of Jesus, the apostles locked themselves up in an upper room (John 20:19–31). At this point, they feel like they've really screwed up. Except for John and the women, they have all abandoned Jesus in what turned out to be his last hours before execution. In this hiding, they are literally and figuratively closed in on themselves, ashamed and scared. When the resurrected Jesus appears among them, he doesn't let them have it for ditching him a few days prior, when he was arrested. He says, "Peace be with you," and gives them the Holy Spirit and the power to forgive sins. In the Catholic world, we call this Divine Mercy. We set aside the Sunday after Easter to celebrate this core attribute of God expressed through Jesus in this first post-resurrection appearance to the apostles. Having conquered sin and death, Jesus comes to us, bringing peace. All bygones are bygones with Jesus. We're freed from what frightens us and separates us from God and each other (sin), allowing us to live new lives. Your record is clean, as far as God's accounting goes.

The mission of mercy that Jesus is all about is clear in all the choices he makes along the way. Even his suffering has a loving purpose. Easter is the central Christian holiday (theologically, that is; Christmas was later elevated culturally because of the gift giving) because it is the completion, the victory, of Jesus in a series of decisions to reach out to us. These decisions were not pronouncements from on high but revelations in lived experience among us. Jesus is God who decided to take on our flesh and blood to express mercy to us in person.

Jesus *decided* to die on a cross. Jesus didn't decide to die painlessly. He wasn't going to diminish real suffering by not submitting himself to it. Jesus doesn't seek to minimize what we think is holding us up in life; he wants to subject himself to those struggles with us. Our problems are real. Our pain is real. Our persistent outward and inward torturers are real. The best way to console is not to insist some good will come of troubles, even though it might, and in the case of Jesus, it did. Effective consolers are like Jesus this way, in that they know they have to be present as friends, as brothers and sisters of a human family, confirming the sufferings felt. We can't console away the discomfort of suffering. We need to experience it without resigning ourselves to nihilism. That's why Jesus died by crucifixion. He wanted to relate to our suffering and use that to be there for us in every kind of hardship, the stuff natural to life too! That crucifix is Jesus saying, "I know what you're dealing with; I'm here for you." It's solidarity with us rather than simply trying to comfort away all the difficulty we do actually face.

That's quite a friendship! That's the mercy of Jesus. That's New Life: seeing through the lens of Christ's mercy. Where there is mercy, there is personal solidarity in all the ugly stuff of life. In the mercy and solidarity of New Life in Jesus, we can stop that ugliness from ruining our relationship with God, ourselves, and others. When we look at the world through mercy, there are so many new avenues for peace, justice, and solidarity, as well as patience with ourselves on the personal level. From Easter onward, mercy can prevail where it takes root. In other words, both our vertical and horizontal relationships can now grow without any outward or inward blight. Easter is the celebration of this. Easter is all about how Jesus helps us overcome all suffering, sin, and guilt. It's not a rejection of dealing with any of those things but the freedom to overcome them and grow. Jesus gives us the tools to overcome the difficulties underneath our struggles. (I felt the need to make a joke about how he was a carpenter there, but I couldn't quite get to one.)

Brief sidebar: Outward and inward is an important little nugget here. We'll get deeper into this later on in the next chapter, but for now, consider this: outer freedom and inner freedom both have an effect on how we might live a New Life. If we are not right within ourselves—in other words, if we don't properly love ourselves—it's hard to find a healthy relationship outwardly. That's true with Jesus just like with others, the difference being, Jesus can help with that inward stuff more than another person might be able to. We may be able to put on brave faces, but if we are not free of what might hold us down inwardly, be that any kind of addiction, depression, or other personal suffering, any outward expression of our New Life may be undermined. If we are outwardly oppressed, whether that be institutionally by various modes of injustice or personally by a toxic relationship, our inner freedom and peace will struggle. Jesus wants to heal all these inward and outward ills with us. He can come to us, bringing that merciful New Life he showed the apostles, by many ways. This is what we mean when we talk about transformation. Jesus can bring about powerful transformations in us once we're converted to his New Life. Sidebar over.

What we're talking about here is transformative relationships. From mere acquaintance all the way to intimate relationship, we are made better for sharing life with others. An outwardly effective New Life begins where we grow for encountering one another. Our selfish inclinations to be locked in on ourselves set aside, we can live more fulfilling lives. This kind of enlightenment is like Second Man, in that it is pre-Christian, lending itself to a certain base state of human existence that grows groups and binds together. Community grows this way. Historically, humanity's first communities grew because of agricultural surplus, but you know what I mean: people need to be giving enough to live together for that to happen. Sharing happened in those places, even if at a cost. We need to be loving with each other if we expect to get anywhere as communities of human beings.

Jesus Christ shows us the epitome of self-giving love and therefore the greatest heights of a New Life that enters into something more transformative. We might think of that divine mercy of Jesus bringing peace to us in spite of our shortcomings as the epicenter of conversion. Conversion is that transformative grace we're talking about localized in your own story, through a few events but also through the ongoing process. New Life is what follows the transformation . . . and conversion again . . . and more transformation. It never ends, no matter how long you've known Jesus. New Life is, in the most accessible understanding, the virtuous cycle in which we grow into better people. Conversion and transformation, the cycle of New Life.

Figure 3: Cycle of New Life Chart

I can think of at least half a dozen turning point moments in my life like this. If you're old enough to have some time to look back on, you have your own version of this that you can see. We have turning points where we're converted into a new way of thinking and are transformed as a result—at least, we're transformed if we're willing to be. If we truly integrate whatever the new information is into our way of living, we grow and develop as people. This isn't just with religious things; this is true with most complicated things in life. In the first couple decades of life, this cycle is a constant as we are primarily learning new things. As we get older, we have to pay attention to keep this cycle going by looking at things in new ways and opening our hearts to new realities in a changing world. When someone really becomes out of touch and begins to regress in some way or another, it's because they are struggling with the cycle of New Life or outright refusing it. Let's connect this back to a practical example.

The Map of New Life

In the introduction, I brought up the born-again movement, a latent form of Protestantism's greatest revitalization of Christian faith: the personal relationship with Jesus. Born-again status in some communities becomes an in-crowd versus out-crowd thing. I just want to be clear here that the more relational your experience with Jesus is, the less it is about social status. Jesus wanted the Pharisees to pray in private because he knew public practice of faith so easily devolves into performance. When we make a show of our practices, they lose some sincerity and often all their authenticity. Such an arrangement actually begins to distance ourselves from Christ's charism. Yeah, the guy writing a book about Jesus is decrying the damaging effects of public displays of religion. You got me. I bring it up because you have to meet Jesus first, one-on-one, the right way for you before you'll catch any feelings. He doesn't want to be your sidepiece for popularity at parties. Friends don't use each other.

This personal encounter, conversion, and transformation in Jesus may not feel right quite yet. That's okay, we've got a lot of book left here. But if you sense a discomfort with this related to how Jesus and Christian faith has been presented to you in the past (I imagine bringing up the born-again movement here might have awoken some religious trauma in some readers), you need to know that Jesus also uses sacred deconstruction to bring about New Life. Yes, the way Jesus and the faith built around him has been presented to you may itself be an obstacle to you encountering Jesus and then being truly converted and transformed. This is a common experience. Jesus himself was deconstructing his own faith, to a degree. What you may need to truly enter into Christ's New Life is a process of sacred deconstruction—that is, investigating how and why things were given to you the way they were; deconstructing the cultural, sociopolitical, and power dynamics involved; and then reconstructing a relationship with Jesus afterwards in a healthier, informed way.

In the same vein of sacred deconstruction, you also might need to allow yourself some anger. For newcomers to the faith, questioning God will come fairly easily; but if you were given a whole bunch of preconceived notions, you may feel this is awkward or sacrilegious. It is, in fact, how many saints and biblical characters got their stories going. We cannot be afraid to say to God "But why!?" That same summer of 2011, I spent no shortage of time fighting with God; I'm talking yell-fighting, crying, and a whole lot of sarcasm. It ended up being the most transformative spiritual experience of my life. In the metaphor of God as a loving parent, such sincere emotional expressions reconnect the bond, whether or not there's a whole lot of love in our expression. No matter how bitter and harsh it may be, it is an act of faith to initiate such an exchange in the first place, and indeed, it's a very ancient, special form of prayer. There are whole books of the Bible dedicated to complaining to God—I'm looking at you, Ecclesiastes and Job!

As I increasingly got engaged with my faith as a preteen, I was also very interested in sharing it. I can already feel the cringe coming on. My mother will tell you of a boy from down the block who would literally come over and sit on my porch so we could talk about Jesus. As we were twelve-year-olds, you can imagine these conversations weren't wildly concise or informed. I would sometimes send my porch friend home with printouts of the Beatitudes or other teachings. One day, that boy stopped coming. He had a troubled family life, and as best I can remember, his family moved away. Evidently, our porch meetings were an escape for him. At that age, I felt a bit betrayed by this, thinking, how could this just be a fun leisure activity for this kid I thought was my friend! I had to learn some canniness for life's difficulties, for one, but also the fact that just because something exists differently in the mind of others doesn't mean that nothing is sacred or meaningful. We find our way in life differently based on who we are, what time and place we were born into. Similarly, we find Jesus in different ways.

Sometimes, the first way Jesus is presented to us might not take. We'll talk some more about these dynamics of evangelizing Jesus in chapter 5. For now, what I'm trying to say is, Jesus, with the New Life he can bring you, is not a monolith. It's not my way or the highway. That's not Jesus. Jesus reaches out to us, and if you met Jesus in an unhealthy, unhelpful context the first time, that doesn't mean he's not still there to be met through other means. It is a liberating feeling to see Jesus in spite of the cultural milieu that we inhabit. It is also liberating sometimes to see him through a different setting. There is something deeply holy about cutting through the bullshit of unhelpful cultural settings, and indeed, Jesus is already shoveling through it toward you. Frankly, I'd be worried for his back, with all that shoveling.

Jesus wants to be yours sincerely. Jesus wants to be yours in a healthy relationship. The New Life we can live in him is not a matter of feelings as much as it is action. When Jesus really breaks into our lived experience, we are transformed more and more, day by day, for having that relationship and . . . here's the kicker: doing something about it in concrete ways. New Life is a cycle of conversion and transformation that also works in horizontal relationships—that is, in how we work with and relate to others.

I was once on a service trip in Camden, New Jersey. The religious brother we stayed with was called an oblate of St. Joseph. Most of his brothers in that order only visited him occasionally, as his ministry there was something he only was needed to do. He helped run the local church, but he was also a bit of a street savior, helping the hungry and homeless in that downtrodden community. For perspective, Camden was, for years, the most economically depressed, drug-riddled, violent city in America. Walking down the street, you could see discarded syringes, and like many similar cities, it was hollowed out by decades of white flight. Our oblate friend was doing work in this setting by himself, and doing it fairly well, if I might editorialize, since he still was able to host retreats and service trips, on top of being on a first-name basis with almost everyone on the street.

I bring up this wonderful oblate to illustrate that faith has effects. Yes, Jesus saves, but faith without works is indeed dead. Consider faith as a road map for New Life. The opposite of faith is not doubt, its selfish certainty. When we lack faith, we're closed in on the self. That is, like we laid out last chapter, being self-giving is the step out of our natural survivalism into the unknown of relationships with other people and God. We're generally closed in on self-preservation at best and self-obsession at worst. When we decide to have faith, we are opening ourselves up to the adventure that comes from the acknowledgment of a being infinitely more complex than and beyond us. Take the higher being out of it for a moment, and consider making choices in faith, illogical though that sometimes may be, as the simple admission we don't have all the answers. If we have all the answers in life, we don't need God—or anyone else, for that matter. Faith is something everyone displays when they make a choice in situations in which they know they can't have all the answers beforehand. Faith is just opening your heart on a very basic level. Christian faith is, in a broad philosophical sense, attributing that kind of heart-opening faith to a loving God who also became flesh to do it with us.

What emerges once we accept living in faith is something of a road map; that kind of heart-opening faith, if held sincerely, leads to an innate humility, which causes the purest kind of righteousness. Yes, I am going to visualize that here for you. The oblate we stayed with in Camden was a righteous person, if I've ever met one. If we can be humble, many great things can grow out of that, including the actual, real world, not a cartoon kind of righteousness. That is the kind of righteousness that just wants to do things the right way: for God and others. Many people of good will, regardless of the religious dimension, seek righteousness this way. Humility has to come first, and faith is often how one gets there. Righteousness leads back to humility in a way because if you think you're so righteous, you probably aren't humble. That then leads to a kind of conversion, insomuch as this is where God can bring us into specific faith in his Son, Jesus Christ. God has his ways to convert you, tailored to you specifically; but often, that comes after a kind of prerequisite faithful openness, which in turn instructs a thirst for righteousness. Faith is openness to something we can't predict though we're in a personal relationship with it. Yeah, that's a little wonky; let me insert that visualizer.

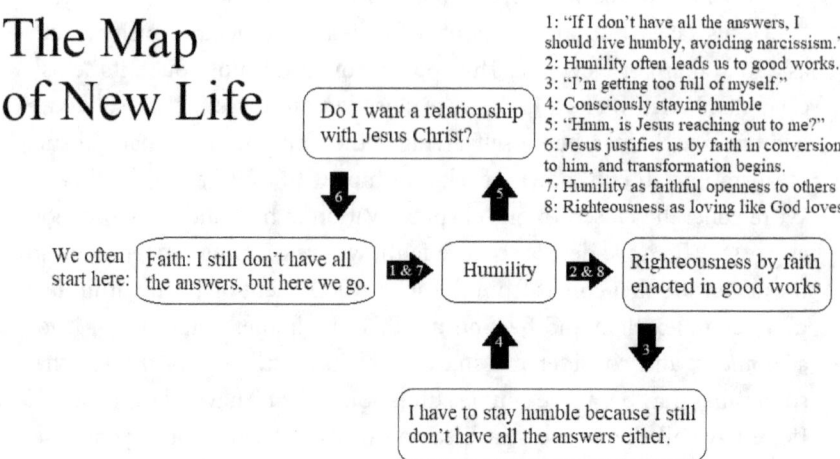

Figure 4: Map of New Life Chart

Notice that there are a couple loops in this map. We can go around the map without ever necessarily bringing Jesus into our lives. When we do bring Jesus in, however, we take a familiar path through the eyes of mercy. This is how New Life in Christ feels so different but somehow so similar to any reasonably compassionate life as well. You could even overlay the Cycle of New Life from earlier—conversion to transformation and back—over that 5-6-7 circuit. Also, take note that although this looks complicated, it all revolves around humility. It's somewhat remarkable that, religion or not, we innately know being humble is some divine quality. This is why self-reflection is important to New Life in Christ. Without the reflection, which prayer frequently brings on, we often find ourselves missing connections in our lives.

Before I finish illustrating this map for you, another quick sidenote we've already dabbled in a few times: faith is not a shrinking to unfounded belief. I may lose count of how many times I write this through the course of this book. Faith is not an effort to reduce us to folly in order to submit to God. Faith is an informed relationship with someone you know, someone you have met personally, perhaps after an aforementioned sacred deconstruction. I think about St. Paul this way after his days of opposing Christian faith came to a sudden, dramatic end. We tend to paper over the fact that he just ran off to Arabia for a few years after that wild conversion experience where he saw the now-ascended Jesus, went blind, and fell off his horse. I think Paul needed that time to deconstruct his beliefs about his own faith and then also what he had believed about Jesus. He and Jesus had some bullshit shoveling to do. Faith isn't folly; it's a relationship anchored in lived experience.

Back to the map: converted to Christ, we now are justified by grace—that is, made personally intimate with God, as Jesus's free gift of salvation removes any external barriers between us and God. From this point on, any trouble between you and Jesus arises from either you or Jesus (and any perceived trouble originating with Jesus is likely a straight answer you just haven't wrapped your head around yet). This relationship is made of love. First Corinthians chapter 13 is such a treasure because it lays out this kind of relationship so clearly: this relationship bears all things and keeps no record of wrongs, and all these things because love in its purest form, the love between you and Jesus, is a simple willing the good of other as other. That simple power of willing the good. That's love, doing your best for a person without a reward in mind.

This is, in a way, the completion of Second Man. Self-giving ultimately meets its greatest role model in Jesus Christ. This willing the good of other as other, this self-emptying love, is the cure for the kind of egotism natural in us humans since sin. We all fancy ourselves little gods from the moment we're old enough to make needy noises. Sometimes we hold this off consciously, though it's always there underneath. In Christ-like love, we overcome the all-consuming black hole of self. And this is the destination of my map metaphor but also just the beginning: love, this real kind of love, never ends. This is that mystical participation in Christ, that relationship with Jesus for whom we're trying to catch feeling for. Doing acts of self-giving love, that's the holiness. That's happiness, but that is so beyond feelings and can all grow from the smallest heart-opening seed of faith.

Holiness and Happiness Are the Same Thing

In spite of my own title for this book, I have to pivot here to clear some things up: feelings and appearances can accompany a sincere relationship, but it's not about those things, as tempting as that simple idolatry may be. With the Pharisees and faith performers the world over, feelings are misconstrued as the goal of all this. Feelings as the goal of faith is perhaps the most common misunderstanding of all religious faith . . . well, that, and the general overarching idea that Christianity is just about rules and exclusion. Those two misconceptions are interconnected in an important way: faith as feelings and Christianity as a mere moralizing template for rules and exclusion of therein identified outcasts. Those misconceptions rely on a default version of God that misses quite a bit.

A lot of us imagine this default-version God who is more or less indistinguishable from Santa Claus. As in: a prototypical old dude who is beyond explanation, only vaguely manifested here with us (deism), comforting but, ultimately, brutally moralizing. This default God predominates popular culture because it's not hard to explain: you do good, God is good to you. If you're not good, God will be mean to you. It's your typical old-world superstition stuff with coal in stockings, negative reinforcement, and the like. This default God is not the Christian God, I can assure you of that. Default God isn't worth believing in. That moralizing characteristic though, the rules part, belies a fundamental misunderstanding we have of moral rules in general that can trip up a meaningful relationship with Jesus.

Rules aren't any fun. We've talked already about how relational faith really is. Relationships require some rules. And if you've ever been in any kind of relationship, you hopefully are aware of boundaries. This is why we had that discussion about consent; this is why consent structures apply to relating to God as well. Right relationships require a few rules, but if you're in a good relationship, then no rule is all that hard to follow. In fact, the best relationships seem to have no rules because they just seem so harmonious. They just have made such a reciprocal, peaceful love that the rules rarely need to be mentioned.

Though one never grows out of consent structures, you hopefully might one day grow beyond rules. Real love tends to make rules superfluous because it erodes away our selfishness. Rules, just like good social boundaries, are about calibrating for healthy, fulfilling living. Rules in a right relationship are about magnifying the love already there, which arose out of a consenting relationship. Meaningful rules aren't arbitrary, and the best ones are really just guideposts to a better way. Rules then are helpful if they have some wisdom built into them. That is when rules are made justly and equitably, to be as inclusive as possible.

Jesus's primary mission in coming to us wasn't to establish rules. Jesus wasn't coming to make bad people good; he was coming to raise the dead to life. Jesus knew our aversion to arbitrary, moralistic rules as he delivered his first speech, the Sermon on the Mount. The core of that teaching was the Beatitudes. Eight ideas rooted in . . . attitudes, if you will, to live by. These are not mere rules: they are guidelines for happiness, attitudes to have. In some translations, Jesus's preface to each precept is "Happy are they . . ." These Beatitudes are indicative of his way to true Christian happiness. The Beatitudes are one of the most powerful pieces of the gospel, but they are so often lost in translation. Allow me to attempt a translation for us moderns because they are Jesus's way of telling us happiness and holiness are really the same thing:

"Blessed are the poor in spirit, for theirs is the kingdom of heaven" (Matt 5:3). Translation: Blessed are you if you know God as your deepest desire, not disposed to temporary comfort. When we love as God loves, a self-giving free of possessiveness, we become love embodied for others and the greater world around us.

"Blessed are those who mourn, for they will be comforted" (Matt 5:4). Translation: Blessed are you if you are not dependent on good feelings and impulses but are liberated by Jesus to handle all things with mercy. A clarity of purpose, a sincere single-heartedness, particularly toward God, brings inner harmony to vertical and horizontal relationships alike.

"Blessed are the meek, for they will inherit the land" (Matt 5:5). Translation: God is originator and therefore unifier. His righteousness makes us unifiers when we are humble enough to desire for good to be done to others. God does not impose; he proposes. That is, our horizontal relationships must be free of unjust divisions.

"Blessed are those who hunger and thirst for righteousness, for they will be satisfied" (Matt 5:6). Translation: Blessed are you if the pursuit of power is not your lord in life. Whatever is your ultimate hunger animates you. Orient it towards righteousness, and you will not be frustrated.

"Blessed are the merciful, for they will be shown mercy" (Matt 5:7). Translation: Blessed are those not attached to wealth and the pursuit of it. Mercy arises from a patient love that just wants to do good for the other. Detach yourself from material fixation because the tangible things don't sustain our souls; they are mere tools for the good works we do.

"Blessed are the clean of heart, for they will see God" (Matt 5:8). Translation: Blessed are those freed from selfish desire because pleasure is as passing as earthly life itself. Don't chase feelings and impulses; they are always mere shadows of greater things.

"Blessed are the peacemakers, for they will be called children of God" (Matt 5:9). Translation: Avoid idolizing power. It diminishes the inherent goodness we all have and makes us greedy in a way that violates the dignity of others. Confraternity, togetherness, and respect for one another animates holiness in all our horizontal relationships, even on a global scale.

"Blessed are those who are persecuted for the sake of righteousness, for theirs is the kingdom of heaven" (Matt 5:10). Translation: Honor only clouds your judgment; seek the good, not the goods. Honor is at best a by-product of good work and at worst a distraction. We shouldn't fear social hardship, as if it can change our connection to God.

You might notice a subtle distinction between the first four and the last four Beatitudes. The first four speak to ways we can grow and become better people. The latter four are more cautionary, warning us of the things that might poison our more virtuous desires with deficient alternatives. One Bishop Robert Barron put it: the latter four can be understood in our modern parlance as the places where "addiction" can creep in.[1] Addiction is a powerful word, but it fits. We chase feelings too often in life. Those last four Beatitudes are warnings against the addictions related to wealth, pleasure, power, and honor. Almost all of the world's most destructive addictions can be traced back to one of those four enticing idols of human nature.

That said, let's talk about happiness. The languages into which the Gospels were first written and translated made no distinction between the words *happy* and *holy*. The word is *makarios* in the Greek, meaning blessed, holy, happy, or lucky. In the writing of the Gospel authors, and surely in the speaking of Jesus when he said these things: holiness and happiness are the same thing. Any distinctions between the two are attitudes we have invented in more recent centuries. Happiness does radiate from life well lived, and that is one and the same for holiness in our own lives and the holiness Jesus teaches.

New Life is holy life and therefore happy life. It's not just some collection of feelings designed to reinforce religious practice. Religious practice has a place in worship, of course, but the powerful, everyday New Life is about what animates us to do good in that cycle of conversion and transformation. That's the fuel of holiness. Holiness therefore may exist where it appears there is no good to be seen. We can do holy things and not appear holy in any outward way. Works tend to affect the horizontal relationships, those around us, but holiness is that humble cycle always going somewhere better. It isn't destroyed with one false move or even many false moves because it is a movement toward New Life, it's a movement toward the divine, our desire for which is growing all the while as a result.

1. Barron, *Catholicism*.

New Life in Christ is the inspirational fuel of the works we do. What animates you to do good and therefore be holy is the fossil fuel of Christian faith, if you will. It's not finite like that, but bear with me. The holier we become, the more we find new, more ever-replenishing means of doing our good for the world around us: the renewable energy in this clunky metaphor I've unfolded for you. Eventually, we can move beyond the fossil fuels of holiness rooted in feelings and appearances into the renewable energy of thirsting for righteousness and holiness. How about a less clunky example?

In chapter 1, we discussed some basics to lead us here: when we live selflessly, we see each other as fellow children of God, all vulnerable, suffering people trying to find their way in the world, needy in our own unique ways. When we live as second, it enriches our souls and also calls us to more. Living the way of the Beatitudes as Jesus teaches us can naturally flow from being second. Humble service as a truly selfless person entices us to want to be more than just selfless or self-giving. That's holiness growing naturally within us. We yearn for God once we truly live humble lives because we see what is truly needed in ourselves in others. With eyes cleared by self-gift and minds sobered by humility, we see the light of things we can't control, returning us to reexamine the faith that got us there in the first place.

And once again: there is action that results from this. Where the gospel of Christ has inspired holiness and New Life, revolution follows. The gospel of Jesus Christ is explosive.

In all my years of overzealous mansplaining of everything I learned on the *History Channel* in the 2000s, I failed to pass along the zeal for the subject matter that got me mansplaining in the first place. Yes, President Theodore Roosevelt surviving an assassination attempt in the middle of a speech he then finished is a fascinating sidebar over dinner, but if others don't feel quite as excited about it, you lose the purpose of saying it at all. My brother went to college to be a teacher so he could teach about Theodore Roosevelt for more than just the raw excitement of it. He wants to teach for the sake of the good it does for society. Education is a common good; Theodore Roosevelt is just a very fascinating piece of history next to the greatness of the common good. What we're doing, this action I keep going back to that I even called revolutionary, is the common good.

What is the common good? This concept lives within a cluster of broader society-focused theology called, in the Catholic Church at least, social teaching. This concept fundamentally holds that as individuals we have not just the natural inclination but the duty to seek the well-being of all people if we mean to seriously live within a just society. This concept is pillared by some core beliefs of Catholic social teaching: basic human dignity, solidarity, care for God's creation, subsidiarity, the preferential option for the poor, and the universal destination of goods. At least two of those ideas are somewhat self-explanatory, but I think they're worth expanding on because they are so interrelated.

You may notice these principles are both universal and not necessarily predicated upon belief in Jesus. Yes, the work we do, even if we're doing it by way of a relationship with Jesus we've forged, doesn't necessarily have to be exclusively converting people and dunking them in holy water. There is a place for preaching the good news of the gospel, but the oft-forgotten way of doing that is creating a better world for all God's children. As Dorothy Day reportedly said: "I really only love God as much as I love the person I love the least." We'll come back to the straight-up preaching stuff in later chapters. For now, contemplate how it is an act of mercy, of goodness, simply to take care of each other. Just like all of us human beings are inexorably intertwined in the finite span of life we have to live, so too must we attend to some common goods that affect us all therein. This was true before the globalized world, and this will continue to be true forever, no matter how much we fail to see the need for solidarity among all of humanity.

Human dignity is a universal truth, regardless of where each of us finds ourselves within the trappings of life. We are, even without belief in a supernatural being, imbued with some dignity just by virtue of being humans (*imago Dei*, in Church speak). We also all share this same earth, so it's incumbent upon us to protect it in caring for God's creation. Subsidiarity is essentially Christian faith's affirmation of representative governance: people have the right to participate in decision-making processes relevant to them, particularly at local levels, where they can have a bigger impact. The principle of solidarity feeds directly into common good, in that we are all one human family and have to bond together in the obligation to promote everyone's rights and development across the world. This is local and global: working in our specific context of time and place while seeing where things on the worldwide scale come to bear. In a world as interconnected as it is today, this requires a mindfulness for the local, balanced by the more universal reality that we are inseparable from others on the global scale as well. In the words of Pope Francis: "We are bound by bonds of reciprocity."[2]

Finally, the last two are connected: the preferential option for the poor holds that since God chose to come among us in the form of a poor guy in a backwater country, a guy named Jesus, we ought to take care of the especially poor and needy with an especially attentive approach (hence the morally devastating declaration Jesus gives us in Matt 25:40 that he is in fact the neediest among us). To anchor this one even more explicitly in Jesus: we tend to see God from the peripheries of society much more clearly. For the oppressed, God is most visible. The universal destination of goods is the one that, even more than the preferential option for the poor, really upsets the wealthy and well-to-do in society. It holds that everything beyond our needs and the needs of those we're responsible for belongs to those who are in need beyond us. In other words: private property, business, and all the doings of a free economy are all fine for their common good purposes, but when they are greedily held up and hoarded away for the benefit of a selfish few, they are holding up the will of God. The universal destination of goods is, in a word, to those who need them. There is no dancing around this one: God hates greed.

These principles aren't unique to the Catholic Church; I think they're simply best expressed in Catholic theology. Forgive my bias. Also forgive me the usage of the words *duty* and *obligation*. Perhaps it's too early in the journey of this book for those words. Allow me to dissuade you from the notion that I am another inaccessible religious zealot. The grand question here that branches out from being second and into living a New Life is not the why of religion; it's the how. Catholic social teaching is a framework to think in a more global sense: how do I give of myself?

Living up to the demands of service to others is hard. You must understand, I have rarely responded with a coherent or consistent answer in my own life either. New Life is not an end; it's a state of matter. Holiness is always this cycle of New Life: conversion, transformation, and conversion again. We all struggle on our way to holiness and doubt whether we can do it at all. In fact, "a faith without doubts," as Pope Francis says, "cannot advance."[3] This is to say that our doubts can keep us humble and hungry for good things, resistant to the evils that can arise from self-righteousness, fundamentalism, and a belief in our own religious goodness

---

2. Francis, *Let Us Dream*, 107.
3. *Vatican News*, "Pope Francis."

that always equates to selfishness. If we're self-assured without doubt, then faith fades and selfishness expands. If your faith doesn't challenge you to do more, to act, then it's dead. In the ostensible words of St. Óscar Romero: "Aspire not to have more, but to be more." This is a challenge we have to embrace with Jesus if we are truly to live in his New Life.

The fragile self is at the root of a lot of our more belligerent selfishness as social animals. We otherize and make enemies out of a sense of self that often comes together as a tenuous collection of our favorite things, behavioral norms, and closed support structures. Humility demands we don't jealously protect the fragile, isolated conscience we sometimes express. Even this state of affairs points us to New Life in Christ because Jesus's whole shtick is getting out of the closed inward-looking self to go out to others. We become beleaguered, defensive beings when we isolate ourselves from others. Matthew 7:12, that Golden Rule we learn in grade school, shows us something that many adults today struggle with. We have to be what we want to see around us. Do we want to be heard? Let us first listen. Do we need encouragement? Let us first give encouragement. Do we want someone to believe what we know is the truth? Then let us demonstrate its truth with our own actions first. Action.

Hearing God

When I say I think someone "needs Jesus" in the tradition of the hilarious meme, it's almost never upon seeing some kind of moral wrongdoing that offends me. I was raised too down-to-earth for that. I think folks who "need Jesus" the most are those who guard the borders of their tribes, their curated echo chambers, so jealously that it's evident what's important to them isn't personal or societal growth. What's important for the fragile self is closed living: tribal living in a state of regression to ever smaller orders of community. Jesus never permits us closed living. Indeed, God's voice is the voice of unity and togetherness. True followers of Christ, those who have truly found him and his New Life, are openhearted in a way of love, a way that is converted anew for every encounter with another person. The real Jesus who brings New Life brings change of all sorts as a gift for our continued maturation and development as people. Change is a constant that God gave us. Don't demonize it.

We're supposed to go places to which we're not accustomed in our new lives for Jesus. Every priest I've ever heard preach about the Magi and the gifts they bring to baby Jesus will never miss a chance to mention Matt 2:12 if they can, even if it wasn't directly included in the Gospel reading. This is the verse that states the Magi "departed for their country by another way." It is so easy and obvious to any listener, both the literal and metaphorical meanings at work there. They literally went back a different way to avoid giving up Jesus to a murderous tyrant in Herod, but they also spiritually went back a different way because they were changed by their encounter with Jesus. Mind you, at this point, we'd be talking about the newborn version of him, who might've spit up and soiled his undies when they were there.

This is truly where a more agreeable, worldly, even agnostic practice of Second Man can take the proverbial leap of faith into Christianity and the sincere, personal encounter with Jesus. Homilists of Matt 2:12 almost always pose the questions of commitment: are you giving your all to Jesus? Are you setting Jesus aside by prioritizing more important efforts in your life ahead of him? Are you, like the Magi, willing to brave distance and despots to meet Jesus and live your life with him?

The Magi don't just belong to Christmas and the nativity story. They also belong to a little feast in early January called Epiphany. That word is used there for a reason. It is synonymous with a sudden revelation, a profound realization or "a revealing scene or moment" in the definition of the *Merriam-Webster Dictionary*. It's important to understand the epiphany of Jesus did not occur for the Magi by accident: they searched for him, and they found him. To cross into New Life in Christ, we have to stop waiting for a touching moment and go pursue that epiphany experience with Jesus. The intentionality of your epiphany will not go unrewarded if you have your eyes trained for God's voice in it. How do I give of myself? Am I prepared to take a personal risk to meet Jesus and never be the same? In such a vast world with myriad experiences, sufferings, and ways of life, how can I give of myself and leave a mark in a meaningful way? A good starting point is making your own epiphany and giving Jesus a chance to make a meaningful difference in you.

As we go over these sweeping principles of living in Christ, it must be noted that zeal is a secondary characteristic for which one hopes as a by-product of loving God and others. It's not how hard you pound the table, it's about what's on the inside, to get super corny about it. My personal zeal for these kinds of things can be an obstacle. You don't have to be springing to your feet shouting Jesus at anyone who looks remotely downcast. That might be counterproductive in most company, actually. It rarely strikes to the heart of encounter and genuine conversion, in my experience.

My maternal grandmother is a devout Catholic. She posed the prospect of pursing a vocation for the priesthood to me as soon as I showed any interest. A lot of people look at anyone under eighteen who has an eye for religion in the Catholic Church and think "That guy looks like a future priest!" It's not a terrible supposition, but it's rooted in the world in which my grandma grew up more than my own. There was a time in the Catholic Church (before the Second Vatican Council) when the Bible, worship, and all the faith's acts were explicitly in Latin only. In that world, many young men with an eye for the faith went into the priesthood because that's how you did what you could for that Catholic world, if you really loved it. Putting the Catholic Bible, liturgies, and all the surrounding accoutrements in native tongues made it personal for anyone with a set of ears and a functional, educated, and sufficiently literate brain. In a way, us Catholics finally caught up with the rest of the Christian world. But let's get back to my grandma in particular. Her suggestions brought on a question that is crucial to hearing God.

Her hopes of me as a priest were not just rooted in a world where that's what you did if you had a special passion for the faith; they were rooted in her seeing a way for me to give of myself to others. How do I give? It's a question we ask in big ways and small ways. It's a question we answer in some measure every single day. New Life is engaging in all the awkward milieu of that: the probing conversations with trusted advisors and trial efforts and various jobs. Although it was awkward, and sometimes I felt embarrassed as a teenager, for my grandma wanting a life without girls for me, the intent there was beautiful. Though that specific vocation is not where I find myself today, I certainly have known a great many priests already in my life who have helped me on the journey of holiness, the journey of New Life. It's like my grandma knew something, even if I wasn't to be a priest. The ones who truly love us, deeply and sincerely with a reciprocating love, can act as God's own voice for us. Sometimes, in fact, we hear echoes of real humans we know or once did in the machinations of life. The voice of Jesus Christ is never far from us and especially in those who seek to give.

Hearing God: that there is worth some more unpacking. Essential to living a New Life in Christ is this concept of hearing God. I mentioned earlier that prayer is just thinking with another. Formulation of plans is prayer in a way. The "with another" part there is absolutely essential. And when the other is God, who is, in the Christian understanding, at least, "the being of which no greater being can be thought" (per St. Anslem of Canterbury),[4] then it can get headier than your average discussion of the weather. God is, though so unbelievably grander than our brain's comprehension, knowable and hearable, if we so train ourselves.

God is love, in the Christian understanding. He *is* love. That is to say, in his very being, he is the embodiment of love. Such a being wants to know us in spite of how unknowable he may be in a completed empirical sense. He reaches out to us! He is love! Hearing God, not just in prayer but in the mechanics and circumstances of life, requires knowing how he speaks. How do we know anything of that sort when we're talking about a divine being of which no greater being can be thought? God is, in the Christian sense, mysterious. That's why when Moses asks who God is at the burning bush in Exodus, God simply responds with "I am who I am." God is not captured by any words we have and therefore not to be encapsulated by us in any way. But don't let this fool you into believing God is unknowable. God is, particularly in the Christian tradition, very accessible and pines to know us on a personal level. How we hear God personally always springs from . . . well, the personal, as we have so intensively gone over. That's why it's such a difficult thing to write about. I can't tell you how you hear God. I can only give you the tools Jesus gives us.

(Shoot, I still can't call a carpentry joke to mind.)

Perhaps the best starting point here is to talk about God's various names. "I am" is probably the most accurate one because it is indescribably vast; but different titles allow us different insights into who we're talking to. Take the title of God as our Creator: he knows us like any builder knows their final product. But yes, we are not final products. Life is a state of constant change and growth. God created us and the circumstances into which we're born, knowing this. One name for God the Holy Spirit is Paraclete, or Advocate in English. There is a certain richness to thinking of God as our advocate via the Holy Spirit. God's voice to us on a personal level is unique to each of us, but he gives us the book on him— or, should I say, many books and countless other resources to know him. Any two beings need to know each other on some basic level to communicate. While I hope this book may help with that getting-to-know-you process, the pinnacle of all such works to help you know God is the Bible. The Bible is the sun from which the rays of all other worthwhile Christian spiritual writing emanate. All Christian traditions of knowing God

---

4. See Anselm, *St. Anselm's Proslogion*.

spring from the biblical tools we are given for knowing God. Even though the Church assembled the Bible, even it recognizes it was just collecting the right parts to envisage a primary source of knowing God.

I could write a whole book about how to read the Bible, but for the sake of brevity, here is a very hyper-condensed guide to reading it. For one, you must understand the Bible is actually a library of books. Some books within the Bible are just poetry, others are full-on history lessons, others are letters, still others are artfully told mythology or teaching stories that don't really pretend to be factually true. Moreover, the *message of the Bible* and the *contents of the Bible itself* are two *very* different things. The Bible contains abuse, racism, sexism, slavery, adultery, and almost every evil imaginable. Those are not to be thought of as "the message of the Bible," because everything outside the primary goal of love for God and neighbor is fundamentally not the message of the Bible. Oh, look at that: Second Man in biblical form!

Those two religious principles that Jesus gives us and that the Old Testament foreshadows fundamentally define everything in the Bible you can interpret as what the Bible actually teaches. Obviously, biblical interpretation is one of the most contentious issues in Christian thought, and many people have used the existence of an evil like slavery in the Bible to justify it in the present. You can do a DIY Bible translation and blur the line between content and message all you want, and that doesn't make it the gospel message of Jesus. Who has the final say on the true canon of the Bible, as you can imagine, is accordingly a very contentious issue that's ultimately a matter of what denomination you select. I am Catholic and would point you in that direction, but let's keep this as inclusive as possible.

Within that primary goal of love within the message of the Bible, to love God and your neighbor, two themes seem to run throughout: the sins of idolatry and oppression of the poor and marginalized (Isa 1:23, 10:2; Jer 5:28). These two themes match those two facets of that primary goal of love, and almost all prophesizing and teaching in the text of the Bible could be put in one of those two categories. I bring this up because we tend to differentiate an Old Testament God from a New Testament God. Yes, there is a certain evolution to salvation history that looks very different in the Old Testament but we exaggerate what these differences mean about God's nature. When we make the God of the Old Testament into a different character, it also reinforces a certain anti-Semitism that crops up time and time again in Christian history. Moreover, whenever we make the prophesizing and teaching of the inspired word of God into an object of a past time and place, we lose the power of it. These two themes are eternal in the human experience and are fundamental to the Christian worldview. Context matters, but when God speaks in the Bible, he's talking to everyone down through the eons; and when he's not, it's pretty obvious with some basic anthropological knowledge à la mixed fabrics and pork consumption. Don't overthink it: context clues let you know what's relevant.

You also have to remember when reading the Bible in your own language that it has been translated through at least four other languages before it got translated into your language. There are whole passages that rise and fall based on translation. Most of the New Testament was first written in the subtle language of ancient Greek before being translated into Latin. About a thousand years after that, it was translated into the older versions of several European languages like German, French, and English before finally being translated into modern languages. That game of telephone, particularly before the printing press, led to some mistranslations. Take things with a grain of salt and consult translation notes accordingly. This researching of the text can prove to be a spiritual good all its own, if you're patient with it. No matter what sect you decide on joining, we all uphold the truth that the text is inspired by God nonetheless.

Additionally, in chapter 6, there is a sidebar about biblical fundamentalism. I won't go into it at length here because it requires some context we'll get to later in this book. For now, it's worth understanding that the "plain sense reading" of the Bible, that is, reading the whole thing literally as if all the context I just gave you is an irrelevant perversion of God's word, is only about 150 years old. Yes, the idea that you just need to read it without thinking any of this may require some additional clarification dates to about the 1870s. The belief of *sola scriptura* (Scripture alone), on the other hand, dates all the way back to Martin Luther and the Reformation, but that's a different thing, and we'll talk more about both in chapter 6. I've already admitted to my Catholicism but understand that even most Protestant groups don't look at the Bible through the fundamentalist lens. Biblical fundamentalism is a feature of contemporary Evangelicalism and the most fringe churches of what we call low-liturgy or low-church denominations. Biblical fundamentalism lends itself to certain interpretations and generally allows any preacher to say just about anything they want, rejecting any higher religious authority that they can deem against God's own word.

With those important contextual notes out of the way, let's look at the structure of the Bible: Old and New Testament. The Old is essentially how God tried to bring salvation to humanity before Jesus, while the New is really God saying, "You know what—I'll do this myself." God's breaking into human reality in the form of Jesus is the turning point of the Bible. The whole Old Testament can be thought of as prelude to that momentous event. To break it down further, the Old Testament's first five books are the origin story of the nation of Israel into which Jesus would one day be born. That's followed by eleven history books, three prophets in the Jewish tradition, and then seven books I really consider the jewels of the Old Testament (Job, Psalms, Proverbs, Wisdom, Ecclesiastes, Song of Solomon, and Isaiah), before the homestretch of sixteen books comprised of more prophets, a bit more history, and at least one book that heads back into practical poetry in Lamentations.

The New Testament is where you're going to want to begin if you've never read the Bible before. The first four books of this part of the Bible are the God-spells, or Gospels, the whole of the Christian religion reveres as essential. They account the specifics of Jesus's life, ministry, death, and resurrection. I'd recommend Mark first, but which Gospel you start with is one of those personal points of self-understanding. Generally, John's Gospel is for big-picture folks, Matthew is for those into historical detail and continuity, Luke is the most practical Gospel, and Mark is caked with the most expository exegesis (interpretation of meaning) of them all. The Gospels are followed by Acts of the Apostles, which can be thought of as the first . . . well, acts of the Church. Then the remaining twenty-two books of the Bible are primarily letters from apostles and missionaries to various early Christian churches.

If I can add one more contextual detail: consider the whole Bible, but particularly the New Testament, as a document brought together by a formal religious body in the Church. That is to say, we believe the Bible is the perfect revelation of God's word to us, but it was also composed in this final form by a formal body of the leadership of the Church. To be specific, part of that formal body of Christian leadership still exists today as the Catholic Church. That's me advertising my own sect, but I also bring it up for a less sectarian, practical reason. People decided which texts floating around at the time would be canon and which ones wouldn't. After the Protestant Reformation, the Reformers would subtract certain passages and whole books.

The relative wisdom of adding or subtracting from the canon of the Bible aside, we have to view the Bible as both the inspired word of God and a flawed human document. Both are true at the same time. As the content versus message distinction implies, we have to be careful not to miss the forest for the trees with this. That's why most Christians don't subscribe to the "plain sense reading" of the Bible. It is a book brought together by people with their frailties, preserved from error in that construction only by the Holy Spirit. But yes, it is a bit of a slippery slope. Where you draw the line, what kind of interpretive lens you apply, is ultimately a denominational choice for you to make.

Biblical understanding will always take on an interpretive lens. Unless you yourself are each of the Gospel writers, there will be interpretive work done reading the Bible. Obvious though that fact may be, the struggle for understanding can lead to discouragement. There is a reason the Bible wasn't first translated into the vernacular languages until the fifteenth century! We lean on sermons and homilies to convey studied meaning—and indeed, our churches provide us with context and meaning—but this is also personal. Revelation isn't just something that comes to preachers and the magisterium of the Church. God speaks to us personally through inspired text if we are prepared to listen. Yes, I mean to say, God speaks to you specifically through the text of the Bible, if you are so prepared. How could I mean that after all the context I just gave? God speaks to us in a day-to-day way through Scripture if we are so prepared; it's called personal revelation.

Once you read enough of the Bible to get to know God and his human incarnation in Jesus Christ, you find yourself having a general idea of the personal and universal "who God is"; though, of course, God is such a profound higher truth. That canonical understanding, combined with the realities of your own life, allows for your own day-to-day interpretative abilities of how God is speaking to you in your circumstance, which is the most concise way to say "This is how you hear God." I cannot possibly put enough asterisks on that last sentence. So much of this is personal, while so much of it is also the canonical interpretation of Scripture and tradition that your own particular denomination and congregational life mediates. Misinterpretation can lead to some terrible things, so if you think you may be going down a negative path by way of Scripture, please reach out for some help. Consult later wisdom and reflection on the Bible, as well saints and other holy people. God's voice is love; remember that when you're listening for it.

This personal, universal, and canonical knowing "who God is" that helps us to listen and converse with God could be called one's conscience. I've already used that word several times and not defined it: conscience. It's a wisdom for right and wrong that is often informed by this hearing God we've just gone over. It's a religious concept that is so well known that it ceases to be a religious concept. Like I said last chapter: I'm not of the mind one needs to be religious to be a good person or to have a well-formed conscience. People of good will, whether they're religious or not, often do. I've met nonreligious people with better consciences than some clergy. To the degree conscience is described in Christ's New Life for us, a well-formed conscience can be a fountain of the thirst for righteousness. If we can avoid becoming legalistic and overly guilty, we can use our own conscience to develop that thirst and the love of Jesus that it can induce when we consider him our goal in all this.

Very quick sidebar: I'll circle back around to guilt next chapter because there are many of us who would be skeptical of the concept of a conscience at all. They think guilt is always and exclusively a toxic thing to be avoided in life. If your conscience never makes you feel guilty, then it probably isn't a well-formed one. The idea that we should never feel guilty about any of our actions if we're living our best lives can be just as harmful, if not more harmful, than a conscience convicting us of guilt all the time. Sidebar over—for now, at least.

But to bring it back down to a bite-size proverbial understanding: hearing God is how we reach toward his divine life for us. This is the navigator of the New Life this whole chapter is about. Prayer has a lot to do with this, too, but we're not to the end of this chapter quite yet. There are still some nuts and bolts we should touch on here.

The Soul and the Infinite within

Don't read into this whole concept of New Life in Christ as if it is a narrow destiny into which you'll have to fit. Sometimes, when we read religious texts, we are seduced by the cynicism of the simple. Half the Protestant Reformation was built on the concept that the Bible and only the Bible represented God's revelation to us. To be fair to Protestants, that thinking arose in a time when literally nobody except highly educated clerics read the Bible—or read at all, for that matter, so it was a smart, liberating concept to make literacy a moral crusade via religion.

Martin Luther's assertion that we can encounter God for ourselves through the text of the Bible was revolutionary and really drove up literacy in the biggest way ever seen.

The temptation to simplicity of theology is seductive but immediately ineffective for us individual thinkers of the modern world when we find ourselves reducing all religion to an ethical code or generic calls to good will that are indistinguishable from any legal code of conduct. If religion were just ethics, then Jesus would have made a few updates to Hammurabi's Code or the Levitical Law and retired back into the carpentry business. The opposite is problematic as well, when we suddenly find ourselves thinking we just have to follow rules to be holy. We went over this problem earlier, but it bears repeating that as a point of New Life, as a point of living with Jesus, things change in an intentional way. Some people interpret this as rules, when it is probably more comparable to an athletic discipline, a spiritual athleticism or training, if you will.

Truly holy life does not arise from the mere following of rules, though discipline can be transformative. Holiness arises when we embrace God's work in our lives and in our souls, understanding that the only reason God is working in us in the first place is that he already knows us and, moreover, that He wants to be with us. Jesus is the evidence God desperately wants to have a relationship with us. Don't oversimplify New Life in Christ. Don't put Jesus in a box, no matter how nicely you decorate that box or how much you worship it. Jesus and his message are always more explosive than the various ways we domesticate him.

There is a lot to be said here about God having a plan for our lives and the subtleties of that deeper, very religious reality. As we climb the rungs of God's Canon in My Life, the journey gets more personal and less abstract. The easy literalism of Second Man is going to turn into the more complex orbits of what you really want out of your own life. That question may bring on some existential dread, and I know; it does for me too. But that's where our encounter with God really is. The conversion of our hearts and minds wells up from encounter with God in ways that engage the depth of our souls. We are confronted by existential sensations at the gates of the unknown.

How do we go out into the spiritual unknown? Who are we as spiritual beings? What are we even in the grand scheme of things? How do we receive Jesus, his New Life, and all this holy happiness I keep talking about? Let's define the soul.

We millennials have been taught by a surge in young adult fiction that we are special and deserve trophies. Just kidding, this isn't that kind of book. No patronizing discussion of trophies and participation or entitlement here. We are special. We are, just like all human beings, special, made in the image of God (*imago Dei*). That specialness points to something, though. It's not specialness for specialness's sake. It's purposeful. The likes of *Harry Potter* (2001–2011) and *The Hunger Games* (2008–2010) taught us two primary lessons in this vein: one, adults are always the bad guys. Okay, obviously, this one isn't always true, assuming adulthood doesn't drain all the creativity and hope out of you. And two, we learn everyone has a human dignity that cannot be diminished, which is—to use a very YA term—infinite. *Perks of Being a Wallflower* (2012) even has a recurring line of dialogue about this. This metaphysical infinity, the fountain of the dignity that makes us human (which, if it's disrespected in any of these narratives, that's when you know who the bad guy is), is the greatest hint at our maker. Our souls are the dignity, the metaphysical infinity, the infinite part yearning for an infinite God. These are Christian narratives, it would seem.

The whole philosophical concept of infinity and an infinite God is a complex discussion and actually a proof of God's existence, if you want to dive into it. I won't here because I want to focus on the soul itself. Our souls, at least in the Christian understanding, are three infinitely deep chambers that yearn for an infinitely deep God. Turns out the being of which no greater being can be thought made us in perfect union with him before original sin; therefore, we have an infinite depth within our souls that finds satisfaction in him. This is where our divine New Life in Christ happens. Enough of the spiritualized mumbo jumbo—what's up with these three chambers? Why are there three? St. John of the Cross wrote a beautiful text called *The Living Flame of Love*. In it, he speaks of three caverns of infinite, unfathomable depth ordered toward God since creation and therefore always yearning for him. They are intellect, will, and feeling.[5]

Our intellect yearns for the infinite truth of the universe and therefore the infinite truth of God, the Prime Creator of the universe. Our will (our core intent or power of choice, in more modern language) yearns for the infinite goodness of life's greatest goods and achievement and therefore the infinite grace that is God the Prime Mover and Essence of being itself. Our feeling is what yearns for the infinite blessings of companionship

---

5. De la Cruz, *Living Flame of Love*, 101–4.

and community and therefore longs for God who is love. God is not only love, but those of us who believe in the Trinity believe he is a community of three persons even within himself! These three chambers of the soul are the specific elements of our being that catch the feelings for Jesus, if you will. Nobody cannot have a soul unless they somehow stopped having will, intellect, or emotion. When these three parts are repressed for any reason, it is the result of a very visceral, practical injustice. With or without God, we are prone to filling these inner caverns with all manner of lesser things, ultimately resulting in dissatisfaction. New Life, divine life in Christ, is about understanding that the depths of our souls are not filled by any passing fancy or even the work of our lives if it's not ordered toward God. Infinite satisfies infinite.

Perhaps this still strikes you as a bridge too far. Have I ever been *ordered toward God*? Could I ever really be ordered toward God with all that constitutes . . . well, me? Being second and this New Life in Christ all sound good on this theoretical level, sure, but how do I really get around some core reservations about God and all the adjacent things about those who love him that quite frankly put me off? To begin to answer some of those questions, I'll have to pass along Jesus's own words: "There are many rooms in my father's house; I would not tell you this if it were not true. I am going there to prepare a place for you" (John 14:2). I believe deep in my core that Jesus means this for us freaks, deviants, and rebels just as much as for the goodie rule-followers who think themselves more worthy. Everyone has a place in Jesus to live happy lives: no moralizing, bigoted preacher can take away what Jesus gives you.

Jesus said those words comforting his followers. He means to be with us all, not just the ones who seem good at it. As St. Thérèse of Lisieux once said: "Just as the sun shines on all the trees and flowers as if each were the only one on earth, so does God care for all souls in a special manner."[6] There is a way in and a place for every kind of person in God's New Life. Intersectionality is in God's parlance: with Jesus, there is a home for you inclusive of all the attributes that make you you. He (or she, if that's your preferred pronoun, because God is beyond these categories we invent) made you the way you are, so why would he torture you for it? There isn't one way to do this. A relationship with Jesus Christ is not merely for the morally upright and societally high placed. In fact, Jesus's choice in friends tells a very different story. Jesus overthrew the societal

---

6. Lisieux, *Story of a Soul*, 2.

order of his time and still does today if it means making contact with his beloved children. Jesus is shoveling toward you.

Part of this is unspeakable. Thomas Merton is a twentieth-century writer many like to bring up as finding Jesus through the beauty of logical yet poetic thought. Part of his journey into New Life in Christ was very intellectual. He read a book of French poetry and found himself in Mass entranced in God's beauty. One of his most notable books, *No Man Is an Island*, details the spirituality he would find after conversion. He said, "Without words, without discursive thoughts, in the silence of our whole being. . . . What is not meant to be related is not even experienced on a level that can be clearly analyzed. We know that it must not be told because it cannot."[7] This book you're reading right now will soon commence with a great deal of difficult topics. Especially beginning next chapter, we're going to talk about how the more nebulous concepts of faith are not, as Merton says, simply "discursive thoughts" or making complex ideas into simpler ones. We're catching feelings for Jesus here, but some part of this you can venture to explain yourself only in your own soul. God invites us into the unknown, into his divine life for us, way out of our comfort zones but somehow, remarkably, still our own all the while, if we're putting our whole soul into it. God gives us everything.

Merton continues:

> But before we come to that which is unspeakable and unthinkable, the Spirit hovers on the frontiers of language, wondering whether or not to stay on its own side of the border, in order to have something to bring back to other men. This is the test of those who wish to cross the frontier. If they are not ready to leave their own idea and their own words behind then, they cannot travel further.[8]

We make things too complex and then reduce them too substantially when we make them simple. New Life in Jesus Christ is a venturing beyond the frontier into what we do not know and what we do not have control of. It is a surrender, yes, but an exploration in another, very powerful way, of the unknowable knowable God who loves us.

Don't worry, I'm not going to flip a switch into condescension. I say this because sometimes we Christians speak of a religion that others don't see. That is, sometimes, we avoid talking about the hard stuff, the

---

7. Merton, *No Man Is an Island*, 270.
8. Merton, *No Man Is an Island*, 271–72.

theologically dense misconceptions that drive folks away from faith in Jesus Christ. I will not avoid anything in this next chapter. I'm not going to sugarcoat these things either; I live in the same reality you do. The same things disturb and drive me to question the very faith and tradition I'm writing about. I won't be handling the rough parts with rose-colored glasses. I won't be rationalizing evil. I, too, don't need the Christ back in Christmas as much as I need the Christ back in Christians. Time to address those things head-on. But once again, let's end another chapter with some prayer.

At the end of chapter 1 I called prayer simply "thinking with another." Let's take that a step further. Prayer is felt as much as it is thought. Therefore, it's a meeting of passions, ours toward God and God's passion for us. That's where the electricity of prayer really is. When we can really sense the intersection of ourselves and another, our intimate self and God's infinite love, the power of prayer is felt. Admittedly, the Second Man prayer was a lot for the end of the first chapter; but as we go on here, you'll see shimmers of prior chapters' prayers. I am a wordy dude when it comes to my expression through prayer, but once again, there are many rooms in the Father's house; there are many ways to access the prayers I give you and thoughts you have buzzing around with the conclusion of this chapter. Just remember that the best kind of prayer is whatever is effective for you actually talking to God.

What works is, of course, unique to the individual, but some things all of us humans have in common. Buddhist tradition speaks of the "monkey mind." This is to say, our brains are always jumping around, anxiety ridden or not, from thought to thought. It's hard to slow down and have a genuine prayer experience when you keep making your grocery list over and over inside the old noggin. Half of prayer is just focusing on the conversation you want to have. Prayer can be a calming influence that allows us to clear the landing zone for a deeper interaction between passions. Don't be afraid to rewrite the prayer I wrote or write your own. You've read enough now to grasp some ideas that may be tugging on your soul in different ways. Express them, if you can, the way you know they make sense to you; God knows your language, and he's glad to speak it with you.

The below prayer is just one writing of a conversation about trust that unfolds between believers and God countless times. If we're to enter into a relationship with Jesus that really constitutes a New Life for us, we have to be blunt. Like I said earlier, getting to a frank relationship with God might require deconstruction or clarifying and venting some anger. This is the openness that is required not just to receive Jesus but to receive other relationships. The conversion of our hearts and minds is begun when we talk to God with that personal passion that doesn't hold anything back. Don't be afraid to ask for something or state something to God, as long as you're willing to hear the response. If you're choosing to pray, you're choosing to go along with God—at least in that you believe he's a knowable being you can interact with. Therefore, tell him you've made that choice, and ask for him to do his part. This kind of prayer—supplication, if you will—is as much motivation for us as it is prayer to God.

> I am about to go out and do this, God.
> You and me together.
> I will do my best, but I am also depending on you to do your part.
> I'll need your help. I need you to do your part.
> I am the vine; you are the branch.
>
> **Amen**

CHAPTER THREE

Gratefulness Is the Key to Happiness

Justice Is the Key to Progress

PERHAPS YOU'VE READ THIS far, and you still have a strong feeling of skepticism. Perhaps you picked up this book with a lot of baggage you thought might hold you back. Maybe the idea of "catching feelings for Jesus" is something you can't *really* imagine for yourself. Perhaps you truthfully don't really even want it. You probably have good reasons. Or, at least, reasons that are relevant to you on a personal level—and this is a personal choice, after all. You read the pieces of the first two chapters that spoke to how this needs to be a sincere relationship caught by feeling, thought, and will, and you're not really there yet. Maybe the title of this chapter looks like it could be your final straw in this venture: ah, now he demands I be grateful for things I don't even want! Perhaps this is your signal the time has come to put this one down.

Let me be clear: this chapter is not a scolding rant by the likes of an out-of-touch puritan. "You ought to be grateful" is an argument for religious faith that fails almost as soon as it leaves the mouth. It certainly hasn't been effective in recent times. Indeed, it's true that "nobody heals themselves by wounding another," as St. Ambrose purportedly said. And yet, religious institutions and, indeed, religious individuals so often use their faith as a pretext for wounding others. Naturally, such hypocrisy drives us away from both the institution and the individuals, insomuch as the toxic qualities of their faith wound others. This is not what we are to be grateful for once we take on a relationship with Jesus. We are grateful for the grace Jesus can give us to reform those evils and heal wounds.

Indeed, Jesus himself said: "You hypocrite! First take the plank out of your own eye, and then you will see clearly to remove the speck from your brother's eye" (Matt 7:5).

But more to the point: gratefulness for what? Gratefulness demands an understanding. First in that understanding is that gratefulness demands self-awareness. We have to be real about what we believe and why we believe it. We have to deconstruct and decenter ourselves to look at things with this level of circumspect. Self-awareness requires some understanding about what exactly is true and false about the thing you may or may not be grateful for. Moreover, before we dive straight into misconceptions and destructive scandals within Christianity, we need to talk a little bit about religion generally, on a theoretical level, because let's be blunt: religion hurts people. Reliably, across almost every example, someone is getting hurt when religion is organized and institutionalized. Why is that?

Healing and Religion's Cultural Embeddedness

Nobody can take back first impressions. Nobody can take back traumatic, devastating crimes. Nobody can easily affect an individual's negative opinion of a whole institution, especially when we're talking about organized religion. There is scarcely any reparation imaginable that would atone for some sins. It's important that I don't come across here as if I am trying to make reparation for the sins of religious institutions. Nothing I write here is meant to be apologetics for a negative experience you might have had with religion and a church that claimed to be Christian. Your suffering is valid. The second thoughts it gave you are valid. You are a valid person, no matter what anyone does to you, no matter what that person says gave them authority to do what they did to you.

That said, accountability ought to be a bare minimum for those responsible for your suffering. Ultimately, I can only offer perspective that will hopefully allow you to evaluate your way in it, or discovery of Jesus Christ in spite of it. Too often, the sad truth is Christians are the greatest obstacles to knowing Christ. As self-awareness often radiates from gratefulness, so too do abuse and violence in the name of Christ often emerge from a lack of comprehension of who exactly he (or they, or she, if you prefer those pronouns) is. Remember the fundamental consent dynamic within the Christian God's very nature.

There is a self-awareness in gratefulness that can elevate religious practice beyond its uglier, nefarious expressions. Many of us younger folks who are devoutly religious as adults remain as such because we have found a certain self-aware gratefulness leading us to Jesus. Any follower of Christ worth their salt needs to be able to see how the beliefs they extol have been used for terrible atrocities and deep, lasting trauma. As a general rule, I steer clear of any congregation, even within my own Catholic faith, that doesn't display any amount of self-awareness for the broader social contexts within and without the framework of the community. How are we to celebrate Jesus among us if we cannot even acknowledge the ways Jesus has been used to hurt others? Such a way of following Jesus requires a destructive level of cognative dissonance. Such fracturing of the conscience is opposed to the gospel of Jesus Christ.

Before I get into all this stuff about culture as a lens to understand why there is so much corruption and . . . for lack of a better term, failures of humanity among religious leadership, let me just make clear: accountability followed by reparation, reconciliation, and reform is what is needed. When evil happens, particularly by way of those in positions of power, it is always a sin against the *imago Dei*, the very image of God we are made in light of. I make no defense for abusers and their enablers: I think, generally speaking, they haven't been held to account nearly as much as they need to be for the process of healing to properly unfold. This process for healing is much akin to the cycle of New Life, as it has the power to bring New Life to communities of faith just as it renews us on a personal level.

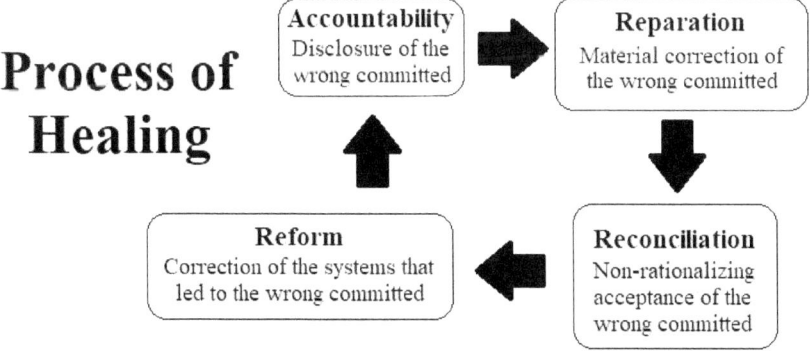

Figure 5: Process of Healing Chart

With any individual or institution, but especially with religious institutions, every step on this process must not only be accomplished but allowed to continue. Each part of this process lends itself to the cycle continuing where necessary. Enablers, not just culprits, need to go through this process as well in order to properly achieve the healing Jesus truly calls us to. Moreover, the way we talk about religious institutions needs to change. The era of the people of God defending the Church from scandal is over; the era of the Church protecting the people of God from the Church is at hand.

In spite of what you may have been told, religious institutions shouldn't be held as inherently sympathetic. Religion is more predisposed to bigotry and oppression than perhaps anything short of mob rule itself. I know that might sound odd coming from someone who literally worked in a Church and is now writing a religious book, but bear with me here. Churches, especially ones that represent the religious majority population of a given region or nation, rarely deserve your benefit of the doubt. That's not because they are always as a rule going to commit abuse, violence, and other crimes; it's because religion will always carry with it the cultural eminence that is attributed to it, both within and without. In other words, cultural clout can and frequently does fracture the real mission of religious faith. Power corrupts us because we're human, and that doesn't stop at those wearing clerics. That fact leads to the aforementioned cognitive dissonance, which allows the conscience to be fractured into rationalizing the doing of truly horrific evils.

Fracturing the conscience happens on the part of individuals and whole institutions when such a cognitive dissonance spreads among clergy and laypeople alike. This is particularly harmful to perceptions of religious groups and religious people because it leads the uninitiated to question whether Jesus Christ can form our consciences well, if they're so often fractured like this. I've seen my lifelong coreligionists leave the faith as they struggle to look at clergymen, wondering, "What did he know when?" Our lapsed coreligionists are right in that it would seem there are multiple people not taking the faith seriously, as to let many abuses in church environments happen. This can lead to a catastrophic chain of abdicating responsibility in our churches. Several clergy and laypeople alike need to simultaneously fail to take Jesus seriously in order to commit the big and little evils the church commits. How does this happen?

Religion is always culturally embedded. Within each religion, there always exists a perspective of believers rooted in where they are culturally and historically. For better or worse, the time and place of culture heavily influence what exactly we practice about our faith or de-emphasize about our faith. This is a crucial thing to understand about religion. The deeper truths that may or may not exist within them may not match up with the actual lived practice of said faith. This is how many "Christian" churches exist that don't look much like Jesus or his message at all: cultural mores often override actual canonical beliefs. This is also why you often see the most heinous crimes committed by religious groups within countries and regions where they are the dominant religious group. Cultural privilege will often fracture the conscience with the seductive hammer of power.

Sometimes, religion is so embedded in the culture that it's hard to tell where the religion ends and where the culture begins. Sometimes, history conspires to say more about religion than the religions in question could ever say about themselves. One example of this is much of the countryside in Spain, where many rural Spaniards express hostility toward the Catholic Church due to its siding with dictator Francisco Franco in that nation's civil war. An even more contemporary, relevant example is the residential schools forced upon the native peoples of North America. Starting in the 1800s up until as recently as the 1990s, the governments of the U.S. and Canada built up institutions designed to erase the culture of indigenous children and enculturate them with Anglo-European values and social norms after forcibly taking them from their families. Not only did these schools abuse these children, but this practice failed to give the children meaningful skills to survive in the colonizing society and caused generational trauma, if it didn't outright kill them, as it often did. Religious institutions, including, if not especially, my own Catholic Church, participated in this evil institution because they existed in the cultural framework of the colonizing governments, so that, in the interest of power, they allowed their consciences to be fractured.

"It was a different time" does not atone for these evils. There is no easy reconciliation for atrocities like this. Healing is hard at this scale, but it's truly shameful when not even one part of the process of healing is attempted. Historical contexts clarify a lot here, and the dynamics of cultural change over time, but I won't lose the lead here: the culture of a specific time and place doesn't justify evil. Nobody gets a mulligan for being a Christian when atrocity x was happening and turning a blind eye to it, just because it was a normal thing at the time. If you believe in the timeless gospel message of Jesus Christ, you have to cut through the false cultural ideologies of your time—racism, sexism, ageism, all the social sins that fracture the connection between each other as much as the connection between us and God. It's hard to view yourself outside your spot in history, but that's what avoiding evils like this requires of us. This is why Jesus's gospel message is timeless: because if we apply it to a time and place, we see how we need to do the right thing here and now. God speaks in and to all times and places.

And there is no hierarchy of grief here. Jesus weeps for the victims of systemic violence just as he weeps for the martyrs and saints. We'll get into this more later on, but know that Jesus is more visible to the eyes of the oppressed than those in high places precisely because he is a victim himself of all our sins, which had their final divine atonement in him. He came to us via a low, oppressed place. He weeps because he knows the agony of injustice and yearns so vigorously to heal it with us and heal us as a society of human persons.

Religion is always a force within broader cultural frameworks. There is always a lot of evil that can come from that. I just gave one big example relevant to where I live, but to rattle off the myriad routes of corruption and abuse that exist in religion would tire the most dedicated historian. They're too numerous and horrible to encapsulate here. Certain religious attitudes by majority churches, and certainly even some minority ones, can often traffic in the toxic fuel of guilt and the otherizing of out-groups who don't conform. Cultural eminence can fracture the conscience of religion, and religion can be used by the culture as a weapon against outsiders. Both lead to abhorrent things. Sometimes, it's as simple as an unequal power dynamic being used to hurt the vulnerable. Many victims of the sex abuse crisis in the Catholic Church were young or otherwise in a subservient place to a predator who groomed them for abuse, making them feel special for being seen by this person of exalted status.

With the sex abuse crisis, we've all seen the failings of the Church laid bare: cover-ups, half-measure solutions, and the worst kinds of institutional failure, all conspiring toward abuse of the vulnerable. Don't let me understate this. This is not just a failure of some corrupt "blue cone of silence" culture among the Catholic hierarchy; this is a reminder that no matter what position those who call themselves Christian hold in a society, they have to be held to the highest scrutiny. We can't protect our churches from scandal as to further support the violence of abuse. We can't look away from our sins; we have to face them head-on, atone for them in doing the actual work or reparation and reconciliation as far as it is possible, and make it a means to become more like Christ. That all starts with being there for the victims. This particular evil requires more than institutional fixes and apologies from bishops on fine parchment. This ongoing scandal requires a reshaping of how Catholic leadership is envisioned and will exist going forward, when it comes to accountability.

Certainly, every place touched by this massive tragedy needs justice. The victims of this nightmare need justice and healing in the fullest possible ways. Nobody who seriously reaches toward following the will of God and imitating the example of Jesus Christ can turn away from a sin of this magnitude. When we looked at the two broad themes of the Bible last chapter—the sin of idolatry and the sin of oppression of the poor and marginalized—we see how both of those core principles within God's revelation to us are violated. The marginalized victim of abuse is being oppressed as their consent is violated, and then the idol of power is used as an excuse to cover up those evils in pursuit of "not bringing scandal upon the Church." Few things are more abhorrent perversions of the gospel than rationalizing abuse in the name of the church of Christ. Religious devotion should not prompt any serious follower of Jesus Christ to participate in cover-ups or abandon the intuition as part of a healthy, formed conscience to hold wrongdoers accountable.

That intuition to hold wrongdoers accountable does not stop at the church doors, and in that acute call to justice is a Christian message: justice is the key to progress. For my fellow Catholics wishing to put this crisis behind us: please don't turn a blind eye to victims because, indeed, justice is the only key to progress with this crisis. We have to reconnect with the meaning of justice in a new way. Gratefulness is the key to happiness, and justice is the key to progress—like two sides of the same coin. We have to be clear in any discussion of institutional sin that what is wrong is wrong, no matter what kind of hat one has attained. Culture change in this respect is desperately needed as a matter of justice and doing right by the gospel of Jesus Christ, if not by basic human decency.

Needless to say, I don't think the evils done in the name of Jesus Christ would ever be condoned by the guy himself. Say what you will about the world of the first century Jesus lived in, Jesus's message was love for God and neighbor. It's fundamentally a moving from self-centeredness to self-gift; the preacher of that message always needs to pay attention to be a liberator, not an oppressor. The true preacher of that message never abuses, only empowers. That message is eternal and doesn't lend itself, in its true form, to institutional evil and injustice. These perpetrators with their fractured consciences treat the deposit of faith within Christian belief as a mere treasure to be protected, a museum to be guarded, not any living good to hold them accountable.

I will be coming back to the sex abuse crisis, particularly in chapter 6, because I do believe it uniquely contributes to a crisis in Christianity in our time. For people my age, we've really only ever known the Church in this state of crisis. If I as the author of this book am going to do any kind of justice with this, I have to reflect on it in multiple places along the journey here. I have to decenter my own experience and look through the eyes of those harmed by it all as much as I can. Guilt is somehow lacking from too many of us who support this Church—and knowing how guilt is helpful, not hurtful, in the reconciliation process is important for us to understand, if we expect others to feel guilty for the actually terrible things they do. One might ask: if Christian faith is all about forgiveness, how does guilt factor in?

Guilt in regard to anything Catholic is a bit comedic because we're well acquainted with this concept of "Catholic guilt." The family I grew up in wasn't that religious, so, honestly, I feel like I missed out when all my coreligionists get talking about their Catholic guilt. That concept is a unique case study in just how cultural religion always is. I went on a pilgrimage to Kenya in 2013 with several other members of my parish in support of a priest from there who had served in our community. Among other things, the experience reoriented my cultural compass when it comes to the spirituality of guilt and holiness. "Catholic guilt," an overly scrupulous conscience that insists on one's own sinfulness, was not something I detected much of amongst the Kenyan Catholics I encountered. Religion in their lives was a source of resplendent joy, and guilt was a passing movement of the conscience toward God, away from fracture. In the Catholic world, one does not need to look far to see where the Church is growing and shrinking and its direct connection to the cultural attitudes in those places. Turns out, perhaps unsurprisingly, that cultural contexts that cause religion to be driven by moralizing legalism and conformity don't readily attract new people.

"Catholic guilt" abounds in the English-speaking world (Anglosphere) with its associated expressions of Catholic faith that now seem to be shrinking in adherents; while Latin America, Africa, and East Asia see their Catholic populations growing, in part because the guilt associated with Catholicism is not culturally moored to them the same way. Scandal and institutional evil of fractured consciences are easier to heal and hold accountable when your whole cultural lens for your faith isn't bound up in a misplaced guilt revolving around who's holy and who's not.

Guilt associated with Christian faith is something that adherents mistake as an external tool, not an internal by-product of a well-formed conscience. Religion by nature lends itself to certain social ills: mob mentality, systemic oppression, and holier-than-thou syndrome, for lack of a better term. As a Catholic, I'll be the first to admit I've seen firsthand how my faith seems to attract puritanical types who want to feel superior to others. Sorry, that isn't Jesus, and guilt as a weapon against others is always counter to any effective telling of his gospel message.

Guilt isn't necessarily something that should be avoided at all costs in Christian spiritual practice. There is such a thing as healthy guilt, when it is, in fact, a properly handled movement of a well-formed conscience. That said, I'd contend it certainly isn't a missionary tool, as those of a more fire-and-brimstone approach would have you believe. We keep coming back to this ugly, un-Christlike dynamic that holiness is some economy of shame and rigorism. Holiness is happiness, yes, but it's the result of approaching God. How can anyone know the truth of your approach to God? Surely, good works flow from holiness, as evidenced by the saints, but holiness is a willful journey between God and people, which is mediated by Church. We should never feel guilty about where our journey toward God is, unless it's helpful on that climb.

But these reminders are disclaimers to the core realization that is lost on us sometimes: Christianity, especially Catholicism, has never been reliant on the relative holiness of its practitioners or clergy. If it were, this book would've never been written because Christian faith wouldn't have survived centuries and centuries of sinful Christians. The Church addressed this problem specifically in the Donatist heresy of the fifth century, if you're looking for an historical rabbit hole to dive down. Guilt is not the purpose of Christian religious devotion, nor is that scolding gratefulness that seems to denote it to so many people. We shouldn't look at the faith as if it's all a farce if ministers *a*, *b*, and *c* are hypocrites. We're believers in Jesus Christ, and priests and ministers are to be servants of him. Jesus was himself fully God and fully human, though preserved without sin. He was perfect that way, and he must have known none of his followers would similarly be perfect that way. He established a church of believers with a mission to spread his gospel nonetheless. He was no hypocrite, but he built a church out of them from the moment he forgave St. Peter.

In all this discussion of the evils done by religious institutions and atrocities committed down through the ages in the name of Jesus, we need the perspective of what Jesus was actually up to. Jesus indicted the mindset of self-justification altogether. In eating with sinners and the people of ill-repute of his time, Jesus was throwing off the kind of religion that needs to violate others' dignity to build up its own. Out-groups gravitated toward Jesus because he gave them a sense of dignity that the religious leaders of his time always failed to. He told them God wasn't exclusively for the privileged, specialized few but was right there among them. He told us that all are capable of knowing God (*capax Dei*) because we are all made in the image of God (*imago Dei*). Jesus empowered and reconnected. He was doing precisely the opposite of what abusers and chauvinists do to cultivate a sense of fealty in their victims. Abusers disempower and isolate; Jesus empowers and integrates.

Jesus was in his very essence not an oppressor but a liberator. If you see a church that seems like nothing but an oppressor, devoid of the liberator Jesus, go there and be that force for Jesus's liberation in that church. To that end, if you gawk at the idea meaningful reform is even possible in the Catholic Church, for example, I'd remind you even in the early church, non-Christian sources like Aristotle were used to develop Christian teaching, understanding, and the integration of all diversity of human relationship with God. This is part of the reason Christmas is on a date that we can be certain wasn't Jesus's actual birthdate: the integration of all people into the love of Jesus Christ. Christianity hasn't remained just a Jewish fringe sect because Jesus made it for everyone. The aim of Catholic belief and real Christian belief more broadly has always been integrating as many people into the family of faith as possible. This involves bringing in some philosophical frameworks and practical traditions that may not have their roots in the original culture of the faith.

It truly makes me sad to see Christians relate to God primarily through defining and avoiding sin, when our faith features the love of incarnation, the hope of the resurrection, and the joy of the gospel, bound up in the idea that all sin is just the lack of something better. Obsession with sin and each other's relative holiness is a cultural bastardization of Christian faith at best and a work of the deceiver at worst. We have to embrace the gospel of Jesus Christ for what it really is: a call to *all* people.

A Call to All People

Believer and nonbeliever alike fantasize about miracles. I vividly remember the CBS show *Touched by an Angel*. It ran for nine seasons in the late 1990s. The concept was basically that one of three angels would intervene in people's lives in miraculous ways. Often, the three angels would build friendships with the human characters, who were different each episode in an anthology format. There would frequently be an epiphany moment toward the end of each narrative, where a character realized this friend of theirs was an angel. There was always a message to do with the divine presence always being with us or something, followed by a light shined from directly above in the fashion of true 90s TV cheese. But the miraculous parts are what made me ponder God more than the angels.

What did it mean that these characters had a miracle done in their life? What did it *really* mean? Sure, this or that about enduring all difficulties in life; but what effect would experiencing a miracle, a genuinely unprovable act that you are told came from the divine, actually have on you? Perhaps this is cynical of me, but it seems like a miracle here or there would actually subvert your free will, as if God were saying: "Here's proof, you disbelieving sinner!" If free will does, in fact, exist, and God is, in fact, the being of which no greater being can be thought, why would miracles be the best way for an autonomous, ensouled being to freely choose God? Yes, God uses miracles readily in the Bible, and Jesus performed them on the regular. But if Jesus is trying to convert and transform our hearts, wouldn't miracles out of the blue force our hand, more than help us get there on our own?

My answer to that question hasn't changed since *Touched by an Angel* was on the air. Yes. There is Jesus's ministry where miracles function as ID for who he says he is, and there are a handful of core, essential miracles for Christians to believe in (the incarnation, nativity, resurrection, and ascension, among a few others); but otherwise, Jesus actually decries demanding signs and miracles, calling it wicked (Matt 16:1–5). It's as if miracles are, more often than not, spiritual laziness when we demand them—an attempt to substitute a real intentional encounter with Jesus for a mere devotional idol. He wants us to choose, he doesn't want us to feel compelled, because he created us to make free choices and established the conditions for a voluntary consensual bond to form. Noncanonical miracles can only supplement that formation; they cannot be our primary engagement with God, unless God specifically leans into the miraculous with us.

This tracks with how Jesus talks about the mission he left to his followers. He sent them out to go make disciples of all nations and spread the gospel of his love and New Life. He forged a mission based on the grateful love of those apostles and those who would come after them. He never said he would take away all our work, only do it with us. The bond of consent and free choice was there from the start. Where the mission fails is where we demand miracles—the toxic inclination to demand miracles and plug in that spiritual cheat code. In that, we become exactly what Jesus didn't intend to establish in the church: just another organization imposing regulation and whatever whim, good or bad, a certain cadre of powerful people might impose.

Jesus calls us all into communion with him, and certainly, he also calls us to be a force for change in the church he established. He knew the failings of institutional religion in his time, and he established an institutional church nonetheless. When we were created, he gave us free will; and when he decided to form a church, he knew he'd have to allow us our own free will again. Why create humans with souls and autonomy if he wanted only robots? As long as the truth of the gospel is in the true essence of the deposit of faith he gave us, the call to all people would be heard by some, if not always the institutional church.

The religion formed around Jesus fails because it is a human vessel of the divine effort to reach out to us. Christ's followers, Christians, sin grievously, as we have from day one, but that is precisely where the voice of God is perhaps the most audible to us: when we fail and sin. There in defeat, our hearts are torn open, and we are able to identify with Christ crucified, if only in dull shades of his fullness. Though the gospel is done great wrong by those who claim to be its vanguard, that truth about who he is is clear underneath it all. Christianity is, at its heart, very simple.

The worship of Jesus Christ, the relationship with Jesus Christ, is with the being who *is* love. God is love. Therefore, Jesus is love, and Jesus wants to love us. Jesus wants, desperately, to *love you*! To love humanity. That is the most basic, sacred truth that is incorruptible by the sins of practitioners and priests. From that, all the other joy of Christian faith springs up. That being who is love threw off the comfort of heaven to become human in the form of a poor child in a poor occupied land. Jesus didn't come as a heavenly conqueror but dropped in at square one, like we all, as a helpless infant. He skipped no stop on the way to solidarity with us.

Over the next thirty-three years of his life, he lived the struggles of human existence. After giving us as much as he could in his ministry, including the legacy of an explicit institution in the church that he knew would contain only in deeply imperfect vessels the sacred truth he embodied, he performed the final miracle of a ministry of love: he was resurrected from the dead, defeating the most primal, existential shortcoming of human existence—death. He is risen! He who *is* love came, lived our lives, gave us all he could without violating our own free will, sacrificed himself so we could throw off our own guilt and sin for a resurrected, divine life in him. That's the grateful thing. That's the life-giving truth that calls us to bring justice to the oppressed and freedom to the captives: God, love embodied beyond all understanding, saves us from anything that could stop us from fulfillment.

The worthiness of any religion or spiritual practice is about the sacred, intangible thing on the inside of it all—not the gross, ugly vessel in which those things are sometimes carried. Moreover, the true power of any religious institution is not in the money it's amassed in its shady bank accounts, or the interpersonal influence of its most public leader, or even the sheer number of adherents to its teachings; the power is in its truth within and the good that does in the world and the souls of living, breathing human beings, struggling everyday with life and its vulnerabilities. This is not to diminish the wrong done in the name of the sacred truth within but only to clarify how sticking by that sacred truth is worth it, even if the institutions that surround it are, very bluntly, not worth it.

Once again, let's make these high-minded beliefs practical. If we are to follow Jesus in spite of the sins committed in his name—a massive step all its own, particularly for those touched by said sins—we need to ask ourselves to look critically at our current time and place: what trends are we adopting now that will be a source of pain and repentance in one hundred years? Every religious atrocity we can list is an example of the devoted embracing a false ideology uncritically, whether that be racism, sexism, homophobia, or any number of social sins. Often, some feature of their own time and place is used to justify it, what their descendants later use in the cop-out "it was a different time" to ignore the hard work of reconciliation. Belief in a timeless gospel demands Jesus's timeless justice: penance (reparation) and liberation. How many evil systems might have never been founded had the believers of that day seriously applied the gospel to it? How often do we justify grave evils using our belief in Jesus? Cultural trends must be purified by the gospel, not the other way around.

This answer is the one Jesus gives us, which we often chose to ignore so as to protect our pride, foolishly and destructively.

Speaking of foolishly protecting our pride, allow me to swallow mine. I promised you it was time to address some things head-on, without rose-colored glasses or sugarcoated explanations. I really believe this call to all people we've been talking about is in fact a call to *all* people. That means everyone. Literally, everyone because God created and treasures each of us so deeply. And as a straight white man writing that, let me put my own privilege out there, in recognition of how all people really is all people. I had to overcome my own biases in life to really come to believe that all people means all people.

Perhaps my greatest struggle with my own faith as a young man was my struggle to contemplate gender nonconformity. I went to college for social work and religious studies, and even after that education, I struggled for the language to address the dynamic interplay of cultural and religious issues at work in how Christianity talks about homosexuality, bisexuality, transsexuality and just people who question their sexuality in a nonbinary kind of way in general. Many of us religious people crave the simplicity of either/or dynamics. The seductive absolutism of black-and-white theology is something very appealing for order-oriented folks who tend to gravitate toward such religious expressions. It's a desire for dualism that truly hurts the complexity of religious faith in general. Holy versus sinful, elect versus damned, the saved versus the lost. But I said I was going to dispense with the anthropology, and you probably get the picture already.

My greatest regret of high school was not asking the wrong girl to senior ball or not getting more involved in the yearly musicals and plays. My greatest regret of those years was my crass teenage religious fervor. I lacked the ability to process the complexity of the Jesus who had captured my heart. I skipped along in the mornings, proclaiming "Jesus loves you" as if a pickup line. I know my sister who shared that building with me for a year still cringes with me at those memories. It's not that the message there was wrong, it was the delivery—and, yes, the deliverer too. I still had not yet gained the proper clairvoyance and decency some years later when I went on the aforementioned trip to Kenya. On that trip, I found myself in a discussion about homosexuality with some of my more open-minded fellow pilgrims. This time, I was at least smart enough to be embarrassed by my ignorance and holed up in my room for an evening. In retrospect, it was somewhat ironic that one of those fellow pilgrims from my parish, one on whom I had a crush for much of high school, came to my door in a failed attempt to coax me out of my disconcerted stupor. God can use guilt to show us the way. I say that out of experience.

I could go into how a deeper understanding of Catholic theology granted me knowledge of the complexity of sexuality enough to process these failings later. I could talk about how the united response of the LGBTQ+ community to the otherizing and persecution to which they are subjected may be the best example of Christ-correct Christianity we have in our modern world. I could say a bunch of platitudes about how tolerance and acceptance are virtues, but that wouldn't be clear enough, and there are better voices than me for that message. Jesus loves everyone. Period. And I think those of us who are allies of the LGBTQ+ community tend to have a better grasp on that dynamic. David Rose, Dan Levy's character in *Schitt's Creek*, the best Canadian sitcom ever, in my humble opinion, put it best when he said: "I like the wine, not the label."[1] I really think Jesus thinks that way. Sexuality is one component part of a whole human being, encapsulating the same soul we all have. As Christians, we are called to love, including those some of us have been stupid enough to make a point of not loving. That profoundly un-Christian inclination to otherize anyone who doesn't conform to our specific imagining of Jesus has done damage of a magnitude inconceivable. These otherizing social sins today are what we'll look back on in a hundred years in horror and shame.

Jesus was not one to give you a purity test on the way in. God loves all of us unconditionally, and he certainly didn't create us to suffer by way of how he made us. It is to disrespect our God-given human dignity to reject anyone of good will. My words of fervent ignorance in high school (and several other instances since) only contributed to suffering for those who weren't finding Jesus at any deeper level. Remembering we're all suffering, vulnerable people who happen to have infinite souls and are loved by an all-powerful God who went as far as incarnation to be with us really erodes away the temptation toward bigotry and intolerance, once you think about that any deeper: God became flesh. Jesus was God embodied in our bodies for all their ailments and inclinations. God became us!

Homophobia is a sin for the same reason racism, sexism, and anti-Semitism are: they pervert God's love into a narrow, exclusive club. God's love is many things, but exclusive is not one of them. In fact, through the course of history, before, during, and long after Jesus's earthly ministry, God goes to great lengths to reach us in solidarity and empowering love

1. Levy, *Schitt's Creek*.

in spite of all the toxicity and obstacles that might stop him (or her, if that pronoun is preferred). He's always shoveling toward us, in spite of what those who even claim to be on his side will say sometimes! This points us to just how active Jesus still is in humanity's ups and downs.

As Catholics, we believe in many, ever-more contemporary miracles, not because of the evidenced truthfulness of them but the power God imparts through them as a result. The perfect example of this is Our Lady of Guadalupe. At the height of Spanish colonialism in modern-day Mexico, Mary appears in the form of a mestizo woman (half Spanish, half native) to a meek Juan Diego. She comes in solidarity, reigning love upon the humble Juan Diego and his downtrodden people. Mary even speaks in the Aztec language and gives Diego her tilma, the cloak of the region, emblazoned with her image and filled with flowers that didn't normally bloom there. Whether or not any of this is provable is beside the point: what occurred over the following twenty years was the conversion of Mexico and, in the centuries that followed, the unifying cultural center of the Latin American world. Did the colonizers use this visitation for their purposes? Yes, of course. Did Mary nonetheless convey the good news of Jesus to a whole people in a way that empowered them? Yes, as well! Jesus is at work in spite of the evils also at work, sometimes parallel to his exact work! The soul grateful enough to notice sees God's work through the historical tumult that may surround it.

Just as terrible evils can come from the fractured conscience spread by a dysfunctional, toxic culture, so too can any evil be healed by solidarity from one another and from God. The justice that Our Lady of Guadalupe represented in her very apparent identity, actions, and the results of her appearance to Juan Diego pushed ahead the gospel message in a miraculous way that didn't subvert anyone's free will—only gratefulness that the culture and people Juan Diego represented were seen and treasured by God. Gratefulness was the fruit of a whole civilization's empowering encounter with God on that hilltop.

This isn't a defense of organized Christianity. It's me trying to tell you the religious truths encapsulated in Jesus Christ's message are not rendered null by the sins of those who claim to follow him. Oftentimes, by both the accounting of the church and history more broadly, those who most wear the clothes of institutional religion fight back against the work of Jesus. The bishop to whom Juan Diego went fought him on it at first. If you do not felt seen, loved, or reached out to by Jesus or his church, then Jesus is, at the very least, devising a way to reach you. If some institution is stopping you from meeting Jesus, that's not on Jesus—or really on you, for that matter. If it helps, deinstitutionalize your faith intentionally. Deconstruct your beliefs and look for where Jesus was misconstrued or his true gospel was perverted. Jesus will stop at nothing to reach us, and we will certainly find him if we don't let anything, including maybe the church itself, stand in the way.

Disabuse yourself of the idea that loving Jesus means loving an institution. Even the institutions I believe Jesus founded I am not going to tell you need to be the focus of our love. Jesus is the focus of our love: Jesus and others. And where the love of God reaches us, and our love in turn reaches out to others, enormous, transformative, and beautiful change unfolds.

Consent and the Divine Yes

Important sidebar: what is sin? That word is used primarily by religious people to describe such a broad cornucopia of things that it, too, becomes a hurdle for belief. How we tend to itemize individual wrongdoings distracts from what sin actually is. Sin can be understood very basically as anything shy of perfection. Nobody is more sinful than anyone else because we're all sinful in our lack of perfection. Murderers' and abusers' sins cry out for justice more, but we are all sinners. In that, it's plainly obvious why we're all sinful—because nobody is perfect, in the wise words sung by Miley Cyrus.[2] Pardon the joke because I understand the unspeakably serious side of defining this. Sin is just a lack of the greatest goods, of which the greatest is God himself (or herself, if you prefer). Recall the discussion of holiness from earlier, and one might recall our movement toward God is our holiness. If God is perfect, then one might realize holiness is movement away from sin. We all move that way at different paces in different ways, even if we don't realize we are moving toward God.

Why are we sinful beings? In discussing holiness and sin, we assign so much hierarchy and competition to them that it's no wonder so much of our existence is occupied by painting each other as villains. Consider this Christian belief about how widespread sin is as acknowledgement of what a wide gulf exists between how good life is and how good life could be. We're not talking about sin as a scarlet letter put on us by God but rather a frequent propensity to put scarlet letters on ourselves and others.

---

2. Gerrard and Nevil, "Nobody's Perfect."

That original sin of humanity is not a stain on us individually as much as it is us having to live our lives in a human context where relationality vertically and horizontally is damaged before we even engage it at all. In other words, our natural propensity toward sinning is not a personality failing but rather a hereditary trait given to us by simply being human. Sidebar over.

A contemporary objection to Christianity's core beliefs is why would a God who claims to be love itself require the gory, violent execution of his self-proclaimed son? If God is all-powerful, why would he even let sin separate himself from humanity whom he loves so much? What kind of *evil* divine being would set about such a horrific requirement?

On all counts: *he did not*. Big misconception here to disillusion yourself of: God did not require Jesus's suffering and death on the cross. We as anguished, tormented human beings needed it, in order to even contemplate an intimate relationship with God as a serious possibility again. If sin is just any act or state of living that is less than perfect, then how could we humans, understanding very well that we are not perfect, seriously approach God? If the God most monotheists believe in is perfect, if he or she is the being of which no greater being can be thought, than anyone who seriously makes an approach at such a being would quickly become well acquainted with how far short we fall. Even those of us who prefer the most optimistic views of humanity tend to be acutely aware that, oftentimes, our biggest obstacle to moving forward is ourselves. How does one overcome this proverbial gap of imperfection?

The only answer is a bridge over the imperfection and, once more, an antidote for sin and all its ailments, including right on up to death itself. God did not let sin separate us from him. Jesus is the bridge. Jesus is that antidote. Taking all our sin upon himself on the cross, therefore becoming intimately in tune with the deepest sufferings of human life, he overcame all our obstacles to knowing him and loving him. Everything Jesus does is an effort to unite us with each other and us with him. The cross was Jesus reaching out to relate to us, whilst not needing to do any of it for God's own good in the strict sense of "needing to." God does not require our sacrifice; God did not even require his own sacrifice on the cross. An infinite, all-powerful God does not need and could never benefit from such things. A God who is love in his very essence could never demand such blood sacrifice because it would be against what he is.

That misconception, once dispatched, really clears the path. The God of true Christianity does not demand suffering. That is a powerful misconception that would lead any reasonable person away from such a God. The only real suffering with a God who is love is distance from that warm love. All other suffering can be redemptive. Hell is cold, heaven is warm. With Jesus Christ in the picture, there is nothing separating us from God if we don't want there to be. The cross is the definitive moment of God saying, if you want to come to me, my door is always open. In that act, he single-handedly made all our sin and its alienating effects irrelevant, as much as we would allow them to be. If you so consent, nothing stands between you and Jesus—or each other, for that matter. That is to say, the power of the crucifix is given freely to all but made personally powerful only in those who consent to it: conversion. Consent is always the mediator of relationships in the bonds of actual love. A free gift you have to accept if you actually want it.

Whether or not you are prepared to accept a gift, the thought alone often brings on some level of gratefulness, even if it's just the thoughtfulness. This is how we're converted. Conversion is where gratefulness animates acceptance and growth as people and a society. I use that word in the sense of conversion to Jesus, but many of us are changed like that when we have these moments of clarity that variable a, b, or c has no power over us. Even nonreligious people will report turning-point moments like that. The gratefulness of those moments hints at that next higher vision: that Jesus sets aside all obstacles and prejudices for us, in order to release us from any such repression.

With Jesus, conversion is the inflection point of gratefulness because it's our recognition that our imperfection (sin) doesn't hold us back. All discord properly reconciled can be forgiven, and new life within ourselves and among each other is possible. In that holy act on the cross, Jesus said to us: all that garbage is nothing between you and me. We can look at ourselves and say through that sacrifice, I am forgiven and redeemed to full potential; through that sacrifice, we may come together, knowing we can achieve divine things. For those who might look at the crucifix as an ugly reminder of torture, we can respond that Jesus chose that act as his profound act of solidarity with and expiation for us.

We defined happiness and holiness last chapter as basically indivisible, but let me just be very clear: this isn't the Holiness Olympics. It's not a race. Sainthood implies some striving for excellence, but even then, it is personal. It isn't a competition because God loves each of us and all of us without favoritism (Rom 2:11).

It's also important to know that we are not God's dogs. Some of us aren't golden retrievers, while others are shivering Chihuahuas. Jesus is not some dog whisperer come to earth to get humanity to finally mush in obedience. This isn't positive reinforcements and negative reinforcements. The Christian promises of eternal life and Jesus's forgiveness aren't dog treats designed for exercises in obedience. A dog doesn't consent to anything; it just wants to survive, and human owners often help with that quite a bit. Such a relationship would not be a healthy relationship with God. We don't cleave to him for some existential, metaphysical survival—at least, in a mature Christian relationship, we don't. Fear of hell isn't a sufficient reason for faith; that's just a hostage situation. I'm probably starting to sound like a broken record on this, but a relationship with God must be a consent relationship.

This is not me using contemporary words to rebrand Jesus; this is actually what it is. When we're compelled by threat, that's not consent. When we're compelled by social compliance, that can be just as sinister. If one is not drawn into a two-way exchange of reciprocal love, then it's just performance. In a Christian world today, beset by self-inflicted scandal and terrible sin on the part of the Church itself, what Christians today must recapture is that sort of grateful and loving consent. Holy consent.

Consent is a profoundly important concept here as we go on dispelling more of the misconceptions that keep us from Jesus. Consider the story of Adam and Eve in the garden of Eden. Even if you're not particularly religious, you get the gist of it. God said there was this one tree from which the primordial couple couldn't eat. The reason that forbidden tree exists at all is not so that God provides us with temptation. Why would a loving God even create the possibility for disobedience and therefore sin? Mind you, this story is poetic fiction, though it is canonical; these are all symbols. The forbidden tree had to exist so free will could. If there are no choices, there is no freedom; if there is no freedom, there is no free will and therefore nothing resembling consent. God didn't make us mere objects in his creation; he made us agents in it, with souls to find him. God did not make us to be holy robots; he made us to be holy humans. We humans, from the very dawn of creation, even before sin, had a choice of God—or not. Even at the dawn of our existence, God asked for our consent.

Adam and Eve chose to defy God and create original sin (original imperfection) and so all the terrible things that arise with a distance from God. God didn't create us to sin so he could judge us: he created us to be perfect with him, but instead, we chose a chaotic world where we could feign supremacy over God. Human history is peppered with tyrants and conquests because we have so often chosen to be gods ourselves. Those fundamentally selfish efforts never work because God is love and we are created for love. When we attempt to be gods ourselves, greater than the one who is love, we fail to live our very nature to love.

Now Jesus has given us the safe space to ask ourselves: will we choose God this time? We find the answer to that one in our own time, in our own ways, with Jesus's help, if we so choose to accept it. And now, finally, is probably the more appropriate time to remind you Jesus claims to be the very Son of God, "I Am" in human flesh. He is either the Lord to be worshipped or a true lunatic. His message doesn't really leave middle ground there. Mankind may try to domesticate Jesus and his message to dull the need to consider consciously choosing God and the revolutionary justice that he brings, but he isn't Elvis. He isn't Plato or Socrates with some good ideas; he is God, or he is not.

Speaking of mankind, let's turn our focus to womankind: Eve is not more sinful than Adam because she took the forbidden fruit first and therefore introduced original sin. This isn't a battle of the sexes thing. It's poetic fiction, remember? The order of fruit consumption doesn't matter unless you're looking to justify sexism. Eve sinned and fancied herself God, just like Adam. To be poetic about it, just like Jesus might be thought of as the New Adam, rejecting sin in his humanity and stripping it of its divisive power, here is now a New Eve for us to consider: Mary, who rejects sin and strips it of its divisive power by her free actions.

Mary, the mother of Jesus, is visited by an angel who does not reduce her to merely a vessel for Jesus's coming. She asks how a virgin could conceive a son, and the angel tells her. Mary wasn't a tool; she asked questions. She then gives her consent. Her dignity is respected, and from it springs not only her consent but also her profound life's work. God shows through his own actions reaching out to Mary that nobody is a mere instrument to him. The relative historical truthfulness of nativity narratives aside here; this is unusual in the history of religion when gods are born. It's not normally a consensual thing. The Greek gods often raped. Not here, not the woman to bring the Redeemer into the world. Perhaps the main reason the Catholic world adores Mary so much is that she responds to this ineffable ask with a yes. She certainly feared what this would mean for herself and those she loved. On a purely practical level, becoming pregnant out of wedlock was a death sentence in her society.

She said yes anyway, before she even knew what her fiancé Joseph would say. She said yes.

The importance of this yes is impossible to overstate. Where Eve said no to God, where Eve said, "I want to be as mighty as you over any boundary you might set," Mary said yes to God's plan. Her song in response is a tribute to the downtrodden and oppressed down through the ages; all those who might be considered second-class citizens are lifted up in Mary and her consent in the Magnificat canticle. Mary's yes is the beginning of the realignment between God and humanity that her son Jesus would complete. Mary's yes was the reorientation of ourselves toward love because God is love. The calculus here isn't just poetry; it's practical. It's liberation.

Surely, we are all sinful because we are all not perfect. Surely, we are all vulnerable flesh and bones with a limited time to breathe. Surely, we want to make the best of that time and strive for the closest to perfection we can accomplish lest we suffer FOMO in our short lives. Surely, the closest we can get to that is forgiveness of sin and salvation by way of the ultimate Redeemer, the physical incarnation of the God who is love itself and indescribably perfect therein. Surely, that perfect incarnation of love itself asks our consent in this—otherwise, it would not be love at all. Surely, our conversion to this is our imitation of Mary, when we, despite all the practical realities and what else that may be tormenting us, say yes to God. Sacred, holy consent. Surely, our way to Jesus is the most practical holy consent of Mary.

I think we millennials have a unique perspective on religious faith that has been inaccessible by generations who have seen religion as an institution for the transmission of theological tradition and cultural mores more than anything else. I think we, the first generation truly engrossed in the milieu of the third millennium, are in touch with the existential dread of human existence in a way that has always been repressed. A generation that insistently throws off every repression does appear entitled, in the view of elders who see that repression as a way of

Figure 6: *The Virgin Mary*, by Circle of Domenico Corvi (1721–1803)

ignoring the struggles we all know as humans... but may not easily have an answer for. A lot of that "it was a different time" discourse is often just a placeholder where a better answer should be put. The need for answers to the biggest questions is such a primal human need that it's very tempting to put down oppressive attitudes to mask the holes in reality we don't know how to patch. If sin is a lack of something better than we can think of many oppressive attitudes as the lack of a deeper understanding of truth. The infinitely deep caverns of the soul cry out for the yes of Mary: a right relationship with the divine infinite being of love.

How many crises of existential proportions will my generation have to face down? Never mind the existential religious questions: how about the impending mass extinction event we humans have brought on?! Forgive me for the generational favoritism, but it is my vantage point of history: if we are to be an honest, open-minded generation of self-care, we ought to acknowledge and attend to the depths within. Generational difference can reveal huge chasms in how we approach and relate to Jesus. Just because your parents, grandparents, or their parents had toxic, otherizing beliefs that they rooted in faith, it doesn't mean they were right or that you should unquestioningly follow suit. No, change is God's inevitable variable, and unlike our forerunners, we ought to participate in the change and therefore participate in God's work.

Recognizing such differences can help us grow spiritually and make a better world. Oftentimes, there is a toxicity we risk falling into at the bottom of these fissures between generational approaches to the divine. Intergenerational friendships can teach us a lot beyond just making us all a little bit more kind. I think my generation is the first in a while to really grasp how holy consent is missing from our Christianity and is desperately needed once again at every level. We deconstruct our faiths in pursuit of this component part that has been neglected so long. Unfortunately, too many of us find it missing and prefer not to replace it, leaving the whole vehicle for our flourishing, known as religious faith, to rust.

I really think the future can be bright for a Christianity that recognizes the ramifications of holy consent throughout the institutional and practical levels of our faith. Gratefulness springs from that conversion realization of overcoming what repressions might hold us back, and from that same realization emerges a thirst for justice. Justice is indeed a part of this, too, brewing under the surface. If we are to consent to the work of love, would it be love if it didn't seek to make the world more just? No, we are called to build that just world, the kingdom of God, right here today, in driving change and participating in God's work that way.

But before we take that dive, let's get a couple more misconceptions out of the way. Naturally, one might be incredulous at the thought religious faith brings any positive change. Let's uproot that misconception as well, so nothing casts shade on the route of progress.

Let's Talk about This Faith Thing

Okay, so we've talked about the importance of the relationship with Jesus, addressed the big crucifix misconception, defined sin more accurately, talked about consent, and asked some deep questions. Am I just going to ask you to be grateful for all this now? No. This is about faith. Oh yeah, you were wondering when it would be time to define the big F-word head-on, weren't you? We've talked faith a couple times so far, but the more serious we get about all this, the more incredible it gets when one thinks faith is some dumb ethereal force. All this talk of consent and justice and whatnot seems empty when the faith statements are coming down the pipe behind them, eh? We've touched on this a couple times, but let's finally bake this cake until it actually rises into something that looks tasty.

We often think religious faith demands we make logical leaps that reduce and limit us as fully formed adults, when so much of everything else in our lives is already built on faith. And before we even get into the true dynamics of faith, let's dispel a couple misconceptions. For one, faith is not blind. It can be if you want it to be, but we usually call that gambling. Whoever started saying faith is blind must have been struggling with some things because almost every human relationship requires some faith. Faith is very much able to see, but the blindness metaphor is a fun image, eh?

Consent informs faith. We're talking about a relationship, after all. Faith is informed consent beyond our regular informational capabilities, to try to put it as concisely as possible. Faith is informed consent, sort of like signing a waiver: you fully know what you're getting into in terms of potential hazards, but you sign on anyway. Faith is the belief in things hoped for, in the Heb 11:1 phrasing, but when you consider how many things you hope for in life, you realize how much faith goes into everything. In that, faith isn't a giving up of the works we do in life: it's the belief that they will all be worth something in the end, even if we can only hope for them for now. Now that I spell it out that way, the waiver metaphor doesn't really make sense. Hmm.

Perhaps a better metaphor would be acting on the recommendation of a friend. The idea is that you have faith in someone you know: Jesus. This is what separates faith from fiction. Faith is grounded in a knowable person. *Knowable* is doing a lot of work in that sentence, I know. The knowing I mean is the knowing of who Jesus is and the ability to communicate with him as a result. This is why I can't shut up about this whole thing, the whole pursuit of this book even, being a personal thing. You act in faith based upon something: a known relationship. Relationships are built on two beings being faithful to each other in different ways. A lot like the way we talk about committed relationships applies here. A lot like the love that hopefully inspires those kinds of relationships, faith is hard to explain. But the title of this book starts with "how to," so let me keep trying.

As much as I may try, I'll never know Luke Skywalker on the personal level one can know Jesus. We're talking faith in a person, not in a fiction. But just as with real flesh-and-blood relationships, consent does not equal control. You may turn the cynical lens up to max and call Jesus a fiction. Putting aside the historical, factual wrongness of that assertion, you or I could seek to control a fiction by head-canon—our own preferred narrative or reasoning for something. Luke Skywalker might be controlled by me if I bought the rights to the intellectual property because he doesn't actually exist. I could theoretically control him. Faith requires that reciprocal, consenting relationship, which is simply impossible with a fiction. Also impossible with fiction: free will.

We're made with free will to choose so that we can consent to a relationship, but that also means we can't expect to fully control Jesus either. If you seek to control a friend or a partner, that goes toxic very fast. Consent therefore informs our faith: we've met the one we believe in; consent to the relationship; and then, perhaps unlike most other kinds of relationships, we have faith the one we know has our best interest in mind, though we can't possibly control them anyway. This is tough because we want to control all things, from that natural predilection of making ourselves little gods à la original sin. But this is not something for us to control. We do not control anything if we join without loving consent. God is just the same. Faith is using our free will to have a relationship. Unlike almost every other relationship, however, a faithful relationship with God has existential ramifications that makes those on the outside looking in on said relationship think you're crazy. And that outward appearance looks that way because we are spelunking down into those unanswerable questions, those aforementioned holes in reality, that pepper our inner life as human beings.

Faith is what draws us into the holes that, in reality, we can't patch. Faith goes where it is called in pursuit of the fullness of truth and mercy. Faith is a big component of that adventurer's spirit we tend to attribute to mere curiosity. Let's bring Luke Skywalker back into this again because I am that kind of nerd. Luke went into the literal and emotional unknown by pursuing the goodness of his father. Luke's quest in episode 6 is essentially to turn himself into the most notorious mass murderer in the galaxy in the hopes he himself won't be turned to the Dark Side or simply be executed long enough to redeem Daddy Vader. That is a whole lot of faith based on the mere fact that one is genetically your father. Luke had faith that the truth was his father could be turned back, and he had the mercy to surrender his own agency in order to see it through. All these great science fiction properties have that Christ figure, but not many give such a stark example of the intrepid spirit of faith that is anything but blind and infantile.

Don't confuse faith with certainty either. Pope Francis goes as far as to say "Faith without doubt cannot advance!"[3] Faith is not certitude, and it's not creative license. To think you have to be logically sure of everything in any relationship is no relationship at all. One might consider that to be a kind of intellectual control, if we think we can control all variables about a person in such a way. That's building a computer: fun if you're into that, but don't call it a human relationship. We can't and we shouldn't seek to control each other because controlling someone is a violation of consent and certainly not a true attempt at reciprocal love.

Now I've already said I don't really believe faith in institutions is something Jesus Christ demands of us as much as faith in the doings of his Advocate to us, the Holy Spirit. To have faith in a church is naturally an obstacle in a sincere relationship with Jesus. This is where faith meets the gears of these onerous establishments that so often fail us. We believe in them insomuch as the Holy Spirit Jesus sends down upon his church is listened to and yielded to as Guide of the whole thing. It's not something that needs to be separate from the frustrating political machinations of any institution to be true. Does not every human institution behave in political ways? Church is a human institution graced by the leadership

---

3. *Vatican News*, "Pope Francis."

of the Holy Spirit containing and promoting our beloved friend Jesus Christ, at the center of an orbit of essential truths we call the deposit of faith. What separates the institution Jesus founds from all the other sinful human institutions plagued by power-hungry technocrats is that if it's functioning correctly, it's being guided by Jesus via the Holy Spirit. Upholding those essential truths in the deposit of faith is a helpful way to pick a church, but we'll come back to that later.

Having faith in the ways Jesus might relate to us through an organized church requires something all faithful relationships have: a willingness to go along and believe in the other person of the relationship, as long as faithfulness and consensual reciprocity are still there. The imaginative grace we grant our friends and family when we go along with their hopes and dreams is this same substance. The technical term for this in regard to the Church among us Catholics is "thinking with the Church." When we talk about imagination as prayer, imagination as faith in the Church, "thinking with the Church" and all that jazz, it alerts our modern brain's skepticism yet again. Faith in the context of institutional religion isn't a belief that people with funny hats won't sin; it's faith that they'll do their jobs and listen to the Holy Spirit. That faith will be violated, but the Holy Spirit goes on to lead another day. We only hope faith between people can be patched up and rebuilt beyond that.

This is why faith is not creative license. Some religions are just great creative works. If faith is a component of a consensual, noncontrolling relationship, then faith in an institution is indeed faith that the core truth of the thing (the aforementioned deposit of faith, in Christian phrasing) is true and beyond our ability to control. If there is no mystery, no risk in loving another person, then faith is simply control. As much as sinful priests and popes may be seduced by mere power, that ain't it. If it's all creative license and was made up somewhere along the way for power's purposes, that's not something worth believing in because it lacks any potential for reciprocal love—truth and grace in lived experience. And that exists in spades among faithful people truly in such a reciprocal relationship with Jesus Christ.

Faith runs deeper than creative fiction because real human beings interact with Jesus, the truth, and graces of the Holy Spirit every day and can attest to it. Faith is a lived experience neither the faithful nor the faithless control. The evidence for that is as numerous as the saints, sinners, and communities down the ages who have continued to form around faith in Jesus Christ. The testimony to the truthfulness there has names and faces. You don't make up things that are right in front of your face, and there is a direct line of faithful people who attest to the reciprocal love that they found and often continue to find in their lived experiences.

You may now be thinking of powerful groupthink or shared illusions or confirmation bias or any number of sociological ways to make the case it could all be made up nonetheless. If it's all made up, then the apostles and certainly Jesus himself didn't do well for themselves. In spite of being part of a core religious mythology, these figures all died brutal deaths. Below is a flow chart of what happened to each of the apostles. Apart from lucky John, everyone suffers a pretty terrible fate in human terms. I mean, it's martyrdom sure, but look at some of this sick, sick stuff: Bartholomew got flayed! Flayed like a main course at a steak house—and then beheaded! At first, you're like, oh, James the Lesser became the first bishop of Jerusalem—boom, stoned to death.

This kind of stuff is why I don't understand the argument that everyone who comes to Jesus does so against their will or better judgment. All the martyrs, all those who still today choose Jesus over life itself, are they just doing it for the clout? Knowing the human experience, it's more feasible at that point to believe there was actually some shared, transcendent thing motivating all these people. Are you going to tell me these apostles went to these ends for a fun, made-up story they felt strongly about? Sure, I don't know how much there was to do in the first century, so maybe starting a religion was just a fun hustle. You might even say grief at their lost friend could drive forward a pretty powerful fantasy that, given the special conditions of the Roman world at the time, could flower into the biggest religion of all time. Sure, that could be the case—but now you're constructing a faith statement, aren't you? Blind faith, I might add, given the historical record.

Okay, that wasn't a trick I was trying to play on you. You may be saying, "No, that wasn't a blind faith statement because it was based on real-world information." You're right, now we're starting to rediscover faith! That is it. You did it right there, trying to conceive of an ulterior motive for this lived Christian tradition. You worked with a belief you had yourself and constructed a theory to believe in. Now, if you tested it, you'd discover there are many plausible historical arguments to be made about the progression of this particular faith in late antiquity, but none rise to a more plausible conclusion than that all these people believed in something that transcended all their own lives and (mostly) gruesome fates. Let's continue on this thread because forming theories in the mold of scientific method is a wonderful, divine thing too.

Gratefulness Is the Key to Happiness

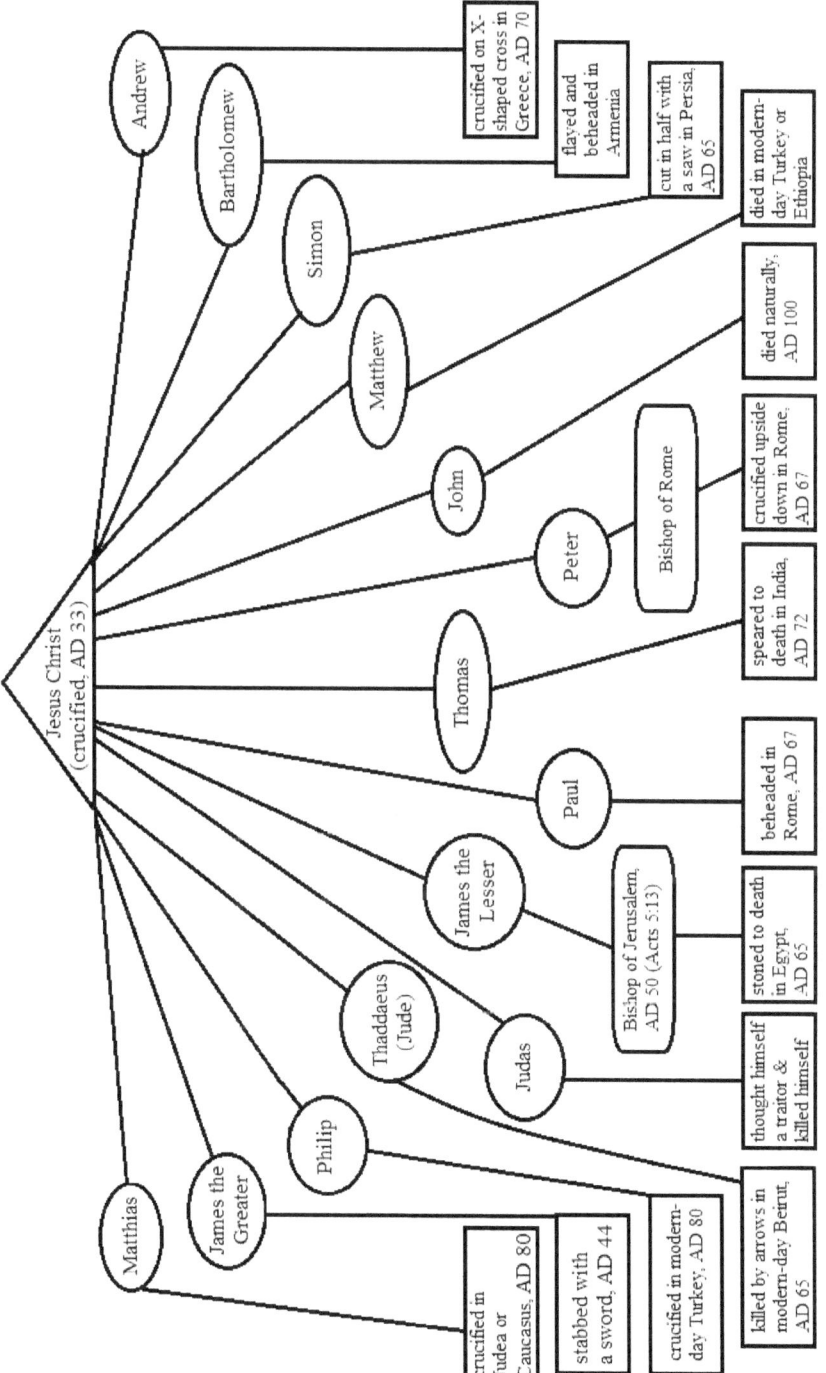

Figure 7: Fate of the Apostles Chart

Part of the beauty of modern science is that it has a really smart way of knowing. Scientific method is a profound treasure, and I mean that very sincerely. I am breathing today only because modern science created a world where being born with a hole in your lung isn't a death sentence. How many billions of people are alive today because of scientific accomplishments? From agriculture to modern medicine, rock-solid inquiries along the testing of hypotheses over and over have created a better world. These things are not to be reduced for the sake of religious faith. Few ideas about religion are as misguided as the idea that technological or scientific advancement is naturally opposed to religious faith. The Industrial Revolution and the modern world it created for us are not forces in opposition to faith or religious life in general, for that matter. Modern science and the scientific method that drives it are not destructive to our relationship with God unless we decide they are. It always comes back to consent. Perhaps modern science has shaken away superstitions that motivate some toward religion, but superstition and religion are not synonymous nor codependent.

I could run down all the religious people, even outright clergy, who are involved in scientific pursuits, but to be blunt, I think that's the lazy way to approach this false conflict between faith and religion. How many insistently enlightened moderns dispense with faith wholesale as superstition and projections of neuroses in order to pursue scientific inquiry as the only way to solve problems (scientism)? How many religious adherents dispense with scientific reasons in favor of crackpot theories that insist that just because God is all-powerful, he did everything literally and only miraculously (creationism)? Some of us do, in fact, use religion as the jumping-off point for some pretty crazy fiction. But TV doctors selling me diets and vaccine alternatives convinced me science can be a jumping-off point for credulousness too.

Turns out, insisting on one form of inquiry and one form only can lead to insanity both ways. The superstitious tendency to look for miracles when they're not necessary poisons the denizens of that pole, while the strictly enlightened are poisoned by their inherent disbelief in everything not subject to the reductionism of contemporary reason. These are two extremes we think are our only options. Far from it. Both perspectives partially obscure the underlying goods they pretend to be faithful to, ignoring that intuitive answers rarely lie at those extremes.

The religious creeds of Christianity are not lists of miracles; outside a core handful, those are supplementary. I don't need miracles to be a

Christian, just like I don't need wings to walk. Dependence on miracles is a sign of a profoundly immature faith. Scientific reason, on the other hand, is not the dogma of ignorance of the unknowable; it is a pursuit in the belief that the universe is knowable! That is very nearly the definition of faith in action. Dependence exclusively on proven facts of physical existence is a sign of deep personal insecurity that can lead to monstrosities like social Darwinism. Faith and reason are two of many different ways of knowing. They are not even particularly different ways of knowing, when you as a person exist in both worlds. They are not rivals. They're not even particularly antithetical, unless we make them.

Just like scientific method gives us a remarkably effective and world-changing way of knowing the universe, so does religious faith. Now, we moderns are predisposed to think of the former as superior to the latter, for some reason. I don't know why. Perhaps because it's much easier from a barrier-to-entry standpoint to think that provable facts dictate all of human existence. Any mature human adult can tell you why that's not true. We have faith the history of the world will trend in a positive direction, though there is a great deal of evidence it doesn't. We have faith our children will grow up in a better world than we did. We have faith everyone we meet is not out to hurt us. Faith is everywhere, and it drives human progress in a certain way, whether or not religion comes into the picture. If we didn't have faith in these things, life would shrink away from us, with little opportunity.

The idea that science will one day solve all mysteries of the universe by the scientific method is a tempting, albeit very interesting, idea. But that idea in itself is an act of faith. Faith is believing the undetected by something you are already acquainted with—hence why it's not blind. Faith and reason are neither opposed nor blind. This is why I mentioned all the apostles' fates earlier. You don't expend the rest of your life running from either mob execution, state execution, or state-endorsed mob execution over some blind faith you have or some shared conspiracy. Such an effort is not worth your faith, never mind your life. You do it because you have faith in the person you know, and you want everyone else you meet to know him too. Just like many scientists gave their lives' work to efforts that their contemporaries thought silly, so too does a healthy faith drive us over the next hill and into the next inquiry, driving forward progress like a gospel of change all its own. You can ask Ignaz Semmelweis about what it means to have faith as a scientist.

Pope St. John Paul II wrote in his 1998 encyclical, literally named *Faith and Reason* (*Fides et Ratio*), that faith and reason are "like two wings on which the human spirit rises to the contemplation of truth."[4] His successor in the papacy, Benedict XVI, put it even more bluntly, essentially saying faith and reason need each other: reason to purify the faith of superstition that reduces us to scapegoating violence, and faith to purify reason of materialism that reduces humanity to mere accidents or sentimentalized by-products of unending chaos. Faith is not devotion to some made-up fan fiction because the originators of Christian fan fiction were just really friggin' dumb if that were the case, and it is not a blind rejection of a more scientifically provable reality. Faith is a relationship to a bigger reality you can't hope to comprehend or control, for sheer magnitude, if nothing else. Faith is going beyond what is known with someone you've met in search of something deeper. Faith is indeed the substance of things hoped for, just like Heb 11:1 tells us.

One more interesting thing about the apostles is they were edgier than you might realize. The whole idea of "spreading the good news" is a very optimistic expression of Jesus Christ, but it's also a political manifesto that would make the likes of Karl Marx, Adam Smith, and Niccolò Machiavelli blush. The classical Greek term the apostles used meaning "good news" was *euangelion*. The glad tidings it would have meant to most listeners of that time would be akin to the messengers who ran ahead of conquering armies returning, to tell of the victory and its spoils. The apostles were in effect saying Jesus Christ is greater than the emperor, for he had conquered the dark powers and death itself, a greater accomplishment than any Roman emperor could ever have dreamed of. Christ would have been, in the honorific terms of that time, a new emperor, greater than any prior. Their faith in Jesus Christ was not the animation of some serene philosophical or religious message; they were doing something very provocative and dangerous in their time in history. It was springing up from a faith in someone they knew, yes, but also a gratefulness to the point they went to their deaths as provocateurs and dissidents. That's a personal calling as much as it is a religious mission. Like we said at the beginning: this has to be a personal journey for each of us.

But don't let me bury the lead here. We're not here just to talk about ancient Greek and epistemology. Even if faith is a worthy equal method of understanding the reality around us, why should I bother with a relationship with Jesus? You have to accept it's useless.

---

4. Opening sentence of John Paul II, *Fides et Ratio*.

Religion is useless. You read that right—I wrote it! Religion is useless, and there isn't even a "without . . . and" coming next. Religion is a useless thing because in our worship we have found faith not in some productive end. You go to work to make money. You build a house to survive the elements. You seek out your life's work so you can die one day, feeling like you did something worthwhile with your time. Friendship, on the other hand, is merely for its own good. Friendship born of extracting a benefit isn't really friendship as much as a business partnership. Love too. It's all self-gift. Really, the whole work of this book is useless because it serves no further end except love of Jesus Christ and others—and perhaps your own general edification as the reader, I hope. Religion is useless, and all the tangible uses we ascribe to it beyond helping the poor and reinforcing human confraternity readily fall into pursuits of the four basic human addictions we talked about last chapter.

Useless things are the greatest things because they are free of agenda and draw us into the stuff that really makes life transcendent, into the infinite depths of the soul. Two best friends are endeared to each other not even really because of the who of each other but because of a transcendent third, which is their shared joy of togetherness. The joy of being together with others is one of life's greatest goods. That is faith. That is what animates true religion: the apparently useless yet profoundly important force of a very real other, uncontrollable being who is known to you undetectedly but very intimately. It's very weird, and that's what is so beautiful about it, really. Jesus Christ, the God of consent, fleshed into our battered reality, is the most beautiful expression of that uncontrollable being yearning for reciprocal, loving relationship with us. It's beautiful in its weird uselessness for us moderns.

Faith is choosing to trust. In the Christian parlance, faith is believing your own experience of God is real. My Catholic readers may call me out for how Protestant that last sentence sounded, but bear with me. Faith is an openness to an infinite God over whom we have not the slightest ounce of control. Faith is believing the creedal truths of the precise faith, yes, but it's also another way of knowing—that is, knowing in the epistemological sense, as well as the personal sense. With Jesus Christ, faith is believing he isn't lying to you. Jesus, unlike any other religious leader, prompted a stark but free choice about who he is. To say he is who he said he is, from day one of his ministry, was an act of faith for those who choose to follow. If he is the Messiah, God made flesh, then that demands our faith and worship. If not, then he is a truly evil man. We punish people who impersonate others for a reason. Faith is a consensual choice, a full-knowledge choice made in something worth believing in. Faith is only worth it when we know who we're believing in.

Justice Is the Key to Progress

And that, my dear readers, is where gratefulness becomes our key to happiness. Gratefulness in this context allows us to contemplate what already exists for us. When we contemplate these things, we see how blessed we are. We also see how much there is left to do. That Second Man inclination toward selflessness may animate us here. Our New Life, our participation in God's divine life, may arise here from our desire for justice in our time and place in history. Once we take an accounting of our blessings, we see where progress is needed. One might call this "checking your privilege" in the contemporary parlance of social awareness. Oftentimes, if you're humble enough to contemplate it, this kind of taking stock of your life and the world around you enlightens the path of justice. This means, on a personal and societal level, that justice is the key to progress.

This chapter comes where it does in this book because gratefulness is the motivator of Second Man and the happiness of New Life in Jesus Christ. It motivates not just the great titans of Christian history but also each and every Christian in their daily pursuits and struggles. In gratefulness, we can see what elevates the people around us as humans, not just other as characters in our own personal life story. We see their dignity, their infinite depth, vulnerable and yearning for complete satisfaction in God. We're all just stinky meat popsicles that yearn to transcend the mundanity of sustaining the meat. If we can't give to each other out of that shared vulnerability, we won't ever accomplish what is of common good: the things that truly advance the progress of society we discussed earlier. Gratefulness and justice are therefore linked. We certainly won't catch feelings for Jesus being grateful for nothing and thoughtless of others. Being second to others is essential to a truly good society; pursuing justice is what that looks like in conscientious practice. In other words, you can't love Jesus and not try to make the world around you a more just place for everyone.

Gratefulness is one of the most obvious indicators of a good person out there, isn't it? Grateful folks tend to be rather honest too. We valorize saying thank you so much because when it's honestly expressed, it actually makes us better people. Saying thank you is my favorite "fake it till you make it" thing. It's so accessible to everyone, no matter where they are in any cultural context. I may not actually be thankful for you opening the door for me since all it did was get me inside about three seconds faster. But if I say thank you enough, I may eventually see the sum of all those three seconds into something notable and worthwhile. The ripple effect of little good deeds like that goes out in all directions and creates a grateful life. There is a level of maturity you reach when you feel inclined to thank those who got you to where you are. For some of us, it's a thank you to our parents and all their sacrifices over the years; for others, it's the thank you to a teacher who informed your life in ways you didn't realize until later; and for still others, it's arriving at a figurative or literal gravestone to pay respect to someone whose sacrifices you never had to endure yourself but for which you're nonetheless so much better.

Gratefulness flows uphill then, eh? It is an activity of first your intellectual soul, then your free will soul, and then the feeling part of your soul, often last in the process. Jesus said, "A wicked and adulterous generation asks for a sign!" (Matt 12:39). The reason for this proclamation of wickedness is that the obsession with signs from God is fundamentally backwards. Unless we're asking for a sign from God out of a genuinely prayerful, spiritual place, it's often us refusing to engage the more complex parts of ourselves. It is often our selfishness polluting our more well-informed prudential decisions. We make prudential decisions, that is, choices based in wisdom and all available knowledge originating from our entire souls, our whole being. Taking that kind of stock of things is a grateful work.

Gratefulness informs our most prudential decisions because it takes stock of why we're here and what here is, in time and space, societally. What is "here" missing? What am I not doing enough with here? How can I make wherever here is a more just and loving place? That privilege-checking or practical introspection plants the seeds of activism, if not the vision for systemic reform. We see through a clearer lens. Suddenly, we find ourselves thinking critically and edifying ourselves and others just because we took gratefulness to heart.

This is going deeper than asking for cheat codes from God in the form of miracles or signs. Remember: faith without doubt can't advance. If we saw miracles nonstop, we'd probably suffer spiritually for it. It would erode away our agency that comes from our free will and make our consent to the whole thing seem less important. Gratefulness for what we can more easily detect in our everyday is so much more powerful when we really attend to it. This is being inspired by God to live an active life toward what we discover as his will through all the realities in which he has placed us. Like an old-timey ship navigator, we have to read the skies and waves for some direction. If justice is the key to progress, that means that we have to read the time and place in which we find ourselves accurately, in order to sail toward what is actually justice. This is a way we participate in God's work on a scale bigger than our own individual lives.

It's working with God in bigger ways through bigger systems and events ongoing in our lives. That's a deep relationship with God, springing up from what may just seem like the mundane goodness evident in our lives. Just as gratefulness helps us love more reciprocally and see more clearly, justice requires critical thought about all the evident realities around us. This is what we might call discernment. Discerning the good and the bad in order to drive toward a better world is the starting point of activism and change-making because it requires us to challenge the status quo state of affairs. Know that this is the way of living with Jesus that goes all the way back to the New Testament:

> Do not conform to the pattern of this world but be transformed by the renewing of your mind. *Then you will be able to test and approve what God's will is*—his good, pleasing and perfect will. (Rom 12:2; emphasis mine)

When you realize discernment rooted in gratefulness often leads to change and justice, it's clearer to see why our relationship with Jesus has relevant power in the world in any day and age. So much is lost then, when we reduce such a relationship to passing signs and sentiments. We like to engage God only with the emotional part of our soul because we think that's the only way to be religious. Just as we said at the end of the last chapter, there are many rooms in the Father's house. There are so many ways to approach Jesus Christ that limiting him to a childish exchange of magic tricks and stunts is rude to him and debasing to you, when you think about it.

Engaging all three caverns of your soul, your intellect and will as much as your emotion, is so important to doing things that matter with our time, energy, and, yes, our relationship with God. It requires some gratefulness because God made us in this threefold way. There is a certain thoughtfulness there that forces us to understand how much we need him—and how much we can be working *with* him. And if that sounds intimidating, rest assured that is a common experience.

It's worth faking it until you make it, I'll say that for sure. I think I speak for a lot of people who have caught feelings for Jesus when I say your initial conversion isn't usually some wild, angelic, biblical visitation in stunning brilliance. It's always ongoing conversion and transformation. I distinctly remember welcoming Jesus into my life as a ten-year-old, saying, "I'll give this Jesus thing a try." Not many ten-year-olds are capable of complex religious allocations, and I certainly wasn't either. Even if you first converted as an adult, you'd probably also concede it wasn't a complex, expansive treatise of a decision at its heart. If it was, then God bless you, but a lot of us aren't dealing with our personal relationships in enthralling prose.

We need God continually to go with us on the journey. We'll get mad at him and even turn away from him from time to time, but you fake it until you make it; and you never really make it until you see God face-to-face in heaven, so I suppose we are always faking it! Well . . . at least, until you catch feelings for Jesus: At some point, it will feel like you're not faking it anymore. At some point, with a grateful heart, you'll realize this is a real, living-and-breathing relationship you're in that is anything but fake. I'll attest to that from personal experience. Gratefulness sustains you along that journey as the flag of the personally relevant element of your hope in Jesus Christ, our Good Shepherd.

Sidebar: a few things about sheep and shepherds. Shepherds don't lead from the front as much as they lead from among the sheep—servant leaders, if you will. Shepherds care for the whole flock, but they also hold up for stragglers and care for each sheep individually and uniquely, learning their little ticks and personality traits. Speaking of personality: sheep also learn to know the voice of their shepherd. They form a bond with the shepherd, even a friendship, if you will. Sheep don't traditionally live in an enclosed space, they're free range by way of a guide—the shepherd. The Good Shepherd Jesus has removed all the obstacles to our consent and therefore removed all the obstacles to our free will with which we were created very intentionally. We're sheep not because we are to follow mindlessly but because our Shepherd has gone before us and made a just society attainable by his own actions, and anything in our way is therefore irrelevant by our sharing in his power, which overcomes the sins of injustice. That is yet another grateful thing, if we can stop making the whole sheep thing into an insult. But let's get back to talking about others: justice is the key to progress.

Justice is truly the key to progress because it demands we restore to right order the balances of our reality. Nothing is more important to God than his precious sheep. He is our Shepherd not because we are to be dumb, submissive sheep but because he gives us the blueprint for justice. Jesus shows us the way gently, suggestively, but not dictatorially. He will always respect our consent, like God respected his mother's consent. Jesus does seek to remove all the barriers between us and him. He wants us to follow him to better pastures. If we're serious about who he says he is, then we must believe he can lead us to a better place—spiritually, physically, communally, and, yes, even globally.

Ultimately, this book is about the personal catching of feelings for Jesus, so this more societally oriented piece is secondary, at first glance. But consider for a moment what believing in a just God (a God who *is* love, as we established, has to therefore also be a just God, by logical extension) means for how we express ourselves to others. Being second is not just a spiritual act; it's an act of justice. Embracing God's divine life, becoming a new creation through it, is not simple self-actualization. It's an act of justice in giving the world the divinely inspired version of ourselves. It's an awakening of sorts. Moreover, as we'll get into, justice at the societal level is also justice at the personal level for those of us who do not get to go through life within the protections of some privileged status.

Being grateful isn't just the means to a happiness that isn't always grasping at something superficial; it's an act of justice. It recognizes the dignity and good of others as equal beings made by God. Gratefulness has a way of organizing and ordering our lives around what we discover really matters and shapes our lives, our happiness, and therefore our holiness. This has stakes for society, the more you think about it—not just the stakes of evangelizing the world but transforming it by Jesus, regardless of how much that world knows Jesus. Jesus is always working in the world, beyond the confines of our perception. God is at work through history in ways we can't comprehend but do sometimes catch a glimpse of. Working for justice and the progress Jesus then shows us is our little way of participating in that divine work.

At Pentecost, God sent the Holy Spirit down upon the apostles in what we might regard as the birthday of the church. More than just the formation of an institution and the investment of preaching ability, the arrival of the Holy Spirit in the human story has a social dimension. The Greek used in the New Testament for Holy Spirit is *Paraclete*. The closest English words for this are what we today would call "Advocate" or

"Helper." This is the part of the Trinity that Jesus says will always be with us. In many churches, the leaders will speak of being guided by the Holy Spirit—the Helper and Advocate Jesus gives to us. When they're serious about it on a practical level, this can have very positive effects.

But beyond the material and organizational workings of communities of believers and churches, I really do believe the Advocate works in human struggles, particularly the struggle for sociocultural progress. As we hopefully advance from a more barbaric, violent civilization to a more tolerant, pluralistic one, the movements of beliefs and behaviors evolve in many ways, conscious and unconscious. I grew up in a time where one threw around "gay" as the punchline to jokes. I remember when it was somewhat normal to call each other "retards." Those may just seem like linguistic, pragmatic changes that occurred over time, but how many people's lives were practically impacted by coming into a more tolerant, just society as a result of the attitude shifts that resulted from those changes? Older readers can come up with more stark examples; that was a very mild example compared to what I think the Holy Spirit calls us to in the grand scheme of change-making. Justice is the key to progress, and a big part of this is working with our Advocate sent by Jesus to make said progress.

The world needs to be liberated from social ills by Jesus Christ as much as it needs to be transformed to knowing him personally. One feeds into the other. That is, the transformation of individuals is lifted up by collective liberation, according to the common good. Jesus didn't just save individuals; he fed thousands and died for all of us collectively as much as individually. We are saved together, so to speak. Jesus knew the broader realities of living in the world affected relationship with God. I mean the guy commented on Roman tax law! He wasn't a spirituality-only kinda guy, as if there weren't a societal context for all this. We are truly foolish if we believe the gospel of Jesus Christ is apolitical. Just as faith isn't a reduction of yourself to foolhardy superstition, so too is spirituality not a withdrawal from all contextual framework of time and place historically. Liberation is the social expression of faith in Jesus Christ.

Jesus can be known to even the most destitute, oppressed person; great saints frequently come from such places as Jesus himself in the flesh did. So much of Jesus's teachings are explicit about the exaltation of the dispossessed and the humbling of the well off. He knew liberation from the ills of civilization was necessary to build up the kingdom of God. Justice for the downtrodden people with whom he ate is the way forward to progress. Justice means liberation from the regimes and systems that violate consent and human flourishing. How do we achieve liberation for everyone? That conversation begins with how we define freedom.

Our modern conception of freedom is born of an individualism at all costs. We miss the subtle truth that freedom that leads to justice is not individualism at all costs but freedom for excellence. Faith purges the banal materialism of reason, this same latent individualistic reason that gives rise to a ruthless independence that only looks inward. Justice becomes difficult without a true freedom that yearns for the common good. Turns out, individualism at all costs will often cost another individual their flourishing or their free will. If we cannot move past the zero-sum trap of perpetual competition, real societal justice is impossible. On an outer level, purely individualistic freedom bites us back when it comes to anything that requires us to truly work together. Freedom on the outward level requires us to look beyond ourselves to what actually is needed among others. Individualistic, aimless freedom will never truly be concerned with others without the chance of some selfish benefit to be had in it. In economic parlance, this is called "no free lunch." As a matter of fact: one of the things Jesus was known for was his free lunches.

Freedom on the inner level, in our souls, is a freedom from sin—from the vices that hold us in a state of slavery to whatever darkness keeps us from doing what we ought. This is a freedom we do not achieve by simply doing whatever we may want to; it's a freedom that calls us to excellence. This excellent freedom is more work than aimless freedom. Ask anyone recovering from an addiction and they will tell you the most powerful, life-changing freedom is not the kind that insists we must be able to do whatever we want. Mastering ourselves and looking to an excellence that frees us from vice is the way of Jesus. Outer freedom then requires the work of liberation—the pursuit of justice that actually progresses society forward, freeing others from what holds them down.

Allow me a brief sidebar to call to mind the beginning of this chapter: the liberation of outer freedom that progresses society forward is often not the forte of institutionalized religion. Granted. We need to work on that. And Christian institutions often lag behind the cutting edge of change in recent decades, at least here in the Anglosphere. This is not just because institutional power is seductive to leaders but because innovative thinkers who can push change forward are often not interested in being part of said institutions (often for good reason). Put bluntly: institutionalized religion is a power structure, and power structures rarely like disruptive forces, even if they are rooted in the faith itself. Some food for thought there we'll come back to in chapter 6. Sidebar over.

Outer freedom demands liberation. Inner freedom demands excellence. The addict may be fully free outwardly, living in a self-determining democratic society with a robust system of rights before the law. Even at the fullest extent of outer freedom, they are inwardly subjugated when they just get by for the sake of the next fix. Extreme as that example is, there are broader ramifications even for those of us who enjoy some level of inner freedom. If we are not fully inwardly free, if we do not grasp at excellence within ourselves, the liberty outer freedom demands will suffer too. This is how dictators who pander to religious people, as they often do, come to power: a plea for support rooted in sacrificing outward liberty for the sake of some imagined inner freedom that is actually rooted in selfish pride.

We need to be inwardly free enough to make those prudential decisions that elevate outer freedom for the liberation of all people. If we're enslaved by a particular habitual sin inwardly, we may become resentful and destructive outwardly. If we're enslaved outwardly by an unjust system that keeps cycles of misery going unabated, then spiritual ailments inwardly likely follow. This is why both inward and outward justice are so needed. This is why spiritual crises effect material and political crises and vice versa.

You can think of the saints as masters of excellent freedom, first inwardly and then outwardly in the way their works affect people. They are the freest among us because their self-mastery, their prudence to the point of virtue, enlightens everything else about their life and works. Most great reformers of history will tell you their work required some faith their movement was morally right and just and could actually succeed among the broader society. A moral clarity drove them forward. Prudence, the obviously necessary expression of self-control and mastery, a feature of emotional maturity, allows us to discipline ourselves long enough to wisely discern how our inner freedom might bring about greater outward freedom and therefore a more excellent freedom for all. Prudential decisions, the ones we make circumspectly without toxic selfishness, allow us to see ourselves in a broader context in a healthier way.

Our world sorely needs excellent freedom and its clarifying effect on justice. When freedom just means whatever I want, the lack of self-discipline there naturally leads to myriad problems personally and societally. The contemporary example that comes to mind for me is mask-wearing here in the United States early in the COVID-19 pandemic: the lack of a concept of excellent freedom caused folks to foolishly take issue with something as uncomplicated as face covering. Aimless freedom rarely brings meaning, and it almost never brings justice. Freedom for excellence—freedom for a cause, if you will—transfigures latent individualism or mere bland selflessness into a thirst for justice. Jesus calls us to bring justice to the world. With Jesus, we need to consciously choose justice over selfishness.

I consider the Black Lives Matter movement to be an even more tremendous contemporary example of this. As a white man who grew up in the suburbs, I had to learn about the world our black and brown brothers and sisters live every day and how it was truly different than mine. I struggled to imagine that in my youth, having dealt with little deprivation of my outward freedom. Moreover, in the tumultuous summer of 2020, it was not enough anymore for socially aware white guys like me just to understand the historical and contemporary struggles of black and brown people; we couldn't just say we aren't racist anymore. The deeper need for liberation was not confronting us. BLM was a movement six years in the making before that, and the struggle for racial equity in this country long predates that. Those of us sitting on the sidelines of those struggles for so long had to discover excellent freedom and let go of the myth these racial struggles only exist in history books. We had to find the inner freedom, the inner strength of an excellent desire for a better society, and act upon it outwardly. We had to take the next prudential step into the *wisdom* that black lives matter. No longer simply not racist, we now had to be consciously and intentionally anti-racist.

Why had we resisted so long? Why had we resisted to say those words that seemed so obvious in their goodness to any thinking adult but that so many of my peers insistently refused to proclaim? Why wasn't our belief in Jesus Christ prompting this epiphany for so many? Knowing simple facts doesn't prompt anything without the wisdom to know how facts can be actionable. Very few privileged people will actively look past their privilege, even if Jesus directs us that way. The Holy Spirit actually needs to be allowed to change us, or we're just going through the motions. On an individual level, going through the motions is seemingly innocuous, if not straight-up lazy. When it comes to outer freedom, to the work of the common good in liberation, it is at best ignorant complicity.

Creating communities of faith in Jesus that are truly welcoming to all as Jesus intended is very much an equality issue. We need to be very explicit going forward: if all are welcome, how are they welcome? Are groups *a* and *b* welcome here, even though that will make group *c* uncomfortable? What does it mean to be welcome in a Christian community? Human dignity demands the church be a welcoming community where everyone can feel as one body united with Jesus Christ. There is a solidarity explicit in the gospel of Jesus Christ—the solidarity of truly excellent freedom to which the gospel calls us. All who love Jesus are united to the calling of a unified humanity that respects and treasures the most dispossessed and harmed as much as the most highly regarded. That requires an intersectional approach that sees every child of God valued as such in light of, not in spite of, all the different identities contained within them.

Identity is a worthy lens in discussing the solidarity to which Jesus calls us. When you are privileged enough to struggle to see where progress is needed in society, entitlement and fragility normally follow. The certain entitlement that comes with aimless freedom, not aspiring to any higher excellence, is something I know personally. When we are confronted by how lazy and aimless our individualistic freedom is, we become defensive. Defensive fragility. I know the fragility that lies so shallow under the surface of those who have never seriously been challenged to think about their privilege in the context of other people's suffering. Credit to the aforementioned youth minister Dawn: she was the first to expose me to more complex themes of human dignity in that very homogenous hometown of mine.

Like many things in this book, a heart for excellent freedom, a mind for action for the good Christ calls us to affirming our brothers and sisters' worth, is something "caught, not taught" for many. We have to be converted to the goodness that is equality and justice. We are liberators like Jesus only when we abandon our domesticated versions of him long enough to tune into where he is working change in the world. If you're coming from a place of privilege like me, you discover the true voice of Jesus has some serious surprises ready to convert and transform you anew with every new piece of information.

What most non-white, non-heteronormative people need, second only to how much we all need Jesus, is liberation from systems of ongoing domination by majority groups. Excellent freedom, the freedom found in Jesus, the freedom justice demands, calls us to dismantle systems of supremacy that exist even within our societies and churches. Perhaps an aimless freedom that has no struggles with racialized oppression leaves you lurching toward an inner bondage to unconscious indifference that stands for nothing at best and exclusion at worst. That otherizing drift of original sin towards selfishness makes us indifferent to the struggles we can't see in our own lives.

The norms that build the very systems of our society, a contemporary, second Gilded Age capitalism, for example, were built on racialized structures of exploitation. These unequal norms we've come to expect thinly veil who is left out. Oppressive systems often pretend to have an order to their ways. That order is often simply an *ism*, be it racism, sexism, or ableism. The expansionism of empire always tries to justify why it ought to be allowed to subjugate others. Too much of the world remains built on, and continues to grow on the back of, exploitation of the least among us. It's the exact kind of thing Jesus is talking about when he points us to the least of these (Matt 25:40). "The rich get richer, and the poor get poorer" is not just a cheap saying; it's true in the dreadful reality of things. We cannot have a faith with which we are prepared to comfort only people similar to us. The expression of a truly vibrant faith in Jesus Christ has intersectional ramifications for many different people. If we can't embrace the liberation of others, our faith stagnates into latent justifications for bigotry. We have to go beyond the gratefulness that can make us happy to the realization that justice is the key to progress, which will make us liberators like Jesus.

Aimless freedom needs to be converted into excellent freedom if we'll be liberators like Jesus. Was it aimless freedom that allowed me and my similarly privileged peers to live in ignorance for so long? Perhaps we were never properly motivated to use our freedom for the dignity of others. I encourage everyone, as an act of faith in Jesus, to consider how the privilege you may have had growing up blinded you from the more convicting parts of the gospel message. We already do this when we embrace humility and decenter ourselves to love God and others. For us American Catholics, Howard Thurman's 1949 classic *Jesus and the Disinherited* is a good place to start with some of these themes the privileged among us may have missed along the way. Thurman's text was formative to Martin Luther King Jr.'s theology of liberation. We have to challenge our own privilege, in order to be more truly Christian. When Jesus's gospel is not challenging us and we're living in aimless freedom and arrogant bliss, we are Christians in name only. Too many of those who still claim this faith live it only in name.

When human excellence is not a goal of freedom, justice is out of reach. Black Lives Matter was a hard thing for people like me to say because our freedom was often aimless, devoid of an eye for excellence and therefore of the liberation of others. The examples get even more personal. Aimless freedom can erode good things in our personal lives. Sometimes, even when all else is right, we shy away from the words "I love you," holding them in such high regard for only the most perfect relationships of our dreams. When we seek no excellence with our freedom, prudential decisions become more a calculation of personal risks than anything else. If we prefer cost-benefit analyses over the risk of searching for reciprocal love, we prevent ourselves from finding real human encounters and connections. Love requires faith enough to take the risk, and justice requires love enough to take action.

This has a lot of impact on whether or not we will meet Jesus at all. If we cannot find excellence in our pursuit of freedom, we most certainly will not find justice. If we do not hold the gratefulness in our hearts enough to see the need for excellence, we will never truly see the need for a relationship with Jesus and almost certainly never catch feelings for him. Jesus's gospel grows in grateful hearts, and it often grows branches of justice in souls where it is nourished and not hidden away or pruned by the intentions of selfishness. Liberation to equal justice for every minority and downtrodden group has, is, and will be accomplished through a sense of excellent freedom.

God is at work through historical events. This is not really preaching on my part as much as it is putting a more global face on theological truths. Just as the self-forgetting nature of Second Man seems implicit across separate cultures and places down through the human millennia, so has an elevated freedom arisen at its greatest moments of transcendent justice. Sometimes, we resist Jesus coming into our lives because we envision him as standing opposed to broad societal progress. This is our latent individualistic tendencies manifesting in a toxic way. The toxic belief in a zero-sum world where either God succeeds or I do is simply not how the Christian God operates. Jesus is the ultimate progressive. Jesus is the ultimate liberator. Jesus is the ultimate activist.

The lens of excellent freedom paints all of religious practice in a different light. Martin Luther King Jr. marched with religious leaders and activists; he himself was a Baptist preacher. The dream of "I Have a Dream" was an excellent freedom, not a merely private freedom. As religious folk have increasingly disappeared from broad reform movements here in America in recent decades, you've seen a perversion of Christianity arise to justify hegemonic oppression in the form of the prosperity gospel and the culture wars. Too many Christians across this nation have decided to hide Christ's light away, as if they can hoard it for themselves. We cannot control God this way. He won't be controlled this way. We offend him when we try to keep his message of justice exclusive. It is a spiritual violence to make Jesus an exclusive club. The being of which no greater being can be thought does not belong hidden away behind a fragile, shrinking identity of supremacy. Justifying some kind of supremacy is always a sin against another.

When we open our minds to God as a bringer of excellence *by way of* our freedom, a world of reform opens up. Think about that for a moment. If our flourishing can bring about the freedom and flourishing of others, what other blessings may God be waiting to bring into our lives? Excellent freedom brings about such blessings as God makes us channels of his holy change in the world, lifting up all his children. Our part in this process requires the critical thought informed by wisdom that forms truly prudential decisions. This is a process we discover with Jesus, with some personal discernment.

Our experience of Jesus Christ is personal. If we are open to Jesus, he'll come into our unique life situation and the factors that influence our world views. He changes us in all facets of our lives. Though many in Jesus's fandom can be quite toxic, the source material here is truly excellent. We have to acknowledge the way our expressions of faith in Jesus have been too toxic to attain to excellent freedom. As an American Christian, I have to acknowledge that our churches in this country were segregated explicitly, just as secular society was. Even today, many church communities have a racial bent to their congregations. Once again: institutionalized Christianity has often struggled with the justice of progress explicit in the gospel of Jesus Christ. But make no mistake: justice and progress are right there in Jesus Christ's message.

The justice Jesus preached is the progress for which good societies strive. Anyone with a grateful heart can see we need it now more than ever. We have seen the apex of individualistic, aimless freedom in our lifetimes. When insurrection and political violence threaten us out of the auspices of personal liberty and a resurgent nationalism that pervades every plane of our identities down to ethnic background, racial makeup, and yes, religious conviction, it means aimless freedom has gone so far as to become militant and toxic beyond parody, to the point of active destruction. When our identities become fragile at the empowerment of others we have truly become so engrossed in aimless freedom that defensiveness is the only choice. We have to reclaim the excellent freedom that

Gratefulness Is the Key to Happiness

reminds us we are not our own—that even in an age of glorious self-determination and belonging to nobody, we do belong to a common good.

Let me repeat the disclaimer here. This is not to say the humanist individualism that defined the last 350 years of history since the Enlightenment is fundamentally in error. No, far from it. Individualism in the political sphere has given us truly revolutionary self-determining democracy. Individualism in the scientific sphere has seen the Industrial Revolution morph into a technological revolution and now finally into an information revolution. Individualism in the economic sphere has seen millions upon millions lifted out of abject poverty. Where just some of the collective good—that is to say, excellence—has been mixed in, we've seen those positive trends enhanced and transformed into something even more restorative. The progress of humanity socially is the result of all these plentiful options of the modern world being opened up to us. With that disclaimer in mind, it now stands to reason, the common good can be considered in a new way, and excellent freedom can open our eyes to such a possibility.

Power will always benefit power. It is incumbent upon lay Christians to hold Jesus to the actors of power overt and covert. We have to initiate the change, the map to New Life, and the process of healing, if nobody else will. That's the call of our baptism, regardless of who holds titles. Nonetheless, life is too short to orient ourselves toward cold, aimless individualism. We belong to our ancestors, peers, and progeny, no matter how we exercise our free will in our short time in mortal flesh. Power be damned: humanity is our prerogative, no matter what the state of affairs is when we arrive on the scene. Jesus Christ knows that because he did that with his life and his gospel.

Transformative beyond Informative

Yes, this is a Christian preaching for an emendation of your concept of freedom. This seems flatly nefarious on a certain level when considering the vast body of evidence that Christian piety has not made anyone freer against the backdrop of perhaps the freest age in human history. Granted. If the last century or so of Christian history has taught the world anything, it is that the teacher is rarely the greatest adherent. In fact, sometimes, we find the moral preacher at odds with Christ's message to the point of being a moral black hole destroying the faith of those beyond even the congregations they head. Where the Holy Spirit is set aside for pursuits of power, this is generally the result.

Perhaps it seems nefarious even after the discussions of this chapter to contend that the gospel of Jesus Christ is a force in modern social justice when it is so often used against that end. I see your point. And I would never venture to defend the moral degenerates of our time, even when they occupy leadership in dioceses and parishes in my own Catholic Church. As much as I may have my recommendation about this church or that church, the whole point of this book is the personal decisions made with Jesus. You have to decide what church or churches you think are worth your time and validation with Jesus. The Holy Spirit can guide us in our prudential decisions, and this is a prudential decision only you can make.

It might be hard for you to separate Jesus and his gospel message from those toxic voices who have preached it in your life. To get brutally honest here: it's hard to catch feelings for Jesus and become part of any formalized Christian church without some kind of attachment to a core truth in this. If I can have any impact on your prudential decision of Church membership, if you choose such a route, let it be that agreeing about who Jesus is and what that practically means ought to be paramount.

Those essential truths, the deposit of faith, as Catholics say, are the rock of your belief. If something in the deposit of faith, something about who Jesus is and his gospel to us, isn't important to you or hasn't captured you in some way, you'll never want to get over the issues in the institutionalized church in the first place. In other words, if there is nothing worth holding onto about it in your mind, you won't feel compelled to engage at all. Our present-day false teachers aside, one does not catch feelings for the one they believe to be the bad guy. If you believe Jesus Christ to be a bad guy, a villain of history and modern progress, you'll never catch feelings for him. That's the blunt truth underneath the goal of this book I can never overcome for you. It might be wiser to consider what exactly you need for your spiritual health this way. After you've made that self-discovery, it will be easier to think clearly about what you need out of a church and its community.

Through the lens of maintaining your spiritual health, we might go back to that cycle of New Life from last chapter: conversion prompts transformation, which prompts more conversion, and so on. That process is the change undergirding the explicit call to justice in Jesus's gospel. To attempt objectivity here as much as it is possible: one will discover potential bonds of reciprocal love and the true gospel of Jesus Christ in principal form where this cycle can be seen in motion. To put it another way, places where change is embraced, not fled from, Jesus Christ is there with people who welcome and trust him. When there is conversion and transformation, you can generally see the Holy Spirit at work. This dead giveaway also allows you to better see false teachers who clearly don't have a grasp on who Jesus really is and one or both of these parts of the cycle of New Life. They're spiritually unhealthy in a way that even those who don't necessarily view themselves as religious can see.

The great annoyance of Christian piety and preaching can seem to be the overly ecstatic repetition of axiomatic phrases and beliefs that don't seem externally relevant. "Seek and you will find!" "Trust in God!" "Accept Jesus as your personal Savior!" The preaching of insistent repetition as a conversion tactic has run its course and played itself out for many modern listeners. People who preach this way are increasingly less effective with modern listeners. Perhaps many who have been raised in and later left the faith, as we'll go into in greater depth in the last two chapters of this book, have seen those preachers speak out of two sides of their mouth—hypocrites not practicing the faith they preach. Even beyond the clerics, there seems to be a social disconnect among those speaking from their faith that has turned off a generation to Christian faith. An elaborative failure has occurred, at least here in American Christianity, as far as I can tell.

As a budding young Christian myself, it was somewhat subversive to see the American football player Tim Tebow take the evangelization of his faith to the point of public kneeling and prayers in a nation already steeped in such performative faith. His professional sports career has in many ways become shorthand for Christians in the American public square today. For all the people that googled John 3:16, I wonder how many were actually persuaded into personal relationships with Jesus as a result? We evangelize in our own time and place in our own way, yes; I don't fault Tebow for doing those things. But the societal connections that make the gospel message relevant beyond theology are rarely communicated this way in America. Pointing others to Christ is only half the mission: even if the numbers of those who found a relationship with Christ as a result of Tebow's witness were high, did it galvanize a sincere gratefulness that brought justice and the transformative power of the gospel message? Did the transformative power of Jesus that brings excellent freedom and its justice to the broader world come from these acts? Just based on evidence in the American football world, I think the answer is no.

An American football world that only a handful of years later chased Colin Kaepernick from the National Football League for making a very straightforward protest for human dignity leads me to believe the answer is no. What separates icons of faith from saints is the effect they have. A vast number of people missed the point of Jesus if they found him through Tebow and later rejected Kaepernick. If the gospel of Jesus you spread doesn't lead to transformative love, it's not Jesus's gospel. Real missionary work is transformative, not simply informative. Recall again the cycle of New Life: conversion *and* transformation.

Prophets of American football aside, transformative justice is a calling of the gospel of Jesus Christ. No longer can preaching the gospel of Jesus Christ be a mere act of emotional education. To the modern person—and, I would venture to guess, many of the people who picked up this book—those who seek for others to know Jesus Christ must show the world Jesus according to how he brings a deeper justice into it. The justice of Jesus Christ must be evident, not just the teaching underwriting it. The "yes . . . and" of transformative preaching must go beyond the mere education of ordinary preaching to rediscover explosive Christianity. The gospel is dynamite, as Peter Maurin similarly wrote.[5] Its truest form cannot be easily controlled. Wherever the true gospel of Jesus Christ goes, revolution follows. Too many of us here in North America and Europe haven't seen the revolutionary gospel in generations.

The unavoidable need for reform arrives here. Gratefulness is the key to happiness, and justice is the key to progress; but the modern person will never know either if Jesus Christ is not a revolutionary character for them. For too long, we've domesticated Jesus and sanded down the difficult parts of his gospel message to fit the quiet oppressions of our culture. Many Christians have regressed into an insular defensiveness masquerading as traditionalism in the Catholic world and Evangelicalism in the Protestant world. This has become so terminal that when Pope Francis writes something like "a Church that teaches must be firstly a Church that listens,"[6] there is a vast contingent of self-identifying Christians with crosses and Marian statues as their profile images decrying a socialist, un-Catholic, schismatic anti-pope aligning himself against Christ! All just because he wants us to listen first like Jesus.

---

5. Maurin, "Blowing the Dynamite," 2.
6. Francis, *Let Us Dream*, 84.

So many of us Christians have become so resistant to anything beyond the scope of our specific Christian practice that we are dividing ourselves within. We prefer a "dictatorship of ideas" over anything resembling Christ's mercy. That dictatorship of ideas and the resulting moral rigorism will often blot out the merciful cutting edge of the gospel that actually brings people in. To put it in biblical terms via Phil 2:6–11, a master is good because he knows how to be a servant. What is more Christlike than that?

There is a lot of cultural baggage to be addressed here as well. When I said toward the beginning of this chapter that religion is always culturally embedded, I meant it as a very important prism for understanding a vast array of problems in contemporary Christianity—problems that turn off myriad fence-sitters and backsliding former religious people to faith in Jesus Christ. I know devout Christians in my social circles who would spit in Jesus's face if he were found among those protesting police violence. I also know former Christians who have found themselves opposed to pretty much all religious faith because they can see it as nothing except a force for oppression and justification for institutionalized bigotry. It would be lazy of me to say all of this is simply my cultural context diluting what the gospel message actually is, but if you want to truly get a feel for the true Jesus, you have to decouple those things.

For example, the preaching of the Argentine Pope Francis is remarkably uncontroversial in Latin American Catholicism. He comes from this cultural framework that is much better acquainted with the contemporary social relevance of Jesus Christ. Catholic belief is often the force behind reform movements in Latin America, even if it is also entrenched among the opposition. In much of the English-speaking world, on the other hand, the social relevance of Jesus Christ is one of our greatest struggles. Speaking as a Northeastern American former youth minister, I can tell you the hardest part of teaching the faith was making it relevant for the teens and young adults of my cultural context. Our culture, long exposed to Christianity, is a hurdle to understanding Jesus sincerely because our Christianity here doesn't care much for the true, revolutionary Jesus as much as the domesticated Jesus who poses no threat to the quiet violence of monolithic suburban churches.

This is to say, certain off-putting elements of Christian faith are rooted in cultural biases that got mixed in with the faith. This is always a challenge for organized religion to overcome, but it is especially problematic right now in history. People are literate and educated enough now to connect the dots. Nothing is hidden—or should've ever been, for that matter. Every cultural sin in the Christian world can be rather easily connected to a dogma or theology by any well-informed enough observer if they're looking for contradiction. The opposite is true as well: rationalizing our bigotries with our religion is in vogue again. This isn't simply a result of the information age; this is a result of Christians not thinking critically enough about our cultural biases and where the gospel of Jesus Christ may be outright opposed to them. Context of cultural embeddedness tells you a lot, and it can help you decenter yourself long enough to make an actual prudential decision beyond the trappings of cultural time and place.

As Pope Francis made clear: we need to listen! That is, listening to our cultural context before we speak religious belief into it. If we do not, we are at best informing, not transforming, with the gospel. More often than not, a preaching ignorant of the real dynamics of the social context actively hurts the spread of God's word. At that point, are we doing anything more than giving a history lesson on Jesus? I suppose historically interested people may catch feelings for Jesus that way, but it certainly does seem to be a limiting force on what could be the transformative work of Jesus Christ in a world constantly changing.

Preachers of all stripes, clergy or not, have relied on proverbial wisdom made brief and edible to the point of reduction to absurdity and cultural irrelevance. My public witness to Jesus Christ is certainly guilty of this as well and speaks volumes on my failures as a youth minister. I do not mean to insistently recite another piece of proverbial wisdom as if saying a magical spell. Once again, I only offer my own words for things so that you might discover your own words in a personal relationship with Jesus Christ.

As you look to that next chapter with its similarly axiomatic title, forgive me for being so blunt. I consider it a virtue, though it does render my witness absurd sometimes. We're at a point in this book where we've looked at the external things. Short of discussing proofs for God's existence and the problem of evil, we've discussed most of the misconceptions, logic traps, and peripheral obstacles you may find between yourself and catching feelings for Jesus. This is about to get personal, if it hasn't already. We find ourselves at a point where you have to come to a personal conclusion about any potential relationship you might have with Jesus Christ. Do you believe he is a villain? Do you believe, less starkly perhaps, that he is an admirable teacher who has been used for evil? Certainly, that is historically true. But what do *you* think?

Gratefulness Is the Key to Happiness

Forget about me, forget about the person or circumstance through which you came to read this book, forget about all the ways other people in this Jesus Christ fandom have really missed the point and done some serious wrong. Forget cultural misconceptions and materialistic reductions of faith. For a moment, consider the one-on-one response. Are you open to Jesus Christ coming into your life and transforming it? If the answer is no, the rest of this book may prove somewhat tough. Perhaps you're just not ready for Mary's yes yet, as it were. If the answer is even a tentative yes, then consider how you can make a willful effort to meet Jesus Christ. This book is just a starting point for your own thought. If the answer was a yes before you even picked up this book, consider how your existing knowledge and faith in Jesus may be in need and how "catching feelings" means something deeper than feelings.

If the answer was no, you are certainly not lost to Christ—not now, not ever, really, if you still harbor an open heart. People of good will are never far from God; nobody ever really is. I'll gladly accept your interested no and raise you a somewhat inside look at Christian struggles at this time and place in history. If you continue on in faith now, even if it's the tiniest bit of a maybe, let that first seed of faith grow as it is nourished. If faith in me the writer and unfunny narrator is the only thing carrying you along, then all power to you, just the same.

Moreover, St. Peter, the rock upon who Jesus built his church (Matt 16:18), was a notorious doubter. For the guy always pictured holding the keys for us Catholics, he was a real skeptic. Peter was just some fisherman whose brother told him about this cool dude who called out to him while he was out in a boat. Even after joining the fold, Peter almost literally drowns doubting Jesus and denies him three times the night the guy was arrested! Peter believed and identified Jesus as the Son of the living God when nobody else would, but he was a real disbeliever most of the time. Even if you doubt it now, you can be like St. Peter—embrace Jesus and find what he calls you to in time. Perhaps this book can both inform and channel Christ's transformative power along that way. Dream big, right? And if I managed to interest you any deeper with the headier culture, Christianity, and church critique stuff, that will remain present for the rest of this book and flower again in chapter 6. I guess I'm doing that serialized television thing: next week, on *How to Catch Feelings for Jesus*!

Prayer after a chapter like this requires conversation. Depending on your experience with prayer in the past, you might be familiar with the more rote variety. That is the kind of prayer that is scripted and is as much instructional as it is practical. The most popular examples of rote prayers are the Our Father, Hail Mary, Jesus Prayer, and Serenity Prayer. Those prayers are very important, especially in the context of organized faith, but without conversational prayer supplementing them, they turn into something more resembling poetic creeds—another great thing that isn't necessarily transformative. Prayer that is truly conversational can have a whole lot more personal power in one's life if the rote stuff feels like mere monotony. After all, God wants to be known by us, and if we want to know God, it follows that we might just . . . you know, want to talk about things. There is a simple joy to just talking to someone who loves you. The more familiar you get, the more informal it can be.

Conversational prayer can be words, but I always found free-form banter helpful because it bridged the gap of composing thoughts and saying them out loud. If we believe in an all-knowing God, rest assured he knows what you're trying to say, even if you can't find the words. Sometimes, prayer can be entirely internal, with our mouth only making vague movements we unconsciously produce. Either way, any written prompt of conversational prayer is often just a jumping-off point. Perhaps it's a question that draws you deeper into a chain of thinking you mean to talk to God about. Maybe it's a prompt that opens your heart to Jesus in a different way than you're used to. This is essentially what guided mediations and examinations of conscience are, but we can talk about those later. I'm going to leave you with a few questions below to prompt some conversational prayer. Feel free to tweak them a little here or there to make them relevant to you. Again, they're just starting points. Don't worry if you finish a long way off from where you started. That's a natural conversational flow, and if you've got that with God, that's a wonderful thing.

One last point on conversational prayer: ignore the need to produce something. Of course, we're trying to produce conversation with God in prayer, but part of interacting with the divine is a release—a letting go of our own control and letting God take us where he will. Just like talking with a person, conversations meander and develop. This is hard for those of us who like to be in control; we need something more definitive! But wouldn't it be awful if all your conversations with God were glorified job interviews or academic presentations? If you benefit more from formal talk, that's fine, too; there is not really a wrong way to do this. Just don't be afraid to pick up on a loose thread here or go along with an ancillary thought there. In time, you'll see God guiding those subtle and not so subtle turns in discussion. I journal conversational prayer with

God sometimes, and that can get rather flowery. You will find more fruit where you haven't gone picking yet. Feel free to wander into the next orchard over, if that's where God is leading you.

- What draws me to or interests me about Jesus?
- What repels or scares me from Jesus?
- Has something made it difficult for me to encounter Jesus, which may not actually be Jesus?
- How far am I willing to go to follow Jesus? What might he be trying to tell me?
- Why does Jesus Christ matter to me at all?

CHAPTER FOUR

Jesus Christ Is the Reason

JESUS CHRIST HAS SO many historical and religious names that we sometimes forget he is actually rather unknown. Hundreds of millions of people claim to know him personally, but we know just about nothing about the guy's life between the ages of twelve and thirty. Yes, I know the contemporary understanding of knowing him personally doesn't really require knowledge of the ups and downs of his awkward teen years or his scrappy twenties. But why not? By the time he started his ministry, Jesus was a critic of the religious leaders of his time while simultaneously having a command of Jewish Scriptures to argue with the best of them. He had a socioeconomic spiritual crisis with those who had set up shop in the temple area of Jerusalem. He called the notorious sinners and social rejects of his society as his closest apostles. He flouted religious laws, eating with his followers on the Sabbath and healing members of societal out-groups. I think the personal formation of a guy like that is an interesting thing to imagine, if you can reconcile the whole God in the flesh thing with full humanity.

I think we lack accounts of Jesus's youth not because they were never given but because the leaders of the early church didn't feel too keen on talking about their Savior as having an adolescent struggle with his identity. Mind you, the oral tradition through which much of the New Testament persisted in for decades before it was written down required people to repeat stories and fact-check them with others. Yeah, it's the telephone game, but it's the telephone game if that entailed passing along Superbowl champion teams accurately among Pittsburgh Steelers fans. Folks are going to care a lot if it's right or not—like, religiously! Returning again and again to Jesus's awkward teenage breakup because he had a nagging intuition he was the Son of God probably felt a bit too sacrilegious. That's a shame, but we've got the essentials of who he was anyway, so it's not hard to imagine Jesus struggling with romantic relationships or family life. No thought is a sin, and if Jesus would later walk among and lead a band of notorious sinners, he'd also go through what they go through in terms of enduring the sin-adjacent world of intrusive and confusing thoughts. There's a lot of space there to imagine a perfect God made flesh living in patently human habits.

This theology is clear and almost universal across all Christian faith: Jesus was both fully God and fully human for the entirety of his life, so he must have always had some idea of his mission and ministry. But given what we know now about human psychology, I like to imagine the teen Jesus only knew the mission of his later life as a somewhat distressing inner calling with which he didn't know what to do initially. That would be the expression of the human side of him. In that, he also experienced panic, fear, loss, loneliness, and all those experiences we think are beneath God's awesome, divine constitution for some reason. This thought exercise here isn't an effort to point out how Jesus was just like us in his humanity, though he was; this is to say, Jesus as a perfect divine avatar of virtue isn't always the most helpful way to envision him. Sometimes, knowing Jesus is much more a matter of solidarity through his humanity.

Non-European portrayals of Jesus fascinate me because whoever relates to Jesus seriously envisions him in a way that looks familiar to them. The vast majority of Christian dogma exists entirely to keep all the essentials of who Jesus is universal across all those who worship him; but beyond those essentials is where we can do some of our best finding of Jesus. Consider that devastating passage from Matthew's Gospel where Jesus says he will say to some "I never knew you" (Matt 7:21–23). Knowing someone is personal and specific to us beyond the dogmas. How would you know God? Where he speaks to you in a private way is where our spiritual imagination can take hold and lead us into a deeper relationship that sanctifies us in meaningful ways. Jesus Christ is yours just as much as he belongs to the mosaic domes and authoritative texts. The domes and texts are all in service of one's own intimate encounter with Jesus, really.

Knowing Jesus

In spite of the more intimate parts of the prior three steps up God's Canon in My Life, this is where the journey got very mental for me. We all battle depressive episodes to different degrees, and how you pull out of them can be an inflection point for growth. Long before any of these steps of God's Canon in My Life, I was just a preteen boy trying to know how to follow Jesus. I would sit down at the family computer writing primers on the Beatitudes, lists of Jesus's teachings, and little Word documents I would print out. That "I never knew you" (Matt 7:21–23) was the most horrifying thing imaginable to me. Once more, how do I approach this relationship seriously, without losing touch with the one for whom I was doing it in the first place by becoming legalistic? Like many things in the Bible, as I was embarrassed to admit back then, there are apparent contradictions to resolve, particularly with what exactly Jesus says of himself and how to relate to himself.

On one hand, Jesus calls us to hunger and thirst for righteousness in the Beatitudes (Matt 5:6) while he simultaneously says he comes to call sinners, not the righteous (Luke 5:27–32). Which is it then, Mr. Son of God? General rule of thumb with the Bible: when you detect an apparent theological contradiction, look for the next level of understanding that clarifies it. In Matt 22:36–40, Jesus is confronted by the Pharisees, who ask him what the greatest commandment of the law of Moses was. They were trying to catch Jesus in a legalistic trap in that timeless, selfish, exclusive righteousness of zealots. As a kid, I struggled with that too. I wrote those Word docs cross-referencing this verse and that teaching to get to the root of it all. What was the prime teaching that I just needed to know in order to live right? In a way, I craved an easy legalistic belief, but at the time, I couldn't put that together—and I certainly didn't know why that was problematic, even after reading about the Pharisees. Our righteousness is the ongoing ascent of New Life: conversion and transformation. What young me and the Pharisees didn't get is that the most basic question, the most basic, most important teaching of Jesus, is only the beginning.

Jesus responds with that beautiful dual-sided rule of life: love God with all your heart, soul, and mind, and love your neighbor as yourself. This is where Second Man springs from, but this is also a gateway to New Life that clarifies what exactly we're doing it all for. This is what necessitates a gratefulness that leads to justice and finally shows how Jesus

Christ is the reason: Jesus knew religion, even one built around him, would lend itself to an ever-increasing legalistic complexity that selfish people would use to make righteousness an inaccessible pursuit reserved for themselves. Complicated rules lend righteousness to a band of self-absorbed fanatics. That's true of religion in general. We can always trace the righteousness one pursues in Jesus Christ back to this central greatest commandment away from those who would seek to wall it up. My own journey with Jesus would go on for a few more years, struggling; there is no satisfactory legalism to be had in such a simple core premise. As you can see by the structure of this book, I still found axiomatic frameworks, but this greatest commandment would always keep me away from the legalism I foolishly thought I wanted from Jesus as an adolescent.

Love God and others. The simplicity of Jesus's calling democratizes righteousness. Jesus isn't a monarch sitting in a castle guarded by legions of moralistic fanatics armed with shame and bigotry. Anyone can search for and find Jesus by way of the two sides of this coin of Christ. When we are lost in one of life's pits of sadness and despair, whether or not being there has anything to do with Jesus, he offers us the simple saving truth that he is the reason. He is the embodiment of loving God and others, and that is what preserves us. When I say Jesus Christ is the reason, I'm not saying he's simply the ultimate exemplar of righteousness and holiness—we already went over all those rules dynamics and the true meaning of holiness back in chapter 2—what I'm saying is, Jesus is the one we always wish we might have. Jesus is the ever-present Friend, the loving Guardian, the patient Partner. Jesus is the Mystery by which one can find the infinite grace that sustains our infinite, threefold souls through thick and thin.

I recall a depressive episode following a college breakup, which sent me into at least six weeks of true dejection: like, I mean, struggling-to-sleep-and-eat misery. I had so botched this budding friendship that I felt I would never be enough to find reciprocal love with another person. What pulled me out of that pit of mental anguish was the simple touch of Jesus's healing telling me I was enough. I was enough because God loves me and made me to love others as well. Jesus Christ is the reason because he calls us out of ourselves. In him, we find a basic self-efficacy that sustains us. Jesus says, "I am with you always" (Matt 28:20), as a promise rooted in why he came in the first place. Whether or not we have attained to whatever standard we built for ourselves to feel worthy, Jesus says, I came to be with you as is. That sacrifice on the cross that we needed for validation was the atonement to end all atonement; there's no price to be paid for your worthiness anymore. Look to Jesus, and you can find what you need. He suffered all suffering with us already and removes any barrier between us.

That can seem like an anecdotal answer. Good for you, you might say. You found Jesus and he helps you out sometimes, what does that mean for the rest of us? That's the transcendent question, isn't it? The answer on that more generalizable, relational level is theopoetics. No, that's not the art of writing poetry about God or even theology as poetry. Theopoetics is this idea that because God makes us in his image (*imago Dei*), and Jesus becomes one of us, he is embodied in all that makes us human. Think of it as rooting theology in the lived experience of people, not the two hundredth regurgitation of something Saints Augustine or Aquinas wrote centuries ago. I love me some Augustine and Aquinas, but anyone who has ever had a transcendent bodily experience like catching that second wind running a race, singing in the shower, giving birth, or any number of other things, knows the divine is not exclusively the unapproachable beyond us. Particularly in Christianity, the divine is right here among us as well, in the flesh. This is what Jesus intends for us to get from his incarnation: coming into human form. *Capax Dei*—we are capable of knowing God and knowing him intimately, in an embodied way, at that. We are not separated from our natural state by God—indeed, his grace perfects nature.

This different approach to theology is another way Jesus democratizes righteousness and salvation. Theology, the study of God, shouldn't be just another cudgel for power or argument with which to win a social media debate. A people's theology is the active component of that "I am with you always." If we are to know Jesus, to study Jesus, and finally to catch feelings for him and live a relationship with him, he must inhabit lived experience with us. Let that sink in. This is why we're here trying to catch feelings for Jesus: it's all about a lived experience.

Jesus needs to inhabit our lived experience with us. No matter what the conditions of that life, Jesus needs to be there with us if he'll ever matter to us in any substantial way. What does that mean in your life?

When we embody Christ like that within our lives and the way we look at the world around us, creativity in us is activated by the Holy Spirit, and we begin to see everything a different way. If God is embodied, then he must so intimately care when you are afraid and alone. If God is embodied, then he must care about the outcast. If God is embodied, he cares so much about the preservation of the environment. Another level deeper: Jesus is embodied, so Jesus is hurt when we are hurt. When black and brown people suffer violence at the hands of bigoted institutions, Jesus is hurt. This is theology unleashed and Jesus active beside us, through us, and into the world around us and all the issues it faces.

But again: who is this Jesus? If I am to find such joy in him, I ought to know him, right? Once again, we remember that's a personal discovery, but what are the broad stokes that make the introductions possible? How do we live this embodiment of Jesus into our reality?

My family was lucky enough to go on vacations every summer when I was growing up. My maternal grandfather diligently saved his money to do this every year in order to take us to the ocean, the source of much of his fun as a kid growing up in coastal Connecticut. When you spend ten hours on a public beach every day for a week, you tend to meet people—or at least, I did. Though I've forgotten many names, certain characters stick out. One guy I met on the beach one summer when I was closing in on high school was a real piece of work. He betrayed you at every turn: stealing your wet sand supply for sandcastle construction, talking over you when you said something on which he had a thought, jumping ahead of you to catch the wave just right. He was my age, and in his defense, most preteen boys can be an ass from time to time. But he had a sibling who told me this was his nicest state. That sibling, a few years our senior, theorized that this time with his family at a happy place on the beach mellowed him out long enough to not constantly fight with her and their parents. For a kid who called his mother Mommy well into high school, I found that frightening. This is his friendliest state?

How does someone like that find peace of mind? How does someone like that live a fulfilling life? Well, in this kid's case, hopefully, maturing into a healthy adult helps. And in any stage of life, Jesus is no substitute for a good mental health check. I know Jesus wants us healthy. That said, I've met kids like this who grow up to be crazy adults too. Some ailments are age- or mental health-related. Some ailments of the human condition are with us always. This is, once again, why Jesus says, "I am with you always." Any crisis brief or ongoing is an epicenter for Jesus to be invited in to fight shoulder-to-shoulder with you or hold you close in love.

We monotheistic people, those of us who believe in one single God, we love to cite the ocean as a metaphor for God. You can't put the whole ocean in a little hole on the beach, which is a metaphor for humanity trying to comprehend an infinite God with our little monkey brains. That image is attributed to St. Augustine. The fifth-century saint's metaphor has a simplistic beauty that communicates a greater-than-all God awfully well. It also reaches for a thought that this memory of the difficult kid on the beach stirs in me: we can, if we will, go about futile efforts in life. Sure, we want companionship, we want reciprocated affection, we want financial security, we want respect—but what is it all for, beyond modest survival at worst and grasping, artificial self-actualization at best? Yes, let's ask the existential questions that torture us. That kid fought for sand on a beach in his most happy moments. The sand, which, like so many things in life, is constantly eroding away.

Jesus is always preached to be this ultimate firmament beneath our feet. The rock imagery isn't just reserved for his establishment of succession rules. The one who carries us and forgives us no matter what is the rock who does not erode beneath our feet. And that image can become problematic the other way when we resist change, eh? He says his burden is light (Matt 11:30), but somehow, no matter how much I make this connection between happiness and holiness, it still is something to be attained. It's still a matter of conforming ourselves to Jesus in some ways. The trapdoor to legalism and moralism is always right there, ready to swing open. How do we reconcile that?

I'll just level with you here: I never met the taskmaster Jesus. I never even met the angry Jesus, though I know why some of us know only that one. At best, people think Jesus is an unnecessary moral guide of a bygone era. At worst, he is used as an instrument of toxic religion that heals no wounds and builds no bridges. The Jesus who gives you tasks for holiness isn't compelling for anyone, even those of us who like a good to-do list. People increasingly respond to religious questions on surveys with a shrug of the shoulders. To a lot of people nowadays, it just doesn't matter to them who Jesus is or if God exists at all. The toxic, taskmaster Jesus isn't really what anyone needs anymore. Once I got over my legalistic streak, I discovered a Jesus who wasn't a toxic force in my life. Perhaps I was projecting a bit in this phase of things, but I imagined a frustrated party host. God's anger and any perceived miserliness therein had a new meaning: Jesus isn't dictatorial as much he is dedicated in his hospitality.

Jesus to me became a nontoxic party animal with a penchant for growing the party at all costs. He wants to set things right, and our resistance to him doing this is like us resisting his invitation to a fantastic party. He'll respect our desire at every turn, like we already established; he isn't toxic. He isn't disappointed in us for sinning as much as he just wants to be with us. An adage I heard from someone in this formative phase of my life went something like this: God is your Judge before you sin and your patient Advocate after you sin. The road to the toxic, taskmaster Jesus begins when we flip that order. He isn't waiting to judge your sins. Your imperfections are immaterial to him. He just wants to make things right, and when you screw up, he's still there, looking for ways to build a solution. He's not going to refuse your entry if you don't have party favors or the right dress for this kinda party. It really is a party because he wants to minimize the downtime en route to the holiness that awaits.

With that party host metaphor established, he's also not the Great Gatsby either, endlessly grasping at a distant form of happiness he thinks he needs but never achieves. This isn't a popularity thing. As we established last chapter, God didn't need to die a brutal death on a cross. God, the being of which no greater being can be thought, gains nothing from the heights of our human virtue. Nothing is added to him by human excellence or subtracted from him via our sinful imperfection. He has no need of us, so our relationship with him is just, very simply and profoundly so—a pure gift. There aren't strings attached; it's an invitation, with a free gift included.

He just wants us to come with him in his divine life for us—as in the party. Angry Jesus, the one who flips tables in the temple and is spoken of via a wrathful God in other parts of the Bible, isn't angry that there weren't enough rams sacrificed today. He's not the greedy type. He asks for mercy, not sacrifice (Matt 12:7). He is actually upset that more people aren't coming to his party or, even worse, are obstructing others from coming to his party. His anger isn't for destruction's sake; it's for redemption's sake. If we can take the invitation, we can find a Jesus who we can know. You catch feelings when you are patient enough to take the invitation and go to the party. And this party never ends. You're never too late. The invitation never expires.

Once we get to the party, the conditions for lasting reciprocal relationship are there. A great friendship can now begin if you're ready to say yes. This is where the theopoetics, the embodiment of Jesus into our immediate reality, is more than moralism or legalism; this is how knowing Jesus becomes something intrinsically valuable in our lives.

When people talk about him as the ultimate Friend and Partner, it doesn't quite get to the root of it, does it? The master-apprentice metaphor does become helpful at one point. I think the party has to come before the master-apprentice dojo when it comes to knowing Jesus. But if you're ready to go to the dojo, I think it's time to ask those questions too: how can we finite creatures hope to do what is our purpose in life without any greater understanding? How do we really find existential meaning? How could Jesus Christ answer questions like these?

Jesus as Objective Meaning

The American founding father and third president of the United States Thomas Jefferson had his own translation of the Bible. He removed any place in which Jesus was divine, did miracles, or proclaimed unprovable existential truths. In doing this, Jefferson made Jesus just another ethical philosopher among the many others down through the ages. Jefferson fancied himself a philosopher-Renaissance man, like many of his aristocratic contemporaries in an intellectual period in which the scientifically provable was supreme. We've already discussed faith and reason, different ways of knowing, and the error of domesticating Jesus too much; these are not the reasons I bring up Jefferson's version of the gospel message. I bring up the Jeffersonian Jesus to point out we're not looking for our own individual version of Jesus that fits our worldview; we're looking for Jesus's version of us.

Jesus is not the meaning that ought to fit into our particular preexisting self-image. Jesus is not simply some ethical teacher. He is transformative for a divine New Life when we fully give him the reins of the infinite longing of our souls. Like the rich young man of Matthew 19, we can keep all the negative, programmatic commandments as basic ethical parameters (e.g., do not kill, do not lie, do not commit adultery) and still not truly engage with Jesus in a meaningful way. We catch feelings not just by way of ethical clarity but by conformity to Christ. Welcome to the dojo, my fellow apprentice.

Allow me to dispel the common misunderstanding here once again that comes from our imagining of a default version of God: conformity to Christ isn't about rules. The moral life isn't an end to itself. It is a means to get closer to God and live in the fullness of his love. And when I say conformity, I'm not envisioning the kind that drains us of diversity and creativity, but rather the kind that allows us to learn a new nature, like one learns how to ride a bike or drive a car. God never asks us to be anything other than ourselves, and in Jesus's own ministry, we can see differences valued and diversity used as a strength. It's a personal conformity within the parameters of who we are—that is, who God created us to be. This is how Jesus becomes our reason: we organize ourselves according to his objective meaning.

If we can't imagine ourselves pursuing conformity to Christ, Jesus, like he did with that rich young man (not unlike how Jefferson must have imagined himself), will let us go live the life we intend because he respects our boundaries. The invitation will remain, but your choice is yours. We can go away finding new reasons, other reasons for doing what we do and being who we are. Many of those reasons will certainly be very worthy in their own right. Thomas Jefferson helped found a nation, after all. If you've read this far, I'd venture to guess you're sufficiently curious about this Jesus Christ to learn more. I'd also extend myself as to say there is a deeper level here yet to be explored, bound up in who exactly Jesus is. We can find many worthy pursuits in life, but is that all there is? Let's get a little bit more existential with it.

Jesus Christ is the reason. Jesus Christ is the meaning of life. Perhaps you saw that assertion coming, like . . . way back in the introduction . . . or when you picked up the book. But I don't say that merely as a religious person. I say that as a millennial with our acute sense for existential dread. So much of the world around us seems irretrievably lost. Long before climate apocalypse became the theme of the mid-distant future, there was always that creeping sense within us that we can't possibly reverse some of the self-inflicted wounds of human existence. Hope is increasingly ascribed to the fancy of the well-off or the naïveté of the suffering.

Jesus Christ, God made flesh, is the reason to have hope. God, again—the being of which no greater being can be thought, the infinite answer to the infinite questions of our souls—is the reason. He abolished the gap between our finite imperfection and infinite perfection in him, bringing a divine life—a divine love, in fact! That love shows us that any finite meaning we make up for ourselves is artificial and may perhaps sate us for periods of time but can never satisfy us infinitely the way only the infinite God can. But what does this mean in less preachy words? Allow me to try my hand at modern translation again.

Affectively—and forgive how dark this sounds—we're all going through life surviving and overcoming various agonies. We suffer by way of the self-inflicted, socially inflicted, and even inexplicably inflicted wounds that make life difficult. Life isn't the intermission between sufferings, of course, but we all carry some things we're dealing with. Jesus doesn't hesitate to heal any wound. He doesn't think you're not good enough because you have a wound, no matter how you got it. This might feel like review at this point, but it bears repeating: nothing you do or that is done to you can separate you from the healing Jesus, except your own refusal. Jesus is there waiting for us.

In all this achieving and striving that we often attribute to spiritual life, we risk missing Jesus in a serious way. We make simple commodities out of relational truths. Jesus isn't someone with whom to make a business transaction for salvation. Salvation is the spiritual healing of being reconciled to God. When you imagine yourself approaching Jesus, don't think of a judgmental look on his face. The most powerful way to imagine Jesus is his saying "Of course, I'll heal you" or "Of course, I'll come into your life." He'll work with us where we're at. He'll be right there waiting for you when you're ready, if you need to deconstruct some things or process some trauma first. The most powerful witness anyone can give on account of Jesus Christ is "This is how Jesus healed me." Nobody who is preaching the true Jesus will say there is any meaningful barrier to entry whatsoever, not with Jesus.

How about I frame this philosophically: how can one pursue Jesus in a way that makes logical sense? Start with the famous quote often attributed to Albert Einstein: "Insanity is doing the same thing over and over again and expecting different results." Einstein would've understood how insane it felt to test and test a scientific theory long enough to uncover its provable reality. Many great thinkers like him report some feeling of madness as they pursued some acute principle. What separates the brilliant from the actually insane is a sense of the overarching reason, the theory of all of which they're in pursuit. Einstein saw something broader forming as he composed his groundbreaking theory. With that higher vision, these great thinkers aren't consumed by a finite part of space-time but rather philosophically connected to what they believe might just be an infinite, eternal reality. For Einstein, it was general relativity. In the spiritual way of knowing, this is existential objectivity: God.

When we're consumed with some finite piece of a finite existence, we're philosophically fixating as to impinge on a deeper pursuit of the reality. We'll always be uncomfortable because that's the state of life without an eternal God. When we grasp at an infinitely satisfactory purpose, we grasp at God. If you don't believe God exists, then the highest purpose of existence beyond reproduction and the utilitarianism of mutual aid that branches off from that is an awe-struck genuflecting before our most determinate, materialistic existence, our emergence from base elements of stardust—"the universe experiencing itself," in the words attributed to Neil deGrasse Tyson. That's the positivistic materialism of which Pope

Benedict XVI warned us that faith needed to purify reason in our last chapter—that is, spiritualizing and lending meaning to things that we believe we can control ourselves. This would be the empirical/rational equivalent of believing your prayers make the rains come. You're extracting spirituality from something that yields none.

Unless there is a bridge between the finite and the infinite, the imperfect and the perfect, an absolution from anything that wedges us apart: life simply has no meaning outside of survival at worst and making each other as comfortable as possible for mutual aid at best. Both are worthy pursuits in their own right but not enough in the pursuit of ultimate meaning. If we finite beings will ever find infinite, eternal, objective truth, the source would have to be that same infinite, eternal truth. For the finite, the infinite is always ineffable.

That's kinda abstract. Let's make a funny example you might imagine seeing in a philosophy class. If you had to count an infinite stock of my favorite bakery delight, bagels (bland, I know), before the opening of your bakery, then the bakery would never open because you'd never finish counting. You can't count the infinite by the definition of infinity. I'd also be sad to not get any bagels, since you apparently have so many. This is the most philosophical proof of God's existence and, in my humble opinion, more importantly, the most coherent logical way to contemplate Jesus as an axiomatic law of the universe. Knowing Jesus in this philosophical way requires that Einsteinian drive against seeming insanity.

If God is the being of which no greater being can be thought, we can never comprehend him unless he made himself known to us through . . . an ambassador, in the form of a relational structure we would understand—a son—and a set of religious teachings: Jesus Christ and his ministry. That would be the source of objective truth, if such a thing is philosophically possible. The greatest human society we could ever build is still absent the final, infinite meaning if we too readily separate ourselves from objective truth. Even someone who believes in God and Jesus as his human form like myself needs to emphasize the *if* there. I'm not saying I know; I'm saying I believe. It's okay to accept those are different things.

Yes, we don't know that objective truth in the positivistic, scientific way; but faith is the personal knowing of this truth though we never prove it in an undeniable way—because if it weren't deniable, there would be no faith or free will needed, remember? See, the more you try to prove God's existence, the more you tend to 1) erode the free will of the relationship and 2) lose track of the God who is, once again, the being of which no greater being can be thought. Those two things don't really require a faith statement; they're just the practical truths forgotten in all our trying to spiritualize reason or rationalize faith. They're different frameworks. Apply one to the other, and it's like trying to drink water with a fork.

Once we wrap our heads around that progression, the question moves fully back into the practical realm of how such an objective truth should be taught and lived and who has the right and expertise to do that. I believe there are right answers to those questions as well (churches), but I'm already on a bit of a tangent, so let's reel it back in: philosophically speaking, Jesus Christ becomes our reason for it all when we accept we're not perfect, long enough to accept something that comes from beyond us. This is why I simultaneously love and hate this idea born of contemporary scientific spiritualism of humanity as a semi-divine interpreter of the universe. It's missing the forest for the trees. We're missing the point of our relative size within the universe while simultaneously pontificating on it—that "universe experiencing itself" stuff.

I'm not going to lie to you: the whole "universe experiencing itself" meaning of life is very appealing. I'm tempted to write fan fiction about it. I think I will, actually! It also drips with the consumerism and greed of our time in history: enjoy your time in the sun! Go experience it all! Seems like it could be fastened in metal, gold-foil script above the gates to Disneyland. Who needs a God or a loving Jesus when we have ourselves, merely collections of billions of electrified cells, apparently, to enjoy what we can? It will be so hilariously telling of who we were to philosophers a couple hundred years from now as they orbit a dead earth beset by climate catastrophe because we just had to experience it all!

Sorry . . . sorry, that got dark. That was my millennial existential dread talking. Jesus wouldn't have me getting so nihilistic trying to tell people about him.

The point here, even for an environmentally conscious "your moment in the sun" meaning or a "leaving the world better than you found it" meaning, is that they may give life a lot of meaning by measure of naked rational facts, but they lack the transcendent reaches of meanings that grasp at a sense of divine objectivity. We can all concoct meanings of life in the Emersonian way that attain to degrees of human flourishing and even give us a very happy life. But such an exercise is tantamount to a truly excellent execution of a hockey game or the construction of a masterfully eloquent poem. It's human flourishing. Splendid though that may be, it's just a piece of something that can have much greater ramifications.

It's beautiful but finite. DIY meanings of life are great material for fan fiction, but they smack of pompous and self-centeredness in a way that I think goes against the spirit of that first human spirituality bound up in the selflessness of Second Man back in chapter 1.

Let's set something straight. Our current age of reason can rightfully wipe away all the superstition from religion—and let us be realistic here—religion would still remain. Even if organized religion did not remain, moral objectivity would. If there is a divinity beyond, reaching out to us out of sheer love, it's not going to be scienced out of existence, in the same way gravity will always exist, even if no sentient being is around to sense it. It's the bone within the meat that is all organized religion. This is a broader point about religion, obviously. Think of it this way: we are not the "universe experiencing itself"; we are the existential self, experiencing the Creator of the universe through many things, including and primarily Jesus. If there is any good in religion, then that's where you should go looking for it: in the divine reaching out for humanity and vice versa. You'll find Jesus there.

I'm not normally the "lost treasure" kind of guy droning on about a past that was actually almost certainly not as good as its conceived of. I think that framework can too readily be a pretext to fascism, the sins of insular societies slowly dying, and an inner lack of freedom bound up in some malignant resentments. But when it comes to religion and philosophy in general, really, we've lost a sense of what objective truth can really do for us. We insist such objectivity can belong only to empirical fact, in an act of faith of which the rigors of said empirical fact could so easily strip us if we recognized the illogical folly therein. We rightfully hope for a better world, in a really default kinda way. We've got good intentions, but we're selling ourselves short in such a materialistic way of looking at things.

This false conflict of objective truth versus subjective experience is a little ironic, actually, because has there ever been a time in human history when more regular people can do math? Pure, factual, unyielding math! Nobody needs to prove $2+2=4$, it's just a priori truth. It's the kind of objective truth that exists independent of experience or observation. It's just true, in other words. Modern science built the modern world on those kinds of truths! Imagine if there were a spiritual equivalent to such truth. If such a thing existed, people would surely have encountered it at some point. Spiritual objective truth would have to meet some standards . . .

Let's imagine what a spiritual objective truth would look like to us. It probably would be as widespread as math (consider the social contract and how widespread self-giving principles of civilization and religion are). It'd have to be something with which a great diversity of people have done great things that are also not necessarily religious ends either (consider spiritual figures like Ghandi leading the way to the dignity of his people or Martin Luther King Jr. spearheading civil rights equality in the United States). Unfortunately, it'd have to also have been used for evil from time to time (consider religiously fueled violence, war, and genocide). Spiritual objective truth isn't fiction; it's the operating system of anyone with an open heart for the things beyond positivistic reality. Make fun of spirituality all you want; it shapes the world.

Let's have a clarifying sidebar here. When Christians (the ones who actually know the Jesus of the Gospels) talk about objective truth and philosophical concepts of objectivism more broadly, they're not talking about the stuff of Ayn Rand. Christopher Dawkins types who mock religion are doing more to propagate the worst kind of religion than they realize by reducing religion to superstition and scientific truth to positivistic materialism. That kind of jaded atheism is often used as a cudgel for those preachers who seek to reduce religion to a simple dictatorial moralism. In a way, toxic belief only makes toxic belief more toxic.

Nowadays, that's the straw man of choice: moralistic religion that preaches authoritarian rule-following while wrapped in a cloak of sins that violates its own morals. I'm talking about many of the people wearing the fancy hats. Knowing this, many bad teachers of the faith will use atheism as a catch-all term for evil in order to not talk about the more difficult issues implicit in their own sins. They often use atheism as a straw man themselves to mask far worse sins they don't want to talk about, like racism, sexism, and all manner of bigotry. To call out such institutional sins in the world today would force these kinds of clerics to face how they've reinforced those things in their own ministries, intentionally or not. For them, it's just easier to say atheism causes all the problems in the world today. It's another scapegoat religious folks seem so good at making. It's a very problematic oversimplification, but we'll talk more about ills within Christian churches like this in chapter 6. Atheism is not a monolith of evil, just as religion is not a monolith of evil.

It bears repeating here that you don't need to believe in God to be a good person. Atheism is not interchangeable with evil. Christian preachers who talk that way lose sight of the Good Shepherd Jesus who didn't condemn nearly as much as he welcomed in. I very intentionally am not going to spend many more words in this book talking about atheism as a concept unto itself. It's hard to fault anyone for not believing in God in a world as messed up as ours. The more common, reasonable, contemporary atheism isn't really about fighting religious people. But on the other hand, the kind of atheist that reduces all deism of any kind to superstition or power dynamics is a cynic at best and a different kind of authoritarian at worst.

Ayn Rand's atheism was a clearer philosophical atheism that arose from her worship of the self-reliance of her fictional John Galt, the archetype for capitalism as a way of life more than a mere social or economic system. She worshiped individualism at the expense of the weak, formulating an objectivism based in nothing but . . . well, her work is rather unclear where her objectivity comes from, other than some all-knowing goodness of the free market. I suppose profitable creativity was her god. Conversely, her atheism recognized all religion as mere superstition against self-reliance. When I talk about objective truth, it is only for the purpose of knowing Jesus as a more universal force in the cosmos, my premise being that a consent relationship with Christ is more freeing and powerful than any philosophy dreamed up by those who believe humanity is not in need of anything greater than its own willpower. Sidebar over.

In the DIY meanings of life, we dream up philosophies that imagine utopia is possible if we just tweak this or that part of human existence or some particular system poisoned by the power-hungry. We might even believe philosophical or spiritual objectivity isn't something attainable. Positivistic, secularized utopia is not attainable, though we may try and try. The kingdom of God, on the other hand, growing out of that relationship with the infinite, eternal God, is possible by his own word. God brings peace, not a philosophy that says hard work is the end-all-be-all of human existence and society. There is a necessity for objective meaning that points us to Jesus, if we are humble enough to listen.

Jesus as Existential Destiny

For fear of getting pedantic, allow me to turn it back to Jesus himself—after all, you picked up a book about him. It's worth considering what living by a spirituality informed by an objective truth of Jesus Christ actually would look like in practice for the common person. How many of us truly plan to be Ghandi one day? God bless you if you do, those are some capital-A ambitions! What would a beyond-observation truth of Jesus Christ mean for the average Joe or Jill? Well, it would look like imitation at best and self-deprecation at worst. To do that, let's talk about a funny romanticized word that Jesus never actually spoke: destiny.

No, not the destiny of Disney movies where two people were created for each other. No, not even the theological predestination of John Calvin or the music of Destiny's Child, which I think is the best of the three mentioned so far. We all have a *christomorphic* destiny. If we are to believe God creates us, knows us intimately therein, has a personalized plan for us, and then finally puts us in a specific time and place in history, we then must have a findable destiny. Don't get too superstitious about this: it's not some astrology forecasting your life's fortunes and failings. This destiny is something more akin to "where you see yourself in ten years" kinda questions. As the phrase suggests, it does entail growing in resemblance to Jesus.

Jesus was, after all, fully human like us but also fully divine and therefore preserved without sin (which again, I must remind you just means imperfection). The pearl of great price, in the wording of Jesus's parable of the same name (Matt 13:44), is this christomorphic destiny. It's the realization to which we come when we embrace Jesus as our metaphysical Advocate and loving Guide in life. This is what we Christians really mean when we talk about God's plan for us. To imagine some chronological list of actions and developments making up your life is a tempting fantasy, but even if that's how God designed it, we wouldn't get to see the schematic of it until we meet him face-to-face. We enter into New Life, the cycle of continual conversion and transformation, which, by God's grace, can ultimately lead to what the Greeks called *theosis*, or the participation in God's nature by doing his will in a substantial way. That fancy Greek word is a concept we'll dive into more next chapter.

Alright, I covered a lot of ground real fast there. Let's put it a different way: our Christian destiny (christomorphic destiny) is ultimately about finding our own sainthood. How will we imitate Christ? How might we craft our doings in the grand scheme of God's plan? The saints inform us of the many ways to God but also of a more basic truth that a life well lived in the Christian understanding is pursing the holiness that is synonymous with our happiness. Once you've caught feelings for this guy and believed he is who he says he is, you're gripped by a desire to reorient yourself to such a wonderful truth. We are not to conform to some outside builder trying to construct our lives for us but rather to find that divine self-image because doing it is the pursuit of holiness. I phrased it that way very intentionally. The pursuit of happiness, as we

Americans harp on and on about, is really the same thing as the pursuit of holiness, just with a vaguer understanding of who God is and why he even exists. When we pursue holiness as Christians, we're not pursuing our own exaltation; we're pursuing Jesus Christ himself. And this isn't a betrayal of who we are at all because it's exactly what we're made for.

The christomorphic destiny of sainthood demands we discover our cruciform identity: who we are, with Christ as our exemplar. That may seem like me just throwing more churchy phrases at you, but consider the practical dynamics of our christomorphic destiny. We find who we are to be with Jesus at our center in order to find the destiny we were created for, so to speak. If we want Jesus and we want him as our Center, our Guide, we look to his sacrificial example, his cruciform example. Saint Aquinas allegedly put it this way:

> The passion of Christ completely suffices to fashion our lives. Whoever wishes to live perfectly should do nothing but disdain what Christ distained on the cross and desire what he desired, for the cross exemplifies every virtue.

Jesus's example is what shows us the way when the going gets tough. In that toughest moment, Jesus accomplishes a great mission, which to many looks to be just a gruesome defeat. Who are we, once we've desired and to some extent found the pearl of great price, a life rightly ordered by God that is nonetheless indelibly very much our own as well? How will our lives express Jesus's glow of love?

Let's ground this in practical life. Long before I was even going to any youth ministry events in my church, I found myself helping out with the Mass. This was occasionally helping bringing up the gifts, but more frequently this looked like my dad and me helping out with the offering, taking those money baskets on the long poles down the aisle before

Figure 8: *Figure of Christ,* by Heinrich Hofmann (1884)

communion. Funny personal sidebar: my first crush was the result of one of these collectors missing me, not saying hello, and then stopping, turning around, and saying the missed hello. I was honored to be thought of and infatuated as a result. She was a girl who went to my middle school, and I would have a little thing for her until high school, when I realized just because someone shows you basic human kindness doesn't mean they are to be your greatest adoration. For a couple years there, she was an angelic figure in my mind. Cringe just went up my spine recounting that. Preteens, eh?

Well, anyway: all this helping in the church eventually led me to become an altar server or an acolyte, as some say. This was fun, and I really felt like I was playing a part in the Mass. Catholic Mass has a lot of specific motions and materials involved; that's why acolytes are necessary. For me, this meant the littlest screwup was the height of embarrassment. I could feel the guilt coursing through my veins, in my bones, whenever a cup wasn't in the right place or a motion was missed. But why did I feel that way? Why did I feel so pressurized by the rituals of my church? Literally everyone involved was as kind as could be. Dawn was there. Pretty much every priest I ever served under was patient and kind. My family went to Mass on Sundays as a cultural obligation more than anything else. It's not like my false moves equated to later punishment. From where was this pressure coming?

I was pressurizing serving on the altar all by myself, fearing I would screw up this opportunity to be closer to him. I had the common misconception many of us have approaching Jesus: he wants me to do this, this, and this, perform a little song and dance, in order to make him happy. That's not Jesus. He certainly works through quantifiable things and rituals—sacraments, if you will—but not as a means of judgment. He just wants us to be with him first and then find the quenching of our thirsts in him. Ah, here is where my preteen cringiness proves teachable! At that Mass when my first crush turned to me for a kind greeting during the collection, in that moment, a thirst that kids often struggle to express was quenched: that universal thirst for basic human kindness.

Everyone thirsts. I was serving on that altar only because I was thirsty for Jesus. A couple short years later, I would be at youth ministry events regularly as my understanding of Jesus matured, little by little. I learned how to depressurize my thirst for Jesus . . . and not become infatuated with anyone who shows me basic human kindness. The question of how we imitate Christ is the personal one at the root of all those fancy words I threw at you a few paragraphs back: christomorphic destiny, cruciform identity, pearl of great price. The answers are yours to find: how is my personality given to me by God for good? How am I best able to relate to Jesus? What can I do to follow Jesus in my own unique life situation? What work am I called to do?

This is where the saints can really clarify our conversation. They provide us with the vast candy shop of flavors of imitating Jesus. If you look hard enough, I promise you that there is one out there who looks like you figuratively and . . . just crunching some numbers here . . . probably literally as well. Just in the Roman Catholic canon, there are more than ten thousand Saints. That's not even counting the ones at various stages on the way to full canonization in blesseds, venerables, and servants of God. The saints show us that this imitation of Jesus Christ is not an impossible task or a cookie-cutter mold but rather a massive mosaic stretching across time and space.

Every Christian saint points us back to Jesus Christ himself, the existential prime reason on whom we've set our eyes here. We Catholics get pinned with a lot of masochism and idol worship when others misinterpret the trappings of these imitation efforts. During the English Reformation, the agents of the Crown melted down saintly images, smashed murals and illustrative windows. Crucifixes were set aside for bare crosses, as they thought seeing the body of Jesus on the cross was too much of a focus on suffering. They did it with a superficial eye for royal supremacy guised in the Zwinglian Reformation's theology of rejecting all visible signs and symbols. Even nowadays, long after religion seems to have receded from society's prime concern, you'll still hear Catholics accused of worshiping the Virgin Mary or idolizing the saints. The truth behind the stereotype is we're the most open of all Christian sects when it comes to different ways to imitate Christ via saints and other examples of virtue. Some of it comes across as oppressive and ugly, I'll admit. But even most Protestants these days acknowledge great examples in the imitation of Christ; some have even adopted Catholicism's formalized system of recognizing saints! It's all in an effort to clarify our own cruciform identities in pursuit of that christomorphic destiny: sainthood. The imitation of Christ is the thing that bonds all Christianity in a certain way, even if we prefer different visions of how to do it.

The common truth is anyone who helps you in the discovery of that identity for yourself is worth a thought because Jesus Christ has an observable power for those who truly engage with him. Yes, a measurable power! We happen to live in a period of history when it's fashionable to domesticate Jesus and emphasize his human side. Certainly, his human side is immensely instructive for Christian living, hence why I started the chapter emphasizing it, but considering his divine side also elevates us, once we're mature enough to embrace it. Christ's example of human life perfectly lived can change us from the inside out. The *how* of these spiritual exercises (shout-out to St. Ignatius of Loyola) is more accessible than you may think, even obvious, after some thinking.

God is great on every different spiritual, metaphysical, and philosophical level, as we established when we defined God a couple chapters back—the being of which no greater being can be thought. When you commit yourself to faith in the belief that God, in the incarnate form of Jesus, is risen, and is with us in every setting of life, there is an incredible, revolutionary power there. Considering Jesus is, in his divine nature, an example of human life perfectly lived shows us a lot to be realized in ourselves. The aforementioned St. Ignatius of Loyola, founder of the Jesuit order of priests (the Society of Jesus), used this funny image of one sitting at a dinner table with Jesus, pigging out, in his famous spiritual exercises. In a charmingly seventeenth-century scene of godly cleanliness, Ignatius insists you wouldn't eat like a pig when you consider the example of Jesus right there in front of you.[1]

Continue the metaphor on a bit further, and perhaps you'd even come to learn proper portion sizes and whatnot from a perfect example of eating dinner right there. This isn't a puritanism; it's imitating Jesus as an objective standard on a spiritual level, giving our lives divine meaning. This gets back to this old-fashioned Catholic idea of unifying our sufferings to Christ crucified. That sounds morbid, but it's why some of us insist on keeping Christ's body on the cross as crucifixes. When we look to that example, when we deeply contemplate it personally and sincerely, we find a way to suffer the Christlike way, the godly way, if that makes any sense at all. After all, we are foolish to not believe suffering is a part of life: how might we imitate Christ even in those difficult parts of life? God chose that method for our salvation and did a great work for us through that suffering. Sometimes, we must endure sufferings in life for our greatest, most transcendent accomplishments. Jesus is there and we're united to his saving work in our own sufferings if we can be open to such a grace.

---

1. Ignatius, "Rules," rule 5.

The aforementioned St. Thomas Aquinas also said, if you want to see true happiness, freedom, and joy, look to Christ on the cross. That horrific image can be hard to digest. Reason cleanses faith of superstition, and so does faith cleanse us of the oppression of the difficulties from which we have found no reasonable way out. Because original sin contorts us out of right relationship with God, ourselves, and others, we must sacrifice in some way to contort ourselves back into the more natural state of relationship with God. It's going to feel like work sometimes, but every good goal will require a little work if it's worthwhile. This isn't reducing the sacrificial act of the crucifixion at all; in his dying and rising, Jesus builds the bridge over our guilt of sin to God. We still have to choose to cross it as individuals. In the resurrection is the ultimate victory of this sacrifice, defeating death itself as a division from God. In our own personal yes is our commitment to share in that victory and set out across the bridge.

But we can also unite our sufferings to Christ and be strengthened for it, even if we can see no light at the end of the tunnel. Even where we see no good to be accomplished, there is something to be discovered in suffering. We can give as Jesus gave of himself and be better for it. Jesus shows us the entire way there, including the most self-giving end of it. You probably won't have to face crucifixion, but the spiritual experiences associated with that and with Jesus's broader struggle are very useful in our own lives. Jesus Christ is the way out of the existential dread that can arise from the myriad smaller dreads of our lives. Jesus Christ is the reason here because he is in it with us and lifts us up therein.

On a profound, spiritual level, we are never closer to Christ than in the gutters of suffering and rejection. It is there Jesus came into this world and lived his life before he ever went into his public ministry. It is there he selected his closest followers. That is why we speak of the preferential option for the poor. It is in being Second Man, imitating the self-gift of Jesus Christ, where we are most sincerely living his gospel and helping those set aside by the world.

If you're driving the struggle-bus today, Jesus may show you the way to master the intrinsic things that may have gotten you there. Anger, vice, and all manner of worldly challenges are beatable with Jesus Christ! This is not some sentimental fantasy that Jesus will be your magic, invisible friend. This is the power of bonding ourselves to the ultimate role model of living and thriving in life, all the way to sacrificial, even happy, death. This is the power of a divine being made human showing us the ways of living, sobriety, and healthy attachments. This is the discovery of our own cruciform identities. Jesus is the existential, objective icon of grace in the storm. We become more ourselves when we follow him.

This is especially where Jesus Christ as our reason begins to transcend simplification and standardization. If I spoke of Jesus's divine nature with St. Ignatius of Loyola, allow me to pivot back to his humanity with St. Thomas Aquinas yet again. Aquinas reputedly reflected on the classic "Jesus is the way, the truth, and the light" passage of John 14:6 by saying: "In His divinity Jesus is the truth and the life. But in His humanity, He is the way." The objective, divine Jesus invites us into objective truth and eternal life, while the human Jesus is our way: the guide to our christomorphic destiny because he chooses the sufferings of life, the oppression of our lived experience. He is the way because he suffers with us. He is with us always, even when we're sure no good is near us. The power of that powerlessness is that often Jesus is the clearest present good in those moments.

Once we have found the way—that is, the pearl of great price of our christomorphic destiny and the personal relationship that allows us to embrace it—we can now contemplate existential truths that give life an objective meaning, that objective meaning being Jesus himself. Once we accept that, Jesus Christ as our existential reason, Jesus becomes not a miserly, angry Jesus, disciplining us like a taskmaster over slaves—no, then Jesus becomes the yoke whose burden is light (Matt 11:30). He becomes a new route for our happy holiness and all that comes before it: our Second Man life, the divine New Life in Him, and, yes, it loops us back around to being grateful in considering this existential reason wants to be known to us and in relation with us. The God of all wants to be our individual way and our vision for social justice. Now that is a profound party, indeed beyond anything Gatsby could muster, if you ask me.

Jesus as the Goal of Our Efforts

Once again, recall this is where the insights of saints affect us so powerfully. The saints are the ones who show us, through myriad different contexts and dictions, how one might welcome Christ's radical, unwarranted love, and then finally give it from themselves as well. Just as we remembered God's house has many rooms earlier in this book, we now consider how the diversity of saints shows us so many personal, unique, and varied ways to approach God—to let him into your boat, in the metaphor of St. Peter—and spread the good news he brings.

We have a soldier saint in Joan of Arc and saints of nonviolence like Francis of Assisi. We have philosopher saints and craftsman saints. Jesus Christ is the way, and if we are on that way, the saints offer us tips and tricks. They may even completely change our methods for traversal. Moreover, there is a simplifying energy when we contemplate how the saints encounter Christ and others. St. Thérèse of Lisieux (the Little Flower) said it best in her most popular prayer: "Jesus, help me to simplify my life by learning what you want me to be and becoming that person."[2] That's a cruciform identity if I've ever seen one.

Saints will never take us off the way that is Jesus Christ that leads to him finally in heaven. That's the christomorphic destiny, and the saints can help us find it quite a bit. While this book can be read as some kind of road map or car handbook, I'd be failing you to not point out why where we're going matters, too, in this. Jesus Christ is the reason, and heaven is the ultimate unity with him. I'd better provide a nice, juicy sidebar on heaven...

Heaven isn't some idyllic retirement community of cloud-bound harpists and perfectly spreadable cream cheese. Our default conception of it as an epitome of our desires here on earth often leaves Jesus as simply the custodian of the place. Heaven is perfect union with the epitome of our desires, but that isn't some wonderland of our own vices with perfectly pasteurized chocolate milk, as I imagine it: heaven is the epitome of our soul's yearnings, which is perfect union with God. It's the fruition of our cruciform identity and, indeed, our christomorphic destiny. Heaven is perfect union with God, so the saints are just those who know they are sinful and have done their spiritual penance, removing anything that might be obstructing their soul's route to Christ during earthly life. Heaven is attainable for all, but don't be mistaken: it's a place ordered around perfect relationship with Jesus.

If sin is just imperfection and we're all imperfect beings, then it follows that few of us would die in perfect relationship with Jesus. This is why purgatory exists. If we're not ready for the perfect union with God in the worship of heaven, we live in purgatory for a while. The saints are people who die and spend the least time, if any, in purgatory. If God is love, as we've established, purgatory needs to exist so there is always a way to him for those who are open to him. If almost all people are likely at least of good will and want to do the right thing in the end, there has to be that purification, as we Catholics say (Rev 21:27; Matt 5:24–25, 12:23;

---

2. Lisieux, *Story of a Soul*, 2.

Mark 9:49; 2 Thess. 1:7–8), for which all such people can pass into full communion with God in heaven. So too, another place has to exist for those who persistently and completely reject God. Remember, God respects our free will and engages with us only at our consent. If you finally and totally want nothing to do with that, you'll be allowed that in the end. I don't even think it's a necessarily torturous place at that—just the boredom and profound resentment of choosing isolation over objective good. Nobody is in hell who doesn't want to be there. Think about that before someone tries to convince you hell can't exist if God is loving.

Before putting a wrap on this juicy sidebar, I'd like to clarify, however, that we'll talk about these last things—eschatology, to put a fancy word on it—more next chapter. I think a different lens is necessary to really wrap our heads around judgment in the Christian imagination. It's so thoroughly lampooned and misrepresented that it really doesn't make sense at all unless you're in pursuit of Jesus. Judgment is a real thinker of a concept, and we ought not lead with it for the uninitiated, certainly not nowadays. Well, anyway, sidebar over.

Back to Jesus: with Jesus Christ as our reason, we realize the splotches of our own sin but also of the society in which we live. Yes, this prompts a call for justice as we come to the understanding of how much our world needs Jesus. This has some fascinating ramifications, the more you contemplate it. Saint Augustine wrote The City of God in the fifth century in contemplation of the fall of the city of Rome in AD 410. The fall of Rome was the greatest tragedy the people of Augustine's time could imagine. For them, it was like everything to which humanity had reached, all it could achieve through civilization, was swiftly lost. Augustine noted Rome was the City of Man, a place built by the conquests of emperors. [3]This is where the critical societal lens of Christianity has something to offer: not in being simply another nexus for power but a power in meekness. Strong men build empires they believe are strong, not aware of the strength of meekness—that is, the first-will-be-last of the gospel of Jesus Christ. The weak man, St. Peter, who failed his friend Jesus over and over, was the weak man on which the church was built. Peter himself was loyal to the crucified Christ, the apparent earthly weakness (a crucified victim of state violence) that brought about divine power. Historically speaking, then, it was the Catholic Church who held Rome together after its secular

---

3. See Augustine, *City of God*, bk. 1.

fall. The church Christ built upon the weak man picked up the pieces of the strong man's fallen empire.

The temporal powers and conditions of the world, political and otherwise, that scare us now are lasting only a little longer than our own lives. To the degree we need to work within the temporal powers of the world, that is not the Christendom we'll discuss in chapter 6, seeking to build another strong man's empire via Jesus. Rather, when Jesus Christ is our reason, our vision becomes circumspect and aware of how possible change is when it is, in fact, constantly happening. Through it all, we can recall real power and justice therein are found in weakness like that of St. Peter and Jesus Christ.

When Jesus Christ is the goal of our efforts, even civilization itself is put into some perspective. When Jesus colors the flow of time and space, the way forward becomes clearer. The truth of the gospel of Jesus Christ doesn't change, but it flows through times and places in history differently like a river bends, meanders, and even falls over waterfalls but never stops being the same river. The unchanging core of Jesus Christ and his gospel remain as we find the ways to relate them to our own times and places along the grand flow of history. Strength in all ways seems to be the theme of people and civilizations who don't have Jesus in mind. With Jesus in mind, we realize weakness, the weak and neediest among us, actually ought to guide our public decisions and policies.

In a world obsessed with power, status, and achievement, we're going to find ourselves doubting the poor Jesus from time to time. That's the paradoxical contradiction. But beyond the power-weakness divide, even the greatest saints struggled with profound doubt, even atheism! We've talked about St. Peter a couple times, but consider folks quite a bit more contemporary like St. Thérèse of Lisieux or St. Teresa of Calcutta (Mother Teresa). Both these modern saints struggled with disbelief in God's very existence later in their lives! Worse, they dealt with a melancholy nihilism that it was all worthless, in their last days. This is not something to hide away, as to preserve the halos of these saintly figures; these are human struggles we need to recognize, consider more deeply, and confront with Christ to grow by them. Existential dread is nothing new, just new clothes on the same anxieties that are older than the fall of Rome.

Jesus Christ is not our reason in spite of the difficulties of it all; Jesus Christ is our reason *because* of the difficulties of it all. We'll always be tempted to run the other way. Jonah, the most secretly funny book of the Bible, illustrates this in a dark, existential way that I think really meets me in my millennial sensibilities. Consider the story of Jonah from the dark humor perspective of it all, and it really starts to read like a Larry David-style comedy.

God essentially asked Jonah to go to the land most hostile to his message through hostile territory to the hostile capital and tell them all they were all wrong and needed the God that history tells us they hated. Jonah was *upset* at God for this. To be blunt, I think it would be natural for any of us to be a tad upset at God for asking us to do something so obviously difficult and dangerous. But this teaching story has entranced us more than most other Old Testament stories because Jonah does what seems like the natural response and just yeets off. Nothing is more human than that response. If we instead embrace the difficulty with Jesus, we can see what he can do. Jonah would bitterly discover this after his prolonged flight away from the mission he was given. And so we can imagine Larry David à la *Curb Your Enthusiasm* theme running through a parade of misfortunes.

Jonah yeets off in the opposite direction as far as humanly possible and endangers everyone around him because of it. The story goes the other people on his ship were horrified of the storm, and he comes out saying he is there defying the will of God. The story of yeets continues as his fellow passengers just yeet him off the ship, and the storm is calmed for it! Jonah then gets swallowed up by what the Bible calls a big fish. We often imagine it as a whale, but that allows us too much imaginary space to envision Jonah setting up a campsite in there and chilling. No, Jonah and his compulsion to flee were literally constricted in there, as a spiritual irony, and certainly he was praying what he thought would be his last prayer in the belly of that fish. And just like that, as the will of God in fish form, Jonah was yeeted onto dry land in the direction of the mission God had given him originally. Jonah would still bitch and moan. Even after this unlikely venture into hostile territory was wildly successful, he was deeply resentful, and the story simply ends with him yeeting himself out of Nineveh to go pout that what God was telling him to do was right all along. He had just accomplished the positively crazy mission given to him, and he's mad about it. He was mad he was wrong. Jonah decided his own pride, even when proven to be foolhardy vanity, was more important to him than even the most successful works of God. The story is so dark, it just ends with Jonah alone bitching. The dark humor there, I suppose, is that we human beings always struggle to swallow our pride, eh?

We need a stoic humility to not demand unattainable heights of ourselves and avoid the pits of bitterness when we're wrong. We need reason to not yeet off in the opposite direction at the first sight of difficulty. On the most superficial, surface level, that's why we need Jesus. When we become pelagianist, self-absorbed buyers of our own hype, we begin to atrophy and degrade. People who think they can be perfect without Jesus, or anyone else for that matter, tend to readily fall into other vices. Remember, excellent freedom has a target built in—gratefulness looking for justice. With aimless freedom in which we believe we can be perfect on our own, ignoring any inborn imperfection, we get absorbed in an inner bondage to some comfort or DIY meaning of life. When we fail to see our neediness and build wild expectations of ourselves and others, our own light diminishes and dies as a result.

Our own unique light can't shine where we are cut off from realistic expectations and practical objectives. Jesus organizes us this way in our individual cruciform identity. Beyond healthy goal-setting (very important in its own right), there is a level of redemptive suffering in the things we truly do in Jesus Christ. This isn't some kind of masochism; we're not denying ourselves for some kind of self-hateful high. Personal growth and progress come from discomfort. Look to any great athlete, leader, or saint in your life for that evidence. To follow Jesus is to sacrifice but not without purpose. We're not slaughtering rams to set the world right anymore. We're sacrificing for a destiny toward which Jesus Christ leads us, one that looks like him—one that transforms reality, even through acute suffering.

Mature adults tend to realize we will suffer in life simply by virtue of being alive. It's an unhappy reality we all acknowledge on some level. Life has as many discouraging lows as it does soaring heights, if not more. But we then often fail to think the next step further. Suffering, just like every other human sensation affecting your mental state, has a purpose in the plan. This is not to make light of the loss of a loved one or a terrible illness. It's not masochistic or puritan. We are never perfected in this life to a state of not needing Jesus. This is to say, if we are to follow a Jesus who made his power known by suffering on a cross and then rising again, we have to use life's trials and tribulations as strength. There is a self-giving muscle attained through enduring difficulties with purpose in mind. All things can be graces of fortitude and fidelity if we let Jesus liberate us from the fears of some kind of corrosiveness in suffering. This is "because he did it, I can do it," but it's also, perhaps more beautifully, "to the degree I can't do it, I can do it through Jesus." Jesus gives us strength, but even when there is no more strength to be gained in some struggle, Jesus is our fallback. It's personal on that level but also so much more.

There was a family in my hometown beset by tragedy after tragedy. The eldest son of this family was my age. He lost his father when he was hardly old enough to remember him. My friend, his siblings, and his mother found the strength to move on and nonetheless treasure the memory and spirit of their father. This strength allowed them to unite their family to a new father and his children, forming a beautiful, blended family. From suffering came a new life that rejuvenated them and those they encountered. Then, when we were in our early twenties, this friend of mine died. Frightening though it was to again lose someone far too soon, his family endured the pain and showed our community what it was, yet again, to be stronger for the suffering. Having very recently finished my time as a youth minister myself in that community, I was devastated, unable to make sense of it, not just because he had been my friend but because I couldn't imagine how to make sense of it. Where I was weak, as this family showed me, Jesus is strong. This strength through suffering is what makes the church one. This is what truly brings together peoples of all differences, a shared overcoming by way of redemptive suffering. This is the key to a united human family: solidarity in all sufferings toward a common good.

This is hardly an answer for the problem of evil. No reason justifies undue loss. I could tell you that evil, the natural kind and the kind that originates from us, are both deprivations of some good and not created things in the same way you or I am. I could go on and on about how these are opportunities for grace. But no answer really satisfies the wounded heart. Perhaps the most compelling thing I've ever read that approaches an answer to this are the words of St. Óscar Romero, who allegedly once said: "There are many things that can only be seen through the eyes that have cried."

Perhaps the most powerful image of Jesus for us in times of suffering and difficulty is the garden of Gethsemane. Jesus knows what's coming, and he dreads it. We so often imagine a Jesus of clear heart and mind. Perhaps he always had that clarity, but that doesn't mean he didn't struggle with what he had to do. He struggled to the point of tears and blood in the words of the passion accounts. He prayed for another way, any other way, to do what had to be done. He certainly felt a sense of abandonment in those prayers. He had the ultimate redemptive suffering ahead of him, and he embraced it. He saw through the tears of anguish the good that had to be done through it. With Jesus as the goal of our efforts, we have the ultimate teammate through all of life's challenges, as well as the greatest fruition of those challenges in the exact same person.

Jesus as the Mystical Body of the Church

I didn't live a redemptive suffering when I was a youth minister. I'll talk a lot more about my youth ministry days later, but for now, just know that it was a wonderful blessing of a job while simultaneously challenging me to my core. I was paralyzed with fear to the point of illness. For weeks on end, I'd see the next big undertaking and freeze in cowardice, undermining the work I needed to do with the courage of Christ crucified. Time and time again, we're reminded there is a divine, mystical good done for each other by suffering difficult things (Eph 3:13, 5:16; 2 Cor. 1:5–6; Col 1–2; 2 Tim 2:9–10; John 15:10). Ask any parent, and they'll tell you they suffered for something worthwhile. I wasn't mature enough to see the forest through the trees in that way. The focus of redemptive suffering would have transformed my work for Jesus, had I been brave enough to go there with him in those years.

It was the self-giving muscles of volunteers and leaders around me who made what did work great during my ministry. I consider this my life's clue, my life's suggestive nod, or pointing finger toward God. When I am most afraid of what I am to do, the mystical togetherness of Jesus Christ, his universal church, and all people of good will are there for me. The ultimate cure for the loneliness of fear was right under my nose the whole time. Unfortunately, it took the difficulty of that job and the death of a friend to really make it clear to me that when all else seems insurmountable, the reason is Jesus Christ. By Jesus, we can manage to continue the climb. Sometimes, Jesus sustains us in ways that I can only describe as mystical. Jesus is a mystical influence in our lives as well.

What is mystical about this? To the degree I can explain it, I default to images at a bigger scale. I'm a visual learner. Folks like me need some kind of tactile thing through which to relate to God. We have this in the form of sacraments. There are seven formal sacraments for most Christians, but I think the broader definition is more helpful for this specific point. There is a sacramental nature to our relationship with Jesus. He uses knowable, sensible signs to interact with us in more sublime, mystical ways. These informal, personal sacraments of our relationship with Jesus may mean something only to you and him. The mystical body of Christ is how some Christians refer to the church community. When us Catholics say the church itself is a sacrament, we're not really talking about the building (although if architecture brings you to Jesus, by all means, please enjoy). We mean to say that in a mystical yet lived sense, the whole church is a sacrament of Jesus's continuing life with us. We are sacraments of Christ's presence to each other as we all worship and imitate the same Jesus who moves us. We know Jesus through tactile reality, in other words, and that is somewhat mystical, if you ask me. Wait, isn't tactile literally the opposite of what mystical means? Yes, but that's the duality of life, right? We do indeed live tactile realities for reasons and by methods and schemas we don't fully grasp.

Jesus Christ is the church in its organic, mystical inclusivity. Jesus is alive and well, and indeed, he *is* the church, alive and collecting all people of good will into a splendid assimilation when the church is at its best. Nobody ought to be trampled beneath the feet of any church of Jesus Christ; they must be brought in, in all that they are, to the sacred community he founded. What can be integrated must be integrated for the sake of the salvation of as many as possible. This is where we are connected into the vast, organic array of God's universal plan in a magnificent way. This is where the virtues of the Beatitudes back in chapter 2 and the hard work of being selfless to others in chapter 1 pays off in a material way. This is where having Jesus Christ as our reason in life makes a difference. Mystically, we become connected in a way that no other truth of life can connect us. A church is ideally a community built in this reciprocal love of Jesus Christ. When it is what it is supposed to be, it's beautiful in an organic way. The mosaic dome of the St. Clement Basilica in Rome describes it in starkly visual terms:

Figure 9: Apse of St. Clement Basilica, Rome[4]

Notice Jesus Christ crucified at the center. It is as if he were a tree within a planter, the seed of so much else sprouting up around him. The doves on the cross represent the apostles, who take his message out like seeds of New Life to all the vines sprouting from him originally. All the little facets of good works worth doing sprout off as branches from that profound good work of self-gift. This is why true Christian faith is dead without works. This is why true Christian faith speaks of a common good. Anything less is a severing of the organic, spiritual way we're all connected. We are inextricably linked as a human family, and Jesus Christ is the completion of human unity by his sacred revelation that self-gift is the greatest organizing principle of human life.

This is the most objective spiritual truth of Christianity. Reciprocity among us vines in this great organism is necessary for the organism to reach its fullest heights. This is why good churches do emphasize a certain coherence and togetherness, in spite of how arbitrary such ways may seem from the outside looking in. It's in protection of this sacred deposit of faith, the sacrament of Jesus, at the center of it all. This is why togetherness, not rebellion, define the true gospel of Jesus Christ.

4. Image courtesy of Globetracks, Inc., at Travel for Kids (Apr. 30, 2015), https://seetheworld.travelforkids.com/rome-basilica-san-clemente-mithraeum/.

We have to think as one church to maintain this sacred reciprocity to its fullest extent. We will all fail—we are human beings, after all—but we fundamentally miss the point when we decide schism and conflict are preferable to unity. Severed vines cannot live true to the love at the center of it all. Jesus Christ provides us the soil and nourishment from which to start. And we are a part of something so much greater than we can see in our little section of vines.

Consider again Christ's closeness to us. He does not require redemptive suffering of us, as if he were some highly enshrined Olympic judge prepared to see if we can do the right number of flips off the high board. He is, at least in the understanding of the Catholic Church, tangibly here with us in the real presence of his sacred body and blood in the bread and wine of the Eucharist. Jesus Christ is made present to us every communion. This is why the Church is a living thing, manifest through people just as sinful as anyone else. The vines will always be covered in dirt, but they never stop being the vines in that they are rooted back tangibly (apostolically) in Jesus Christ and directly to him in the Holy Spirit in the transubstantiation of that sacrament of communion. Jesus gives us his very body and blood in horrifically stark terms (John 6:52–59) to consume and so to become stronger! Jesus is not just suffering with us, we are not just unifying our sufferings to him metaphorically; we are literally united to Him in substance. Jesus is there as the mystical body of the church, present in spirit, truth, and substance.

Allow me one brief fully Catholic tangent while we're in the neighborhood of communion, since I laid down those vibes so heavily in that last paragraph. The blessed sacrament is kinda my thing. The four marks of the true church, to which we Catholics often go back, are one, holy, catholic, and apostolic. The true church is one (Gal 3:28)—that is, whatever is good can find a connection to Christ through the graceful assimilation I mentioned earlier. You can see the many different rites of worship and profession within the church. The true church is holy—that is, by Jesus Christ, who calls the church beyond itself in missionary vigor as well as devoted charity to believer and nonbeliever alike. As long as the church is of Jesus, its sins can be overcome by people of faith and good will by Christ's redeeming sacrifice. The true church is catholic—that is, universal in its ability to transcend national and cultural boundaries to all people of good will. Catholic just means universal in ancient Greek. The true church is apostolic (Matt 16:17–19)—that is, a historical continuity going back to Jesus's authority as a living voice that speaks to every time and place according to how those times and place may come to know Jesus. Catholics, Eastern Orthodox, Nestorians, the Coptic tradition and a handful of other Christian sects maintain actual historical connections back to apostles. We Catholics establish this apostolic authority in the pope via St. Peter specifically. Papist tangent over; there is a *Jeopardy* answer in there, if those four marks don't otherwise interest you.

Jesus will often ask us to do things that are not easy. He compels us to forgiveness of those who have wronged us dearly in the most counterintuitive reality of who Jesus is. Really . . . Jesus can be seen as a comedian. I'd say he's this in a Joker kind of way, but there is no malice in Jesus. He subverts expectations at every turn like a true funnyman, though. Unlike most contemporary comedians, however, Jesus's act doesn't have a mandatory minimum alcohol consumption . . . wait a minute, I just explained the Eucharist—it does! Cathedrals are just expensive comedy clubs in the name of Jesus! Who would have thought this book would contain such comedy.

All kidding aside, Jesus is the reason because nobody delivers the punchlines quite like him. To further belabor the comedian metaphor: Jesus never punches down. Jesus's hilarious subversions offend only those who have resolved to refuse him and those who have something to lose for following him. Again, it's a big rager of a party he wants everyone to be a part of. If we have the assistance of the all-powerful party-master who knows us and the divine plan for our lives, what keeps hindering us from just trusting Jesus and going along with him?

Perhaps one of the things that hinders us is a confusion between truth and mercy. These two modes of Christian faith tend to color perceptions of Christians, the church, and Jesus himself as a result. On one hand, the religion of Jesus Christ is one of endless patience, forgiveness, hope, and redemption, with the most powerful witnesses to these virtues showing his love in stunning relief: mercy. On the other hand, the religion of Jesus Christ is obsessed with the truth of his message, doctrine, meaning of the gospel, the ascetic rising to the occasion of prayer and worship with the most powerful witnesses of these attributes exemplifying a holy life in deep conviction: truth. These two parts are very much in lockstep. There are saints who fit into either category. Certainly, almost everyone fits in both in different ways, though they may lean one way or the other in affective practice and what have you.

This is such a common dividing line for the kinds of Christians outsiders point to as good and bad because it's the gateway to a transformative relationship with Jesus that isn't immediately obvious in casual observation or academic study. In other words: you do both, but the untrained observer will tell you to pick one. The merciful side of Jesus's message is not simply a get-out-of-jail-free card. It's not devoid of further responsibility. It's a calling out, an aspiring to greater holiness. Yes, salvation by Jesus Christ is a free gift, but don't mistake it for a mere detached comfort without the power to purify us as well. The sentimental, domesticated Jesus offers us the easy way out, avoiding the ongoing conversion of a transformative relationship with Christ that leads us to our christomorphic destiny. That false Jesus is beholden to the "sacred me" (forgive the corniness) of our times. That is to say, the true religion of Jesus Christ involves not becoming the best version of ourselves but rather becoming the Jesus version of ourselves. That's a harder effort than the domesticated Jesus, whose salvation for us is ultimately just ornamental to our other mere possessions. If Jesus Christ is your reason, you want his will to be your will. Wait, that's the title of the next chapter! We'll come back to that.

The truth side of Jesus's message, however, is what holds the whole thing together. If Jesus wasn't who he says he was then it's all a scam. We are pitiable people if Jesus was a liar about his resurrection and his ministry at large, as 1 Cor 15:12–20 tells us. If the truth of who Jesus is and what he taught doesn't matter to us at all, we've just reduced Jesus into the Jeffersonian vision: a nice ethical teacher who doesn't really have any power beyond the intellectual parlance of ethics. As someone who formally studied the faith and religion in general, I really enjoy the truth side of things, as it allows me to get to know Jesus in a way that works out the brain. If you ask me, half the fun of having a religious belief is putting it through the rigors of academic study. But I digress, the truth of the matter must always be tempered with the mercy at the soul of things if we are to be followers, not just researchers.

Truth and mercy are not opponent forces in Christian faith. These are not two rival camps; they're just two different elements of New Life in Christ that we must live concurrently to truly follow the Gospel Jesus. They're two sides of the same coin. The same Jesus who calls us to love our neighbor as ourselves also commands: go and sin no more (John 8:11). They color the way forward within the Christian's divine life in Jesus Christ through two different modalities. Our cruciform identities, the Jesus version of ourselves, are not always an easy undertaking, though life with Christ frees us. The journey with Jesus makes us holier (happier) as we go. This is why Christ crucified is an image of joy, even though it appears so obviously to the worldly observer as a place of defeated suffering. Through both the power of the truth of Jesus Christ and the great love of God experienced and practiced through mercy, we find Jesus is our reason—our reason for doing any of this in the first place. The more we realize this, the more we see our christomorphic destiny coming together, as if the one for whom we've now caught feelings has a plan for it all! It is a weird, bluntly obvious, yet somehow exciting realization when it first hits you in your own life: Jesus is the why.

When I contemplated the title of this book, I thought about how it might be misinterpreted—how someone uninitiated in Christian faith could interpret it as an endorsement of a relationship with Jesus Christ that is just ornamental, a relationship that is just another feature of one's personality and emotional life. Everyone has a reason to compartmentalize Jesus into a restricted, private part of our lives. It's easier and less scary to treat him that way. We are so tempted to keep Jesus at arm's length. It's a form of self-preservation because anyone who knows his message knows it can't be an ornamental faith.

Keeping my relationship with Jesus a private affair, at least from my immediate family well into my twenties, contributed to a weird, creeping sense of distance from them that I now hope to resolve. You don't need to proselytize to open your heart to loved ones. You don't need to fear a more intimate relationship with Jesus, because he is patient and gave it all to be with us. In the words attributed to St. Padre Pio: "You don't have to be worthy, you only have to be willing."

Jesus cannot be just an idea hanging from our neck. Jesus is a divisive figure who always prompts a choice and is best understood through an array of historical, cultural, and poetic means, both in the Bible and beyond the Bible, both canonical and very personal. Relationship with Jesus draws us to the edge of our words. Jesus draws us to the borders of ideas and places we otherwise would prefer not to navigate. Jesus is our greatest variable in life when we let him work in us how he would, not how we would domesticate him. I realized I couldn't fit all that in the title and took a breath. I remembered if this book brings anyone to Jesus, it will be to the degree to which they see the true Jesus in it and desire to encounter that guy. I hope and pray this book has endeared you to that Jesus Christ with whom you want to live. We still have two full chapters to go, if you're not quite all the way there yet. Bear with me now as this journey takes another noticeable-enough turn to draw you in deeper.

If chapters 1 and 2 were no-prior-reading-required introductions to the basics of a certain Christian spirituality I called God's Canon in My Life, and chapters 3 and 4 were more challenging explorations of Jesus Christ and the many misconceptions and obstacles to truly encountering him, then chapters 5 and 6 are the windows into the encountered life. That is to say, in these next two chapters, we're going to discuss the mental and spiritual realities of actually living the life—actually living and working with Jesus Christ, day in and day out. What comes after the embrace? What does it mean to actually live the Jesus life? We often neglect to talk about the difficulties of fully living with Jesus, as to sanitize it and not scare off any potentially interested parties. That's unfortunate. One has to see oneself personally living the life, and we do that by seeing how others handle it. We also often lack the humility to admit the parts we're screwing up or struggle to fully live in our own lives. So much of the toxic otherizing attitudes that arise in this faith seem to come from that embarrassed pride that living with Jesus often causes us to face up to. We have to be better than that.

I consider myself something of an expert in such embarrassed pride. I had a lot more to say about my walk with Jesus in the early chapters, and that kinda faded away in the middle two because I didn't really struggle with the misconceptions and obstacles of faith until I was already committed to the thing. I wasn't going to jump ship for any reason by the time I really tackled the problem of evil in any intellectual way or contemplated the consent of Mary. Now that we're getting back into the more grounded reality of this journey, enjoy my embarrassment, explicit in some of the examples I'll provide.

A quick reminder that as you read these, it's not me trying to be holier-than-thou. In fact, my most acute spiritual catalyst seems to be failure, if I really drove down into it, hence this repetition of embarrassment. Me aside, this is about embracing your newfound or long-standing faith, in an active way. This is about how one could ever possibly be about showing Jesus to others when that seems like such a fundamentally divisive and intimidating task. Once you're dedicated to your Christian faith, one of your baptismal duties is being a light of that faith in Jesus Christ to others. It's not necessarily the Bible-thumping, yelling kinda Jesus-sharing you may have been exposed to. How you share Jesus is as personal as how you relate to Jesus yourself. That's where we go next. But first: prayer time!

I only really have one full chapter of the Bible memorized: Romans 12. I had it highlighted in a pocket Bible I'd read on the school bus. It was the King James version of the text, so my recitation is clumsy nowadays with all the "I beseech you" and "therefore" and "thou" of Middle English. The first verse really defined my teenage spirituality, but the second verse seems to be more compelling to my adult faith: "Do not conform to the pattern of this world but be transformed by the renewing of your mind. Then you will be able to test and approve what God's will is—his good, pleasing and perfect will" (Rom 12:2). To discern what is God's will is the great aspiration of anyone who truly wants to love and serve Jesus Christ. In thirty-seven words, Paul writes a road map to it right there. He shows us how we might be able to know what the very will of God is.

We are not just called to bring Jesus to others through a missionary witness; we are called to find the will of God and convert the world around us to Jesus Christ. This is not the work of Crusades or Inquisitions; this is daily conversion to Christ. Jesus Christ is the reason, not the object. We're not giving our friends this hot new show on streaming in which we're engrossed. We're giving them a new perspective on the universe and their place in it, their beloved place in it. Matthew 19:8–9 talks about how the fullness of truth is something we receive incrementally. At first, we may not be prepared for some truth or some good thing, but Jesus will give it to us when we're ready. Is God holding back information and therefore violating our consent relationship? No, he never gives us more than we can handle because he knows us more than we even know ourselves. Overwhelming us mere mortals would be a pretty problematic thing for God to do as well, when you think about it. Knowing his will, knowing him as the central organizing principle in our lives, requires we stay with him prayerfully in order to go along with this unfolding direction as best we can. I'm getting to how this is prayer, I promise.

Jesus Christ is the reason for all our hope, happiness, and holiness. That is what we give others in the missionary adventure. That is what we have to pray for. How do we give people something so complex but also so personal? The answer is there in the good Samaritan. The choice to go outside ourselves, the choice to decenter our own experience long enough to truly care for others, is the most straightforward way to act like Jesus. Let's pray with that.

One heavily underutilized form of prayer is prayer with the scriptures. If you want to get really analytical with it, the practice of *lectio divina* is worth a look. To put it in the most accessible terms possible, you read a passage and contemplate its meaning. Moreover, you ask God for help contemplating its meaning. Maybe you also say: "What do you think I need to learn from this passage, God?" The passage I'll give you to pray on is Luke chapter 10. If you're pressed for time, verses 25–37 are the aforementioned parable of the good Samaritan. Once you start to meditate over its various meanings, more and more of its purpose opens up to you.

I'd also challenge you while praying over Luke 10:25–37 to not gravitate toward a happy ending just because the beaten traveler is cared for by the good Samaritan. Just like in real life, the answers aren't always clean and easy. There really is no definitive conclusion to this parable. Why do you think that is? Why don't we know what comes after that? Should we? What does that say about our willingness to be good to one another? Do you think Jesus was telling us that we have to decide how the story ends? Perhaps the basic human good we do is only the start of what can be.

Chapter Five

So That His Will May Be My Will

My mother passed me the parish bulletin. It was Christmastime 2015. I was closing in on my last semester of my undergraduate time at Niagara University. I was looking for a job and, to be very honest, a bit disillusioned with my degree concentrations. I was twenty-one, and the ad for a youth minister for my childhood parish was as much surreal to read as it was exciting. Dawn, my wonderful youth minister, had an ever-expanding role in the parish. She knew she couldn't devote her whole efforts to youth ministry anymore, and she had the clairvoyance enough to recognize why that merited a new hire for that position. She had been youth minister in different capacities in my parish for fifteen years and was synonymous with the program for the entire community: enough cohorts of young people saw the transformative power of Jesus come into their lives by her efforts to amount to a generation of those professing her effectiveness in that ministry, including myself.

Even for someone who identifies as a very active Christian, there are very few moments where you feel as though the heavens open up with a message for you. Perhaps the Old Testament character Job got so upset at God because he loved God so much while the heavens opened up to him so little. This youth minister job was nothing short of God's will for me at the time. I was declaring my interest in it before I went back to college for the spring semester, interviewed for it by spring break, and accepted it two months before that semester even ended. I was walking off the graduation stage into a job I believed God set aside for me. I was on cloud nine, seeing a career opening up for me. It was quite devastating then when the ensuing five months turned out to be the most mentally and spiritually challenging time of my life.

Without a doubt, that was due to my own immaturity. In case you're not there yet, twenty-two-year-olds aren't the most emotionally or mentally stable folks out there; oftentimes, they are the least emotionally and mentally stable folks out there. I certainly was. It was a baptism of fire I would've embraced excitedly had I been five years older. Immediately, I had to plan the most complicated program of the youth ministry year in the summer service camp that had so shaped my life as a teenager. The parish itself was under a somewhat new pastor who had inspired us all, just before my arrival, to an ambitious new faith formation program that engaged all age-levels in the parish at once. In spite of the scale of that undertaking for herself, Dawn was an ever-present help for my nascent youth ministry, understanding concurrently that I would need help and that she was too recently removed from it to not be involved.

To be very clear, Dawn's help was what buoyed me in that frantically busy summer; but I was also stressed to the point of physical illness in the weeks immediately before that service camp. Youth Ministry was what God called me to do for two years of my life, I know this in my soul. But that doesn't mean it wouldn't be difficult—profoundly—and painfully tough at times. In retrospect, no amount of outside help was going to aid me in overcoming my spiritual unreadiness for that role and mental unhealthiness that was exacerbated while I tried. When you arrive at the point in your relationship with Jesus where you consciously want to do his will in your life, you probably long ago accepted the idea it would be difficult. How it will be difficult is the mysterious question that is more haunting even than what that will actually is. Or at least, that was always my struggle with it.

Dreams of Theosis and Jesus's Call to Mental Health

You've come through the stations of accepting Jesus as the deeper calling of your self-giving; knowing Jesus in continual conversion and transformation toward New Life; accepting a grateful and justice-oriented outlook as a result; and then, finally, some level of surrendering your life to Jesus as the reason for it all. That surrender part is the killer, isn't it? I haven't used that word much because it seems so counterproductive and archaic in modern relational parlance. A surrender doesn't convey me remaining the master of my own destiny. But here I am, telling you such a moment in your relationship with Jesus is inevitable. I suppose it's not a compulsory surrender, so it is consensual, but I said this whole faith in Jesus thing wasn't fundamentally a reduction of ourselves. How does a surrender to Jesus follow with that?

You probably caught wind of this seeming contradiction with all that destiny and becoming the Jesus version of ourselves last chapter. I mean, if we're being honest, the first chapter of this book was called "Second Man"! You probably saw this coming way back, no matter what I've said. Indeed, part of Christian faith is decreasing so that Christ can increase; but the way we do this is not any kind of violence against who we are. For this surrender to be a violence against the self, it would require us to be truly separate from God. We are created souls of his, we're not separate; therefore, surrender to our Creator is much more akin to reunion with a loved one. Surrender is the word so often used in Christian circles because we humans generally struggle to see the agency of God until it's pointed out to us or we have some kind of religious epiphany. This is why clerics arise in every organized religion; some of us decide to point out the work of God among us, while some of us, for a variety of legitimate, personal, and practical reasons, participate in it through the less explicitly religious works of our lives.

This is also how spirituality can exist outside the realm of organized religion; sometimes, we choose to take nobody else's guidance in the quest for the divine. This is also the reason Jesus chose to die on the cross; he wanted to make it crystal clear to us nothing need separate us from the love of God. No image of divine intervention so starkly affects the literate and illiterate alike: God in our flesh choosing to wipe away our guilt in plain-as-day terms. The crucifix is a sacrament of blunt truth.

The fact that moral canniness exists at all beyond the bounds of biosocial utility shows that we yearn for this kind of union with God. Some prime moral arbiter must exist if we sacrifice ourselves and give everything we have to causes and loved ones and finally believe, even outside the auspices of organized religion, that the universe must bend back toward a final moral goodness and justice; some core theological tenets exist too broadly across disparate cultures, times, and places. Somehow, most theologies conceive of some eternal paradise and some eternal separation. So many theologies conceive of god-kings and saviors. So many different religious traditions and spiritualties even have similar symbology and parables. Call these the products of continual collective ideation or another natural intellectual outgrowth of humanity's drive to find meaning everywhere all you want: to the degree a moral perfection exists, it is something anyone of good will naturally gravitates toward. Religious or not, everyone believes in some moral ideal state, even if it is just "take it easy and don't be terrible to each other."

Even the popular contemporary adage "becoming the best version of ourselves" bears the markings of a definitive state of at least some semi-perfection to be reached at some point in relation to some perfection of the self. The moral canniness, the objective truthfulness of Christ in the phrasing of the last chapter, points us to the reality that relationship with God is human nature truly itself. To pursue God in the Christian sense is to pursue our humanity in its fullest form. So we would be wrong to consider surrender to Jesus as some forfeiting of our rights or our individuality. We're made searching for him from square one, and the surrender part is the acceptance of a level of stoicism about who he is and what he'll do with us. We will never have all the answers or full perfection in this life, but if we abide in Jesus, we discover we don't have to. We can nonetheless accomplish life's fullness without perfection.

In all that, we can come back to God as the being of which no greater being can be thought. Therein lies the impetus of the surrender: if a God of that grandeur made me with a moral compass at all, however dysfunctional, and seeks to love me in a two-way consensual relationship, that's a plan I'm interested in, even if it does require some level of surrender on my part. "So that his will may be my will" is the essence of the transformative surrender of Christian faith. When you decide your will, the goals, and desires of your own imagining are secondary to God's will, you've entered into a level of Christian self-giving that grasps at the difficulty of the mission and asks God to help and show you the steps along the way. It is here where personal conviction has become external purpose. We're not abandoning our will, goals, or desires; we're using them in the pursuit of God's will.

To arrive here you have gone beyond the disciplinary basics of the commandments and gone to grasp at the Christly self-emptying that elevates the self-giving of Second Man from mere universal humanistic truth to a more specifically Christian mission. In other words, you're not just going through the motions anymore; you've embraced a personal discipleship of Jesus Christ. Your own goals and desires haven't vanished. They inform your pursuit of God's will because, after all, God put those innate aspirations in you. Unlike the rich young man who went away sad he'd have to give up passing treasures he held so dear, you've now decided to risk it all and put Jesus Christ at the center of your life. Now the hard work begins.

Living in a state of Christian self-gift requires a healthy inner life mentally and physically to the point of showing you how lacking you are in other places. You have to move past misconceptions of what God's intent might be. You have to abandon some crude literalism that you aren't responsible for the facts of your life right in front of you. Take care of your health in all its forms and the well-being of those around you who might need you in one way or another. It also requires the maturity to handle these things effectively with Jesus. Jesus is our partner in the works of his gospel, as well as in the monotony or difficulty of life in general, if we let him in. In the phraseology of the next chapter, we are co-workers with Jesus in life. If he's a good co-worker, then help is help: more hands make for less work!

This is why some devoutly religious people seem self-hateful, constantly attending to spiritual practices as if repentance for sins of which they seem least guilty. It's a by-product of compelling Christian living to seem so obsessed with a right relationship with Jesus. You feel like you need to keep going back to the well once you've fully taken up Jesus's calling in your life. It's a totally virtuous, good desire to have. It's often the clearest sign you've caught said feelings for Jesus! But it does come with the risk you will appear to others like a religious legalist or, within yourself, fall into a toxic scrupulosity that actually hurts yourself and your relationship with Jesus. Hell, I could write a whole book on religious scrupulosity's toxic dark side. But I promised you some more fun ancient Greek, so here's some more fun ancient Greek: theosis.

Theosis is the aim of the soul thirsty for Jesus. Theosis is a gift. Theosis is the conceptualization of the goal of this yearning, this state of relationship, at the point of ecstatic cooperation with God's will where we definitively participate in God's nature. This is not us becoming God in any way but rather us getting to a point where we attain to this kind of unselfish second-nature compunction for doing God's will; and moreover, God connects with us therein to allow us to definitively participate in his work. This does not mean we don't continue to be wounded, sinful beings; it's just the arrival at some reliable cruciform identity fed by the grace of God. This is where we yearn for and increasingly identify with the idea of doing things "so that his will may be my will." Thirsty for Jesus, we grasp at a willful surrender that turns us right back around to do the work.

This is where this fifth step on this ladder of God's Canon in My Life connects back to steps 1 and 2. I mentioned, almost too briefly in chapter 1, that living as second, committing to an unselfish lifestyle, is difficult, particularly when there is a lack of reciprocity. That is the mutually beneficial give-and-take that defines healthy friendships, relationships, and all meaningful human interaction, for that matter. We get distracted by this beautiful core premise of Christian thought that Jesus's whole shtick was to give without expecting anything in return. Indeed, this is the height of virtue: to give recklessly, without assurance of a returned benefit, and it is the beauty of Jesus's work. But even in that work, Jesus was establishing a new reciprocity with humanity. If millennial thinking enriches Christian thought in any way, it's in that the reciprocity of love that Christ also teaches is a mental health lesson. We need a reciprocal love in our lives as a matter of our health. We all grasp at it in different places, but Jesus is the love that finally works when all else fails. Theosis is, in a certain way, the gift given to us when our cruciform identity yields fruits, and as a result, we achieve a steady reciprocity with God.

Beyond just binding Christian communities together for important works like helping the poor or otherwise helping their broader locality, reciprocity must also bind together the sanity of individual Christians. We strive to pour ourselves out completely, but if we don't know how to fill back up again, we can only do so much of God's will. This is a mental health warning straight from the mouth of Jesus to the struggles that seem to besiege our souls. We have to give of ourselves but also develop healthy bonds in order to replenish the joy that lifts us up. God is good, he doesn't give you more than you can handle (1 Cor 10:12–14), and if you think he is, it's probably because you're not taking care of yourself and/or allowing Jesus to help you yourself for a minute too.

A wise man once said failure is not the end. If we are too preoccupied with accomplishing these steps in catching feelings for Jesus or any other pursuit, even if they are for Jesus, we lose the power of New Life in Christ in the first place. We have to have both the fortitude to not be devastated by failure and the willingness to continue learning going forward.

"So that his will may be my will" is a prayer rooted in some stoicism. Even Paul the apostle said he thought equality with God "was not something to be grasped" (Phil 2:1–11). He said it not to confuse us theologically but to remind us to tend to our mental needs. Humility is

So That His Will May Be My Will

a mental health advisory. The bigger your head is, the more vulnerable it is to losing your mind. We're called to be perfect like our heavenly Father is perfect (Matt 5:48), the same way we're called to be good siblings, children, and parents. How do you know you've done so? It's a matter of doing one's best, with Jesus coaching you along the way. It's not a formulaic one-size-fits-all commandment. You only sometimes know if you're doing great, and sometimes you don't know you've screwed up until the failure has already happened.

Moreover, it is a warning against the exhaustion that makes it impossible for us to consistently live in Christ's New Life for us. If we are to say "so that my will may be God's will," we need to know that what we're saying it about is a humble balance of reciprocity within ourselves that then flows out to others replenished by Jesus Christ. We need Jesus to show us the balance of our inner lives, including mental health, spiritual clarity, and physical health too. Only with Jesus showing us a sane inner life can we then seriously undertake his will. And when I say Jesus showing us a sane inner life, don't take that to mean professional help isn't worth it. That's like saying I shouldn't wear glasses because God gave me terrible vision. That's not how Jesus relates to us, depriving us of our needs. Go to the eye doctor. Get your shots.

When I eventually found mental and spiritual stability again at the tail end of that busy 2016 as a youth minister, it was by way of a certain humble stoicism. I accepted my ministry would never be Dawn's, and it shouldn't be, because we're created by God differently. It was the words of a wise veteran schoolteacher in my parish that made that clear to me. In retrospect, perhaps I went too far in that humble stoicism as to exonerate myself from all guilt when things didn't work out thereafter. I don't think I turned out to be a great youth minister in my own right, regardless of how good Dawn was at being one or how difficult it was in my home parish. In the end, God used those years to show me the next step into grad school and a different career I wasn't even considering when my mother handed me the bulletin that December Mass. I hope and pray I showed at least someone the way to Jesus in my time there.

God's plan is seen like a puzzle heavily zoomed in during this life for us. We can't grasp at an immediate understanding of the whole thing; we have to resolve to diligently work with the puzzle pieces we can connect. We suffer the zoomed-in view of the puzzle and the imperfect connection of the puzzle pieces because through that struggling, we come to new conclusions about how the puzzle can fit together. And this is part of where we go outside ourselves. As we slowly put the puzzle together for ourselves, we see how others' puzzle pieces may fit together and consider if and how we could be helpful to others in our lives struggling to put their puzzles together.

Witness by Reciprocity

The loving reciprocity that defines healthy relationships is essential when we're that close to the puzzle. The less and less close we are with someone as we move further out of our more immediate circles of friends and acquaintances, the less reciprocity is important and the more like a bonus it becomes. Indeed, part of friendship is just checking in, even though this seems like the minimum standard for loving reciprocity. There has to be a reciprocity with your significant other, but reciprocity with your co-worker in the next cubicle over is just a bonus.

Others become a powerful force for our spiritual growth once we're properly oriented toward Jesus Christ. Imposing our vision of others' journeys in life is evidence of a fundamentally disordered relationship with Jesus. This is why so many self-proclaimed Christians are really bad at evangelizing and giving Jesus to others. We think we have Jesus as a little gift we can wrap up like a box of clothes and present to them. For one, a relationship with Jesus isn't that simple; and two, others are not merely characters in your story; and finally, another always knows themselves and any potential relationship with Jesus they might have better than you will. Full stop.

We find our own way forward through witnessing to others once we've accepted we don't have all the answers. Don't pretend you have all the answers about Jesus even if you have a PhD in Christology. The practical element is just too personal to instruct, as if you can build such a relationship for anyone else. This is why I have so insistently reminded you the reader throughout this book that you have to discover discipleship yourself. I am no sage. This is why a constant conversion and transformation in New Life is important. This is why servant leadership, going into the trenches with others to do the work, is the key to any outward expression of our love of Jesus. We have to be living examples of Jesus. In the words attributed to one cardinal of Paris, Emmanuel Suhard: "To be a witness does not consist in engaging in propaganda, nor even in stirring people up, but in being a living mystery. It means to live in such a way that one's life would not make sense if God did not exist." Jesus must be evident in us before we can hope to seriously show Jesus to others.

To the degree I was a decent youth minister, it was because the help of others magnified the work I did. Many small things can add up to some great things. Oftentimes, that's the only way great things happen. Doing God's will is a group effort. The difficulties to making God's will our own this way often scare us off and lead us into lesser imitations of the full calling of Jesus. We'll need a retreat every now and again; even Jesus needed periodic rest and reorientation. But too often, when we're faced with the challenges of doing God's will in our own lives, we resort to not retreat and reorientation but to escape into excuse. I see this sin in myself quite a bit in many phases of my life.

Pope Francis wrote in *Let Us Dream* that we tend to flee from meaningful works in a suffering world because of a triad of disastrous escape rationales.[1] Many of us will almost certainly see ourselves in one of these brands of negative escapism: narcissism, discouragement, and pessimism. Maybe you see yourself in all three! In all three of these escapes, we choose a corrosive, regressive self-preservation over working with Jesus and/or others in any meaningful way. With narcissism, we center our lives on our own image. We fall in love with ourselves and get blinded by the glow. When difficulty approaches the narcissist, they feel injustice, as if they can be the world's only victim. Nothing is as counterproductive to God's will as selfishness. Discouragement sees the glass half empty exclusively. For the discouraged person, there are no blessings, only sadness and fear. This state of life makes meaningful work, for God's will and otherwise, very difficult. It's a clear indication you need a retreat and reorientation of things. Finally, pessimism is the most aggressively bitter escape we fall into, seeing how difficult the world around us looks. Pessimism is not only believing the glass is half empty but also insisting anything added to it is poison. Pessimism is an embrace of cynicism to a toxic extent. Nothing positive can grow in a life so insistent that nothing good can come from people or institutions that are not perfect. Needless to say, nothing and nobody is perfect, and these three negative escapes tend to make us wait for a perfect world before we can be second to anyone, never mind do God's will. Perfection is something that comes up a bit too much among religious people.

We don't need to be perfect. We need to be merciful with ourselves because Jesus, the merciful Word of God, was merciful with us first. From

---

1. Francis, *Let Us Dream*, 15–16.

that, we can then enter into doing God's will in a decisive way. The divine mercy of God that undergirds life with Jesus to begin with is the means of doing his will in any meaningful way. If we have found ourselves entranced in one of these aforementioned escape mentalities, all of the content of this book, all of a relationship with God, can seem like a mere obligation rooted in systemic oppression or generational failure of imagination. The burden of obligation melts away when we center ourselves in the headspace that mercy is given to me, so I then give it to others.

This is how that reciprocal love is watered by grace: not hoarding up God's mercy on us but letting ourselves overflow to others with it. This merciful flow reaches to all areas of our lives and our actions in the world. There is no obligation when we find some level of theosis, some love that reciprocates and flows throughout our lives as to be doing, if only a little, God's work in our world.

The word *obligation* seems restricted to the mature among us. Though we enter into marriage contracts, work contracts, and less explicit contracts all the time, we regard the whole idea you *have to* do anything as a bit of a relic of a less free time in history. But what if the obligation arises from within? What if love reciprocates and meshes you to others or some specific other? This is why anyone still gets married, I suppose, decades into a modern world where divorce is no longer the evil that nobody dare utter. Reciprocal love draws you into the desire to obligate yourself to someone for as long as you might live. We don't think of love as an obligation because, ideally, it feels joyous, but it is, the more you really are in love—not just the love that's bound up in feelings but the love that transcends passing difficulties into eternal embrace. Worthy obligations are born of reciprocal love.

If you have children, they are your obligation. It's not some authoritarianism of parenthood; most decent parents will tell you some intrinsic, natural love arises once you have children of your own to care for. But obligation is what it is. This is why we don't look at absent parents as heroes for their commitment to individualism and autonomy; they're just fleeing their obligations. Reciprocal love is a choice as much as it is something given to us, not an obligation. It's not an onerous duty if our heads are in the right place. The necessity of consent is long met when religious obligations are to be embraced. When we use the word obligation then in Christian parlance, it's incumbent upon us to access the level of inner and outer maturity such obligation entails. If one hasn't embraced the holy consent God allows us first, then all religious obligation will feel like oppression.

I preface this brief discussion of obligation in order to say the Great Commission (Matt 28:16) Jesus gives us to go out and make disciples of all nations is an obligation. It's an obligation of our divine life in Christ, but it is just as sacred as how we worship him and love him personally. How do you share your friendship with Jesus Christ? It's an awkward question because sometimes the answer is quite simply: I don't. If you struggle to prioritize such a difficult obligation, consider it as part of your own path. Why does God put some jerk in your path? Maybe that difficult person is there for a reason. Less rudely put: what if someone could benefit from some insight you have? What if, less narcissistically, they present an opportunity to craft a more creative expression of your convictions? Perhaps they force your actions to change in a way that makes you holier and therefore more readily able first to deal with them and second to build more effective social bonds between people in general. That is a sacramental interplay. No matter what, nobody is just an obstacle. Annoyance is always a magnifying glass to a deeper reality. That is a lesson I've struggled to learn over and over again in my life.

Never impose Jesus on another. Like we said earlier, we can't pretend to encapsulate Jesus in any delivery system or know someone well enough to fully comprehend how they would best receive Jesus. However, we should be ready to give the basic answer if asked why we care about this Jesus person. Always be ready to give an explanation of your hope (1 Pet 3:15–16). But we're not often asked such an explicit question, eh? Rarely are we confronted with clear evangelizing moments, regardless of our time and place. But the degree to which the light of Christ shines through you may be all that's needed. As cheesy at it may sound, sometimes being an unflinchingly good person in that uniquely self-emptying, Second Man, Christlike way does a great deal of the missionary work. "This little light of mine" does actually have some power, to put it in the most sentimental way possible.

I hesitate to reduce the work of the Holy Spirit to emotional intelligence, but that working knowledge of people, motivations, and general interpersonal skills goes a long way in seeing the path forward with others. The most beautiful thing of Christianity, that we are loved by Jesus while we are still sinners, while the world is so screwed up in such seemingly intractable ways, is a spiritual medicine of sorts. We experience the beginning of healing when we realize God's love didn't demand perfection first.

Moreover, when we gather together as followers of Jesus Christ, we are not there as the champions of holiness celebrating some place of honor. Triumphalism goes before the corruption of the gospel of Jesus Christ. Rather, we gather together as sinners needing God, not perfect oracles with all the answers. It is in our spiritual neediness we are most identifiable, most connected to the Advocate Jesus left us, the Holy Spirit. Jesus is medicine for sinners, not the commodity of worldly winners.

Gardeners of the Mind and Soul

We've discussed a couple times already in this book that there are many rooms in the Father's house. There are so many different ways to approach Jesus and his divine life for us. The same is true for the missionary calling. There are many different ways to draw others to Jesus without disrespecting or patronizing them, as we so often fear we'll do, talking about religious beliefs. That is why it's every Christian's calling, because we're all uniquely made in God's image with our own strengths and weaknesses as to draw folks in. We too readily have one image of how it's done in mind. It is wiser to think of it as the sum of many efforts or the fruit of a friendship nurtured and built up over time. A friendship that can seem like it has nothing to do with Jesus can develop in ways that open doors neither saw coming. We are gardeners, in a way.

There was a friend of mine in college who was always on retreats and other campus ministry functions. He was an avid reader of religious books, so I hope he's reading this (go, NU Purple Eagles!). His relationship with Jesus was so intellectual that we found ourselves discussing theology into the wee morning hours of any overnight trip. He helped convert me more to Christ with every conversation, and indeed, I found my vocational calling to marriage in no small part because of him. Some people find Jesus in the intellectual pursuit, and God bless them for that! I was always more the emotional type. Theological arguments and treatises were always the recreational part of my faith journey.

That particular friend went on to be a Benedictine monk at a monastery out West. Sometimes, when I look back, I am in awe at having known an actual, real-life monk. Just as we discussed truth and mercy in the last chapter, there is sometimes a relative goodness and badness attributed to those who find Jesus by way of the dogmas and dictations of authoritative Church teachings. The truth way to Jesus is often venerated more highly among existent devotees, while the nonreligious will often focus their ire on these types. Truth and mercy are two sides of the same coin! Let's not forget.

Moreover, the apparent mercy of other missionary styles is just as legitimate. Jesuit missionaries speak of "entering through their door," as in conforming to the cultural contexts that best suit you to bring the gospel to those who might hear it through you. Historically speaking, many lives could have been saved and souls converted if European missionaries had listened to that wisdom and hadn't imposed their cultural norms. The apostle Paul puts it more acutely in 1 Corinthians 9 when he speaks to an obligation imposed upon him in spite of his newfound freedom in Jesus Christ. He says "I have made myself a slave to all so as to win over as many as possible" (1 Cor 9:22–23). He describes an obligation, a heartfelt obligation that is, that pushes him to go to where the souls he can save are.

In my social work education, we called this going to where the client is. We go where the need is, as to do the most possible good. In our missionary calling, we have to not impose our own outline of things if it is not helpful. We go through the way that is most effective. Certainly, we spiritual novices shouldn't expect ourselves to attain to the heights of the apostle Paul, or Jesuit missionaries, or even my monk friend so readily, but this is all to say, there is no silver bullet to bring any given human being to Jesus. It's a case-by-case thing.

Ironically, it can be harder with people you know better. I've always found this to be the case in my own life. Remember: the most powerful witness to Jesus is often "this is how Jesus healed me." We go to where the soul we're interacting with is at of course, and that witness of what has been done to me so readily opens up into a more organic, fruitful discussion (assuming there isn't an intractable cultural gulf between you). With friends and family this can be harder because they might be ready and eager to fact-check your own story for the parts they know whether or not that's an effort to discredit. It's so personal!

We look and see what form of discussion, what part of the soul might be most readily engaged to bring them to Jesus. We also need to simply give them our personal revelation of Jesus and give them their own space to process and develop their own view. We need to bring our flow of things as far as it's helpful. That can be a more effective approach with those you already know, or it might be unhelpful if the friend or family member isn't happy with your acceptance of these things at all. God will use us as long as we follow the two most fundamental commandments:

love for God and love for neighbor. If we don't live by love, nobody will see the loving God through our witness. That's certainly the most important thing to remember in all this.

Let's back it up a step though. We have to plant seeds and till the soil, if you will, before we ever speak Jesus's name into an interaction. Matthew 13 can be an overused passage in this sense: the seeds that fall on rocky ground, thorny ground, or fertile soil naturally lead one to think about the missionary implications of the parable. Everyone is of different soil, if you will. I always conceived of this as not so much a judgmental passage about your upbringing and more as a guide to friendship. Remember, if we've established any relationship, including friendship, it has to be a consent relationship: two willing participants. After all, one isn't really a convert until that first yes. It may be many small yeses over a period of months or years, but that's all of us. We are all always saying yes or no to friendships of all sorts throughout our lives. Consent is really the bare minimum therein. The more sincerity and enthusiasm, the more reciprocal and life-giving a friendship can be. Jesus comes in through these same consent structures through which our friendships and all intimate interactions come. On a personal level, you accept him as a friend before you accept him as a Savior. This has a lot to inform us about how we can be better missionaries for Jesus Christ.

All these different kinds of soil in Matthew 13 are friendships encountered in life. I can think of people in my life who had the gospel of Jesus Christ planted in them, but their family life or any number of other things choked out that New Life—thorny ground, if you will. Others were like the path where the birds picked off the seeds. Some friends have that spiritual seeker's instinct, but the gospel was picked out of their lives by interests and philosophies they found more compelling. The rocky ground were the friends who tried to take up the gospel of Jesus, but the roots they shot out were just too shallow, and life's troubles uprooted it. All these different kinds of friends need Jesus differently. Substitute Jesus's gospel with simple friendship in any of those situations, and you might be able to see various people you knew in different phases of life.

I prefer to be friends with someone, at least casually, before I bring Jesus into the picture. That's not because I'm scared or embarrassed by Jesus. That's because you have to till the land a little while first—forgive the metaphor's agrarian utilitarianism. This is not using someone until you can give them Jesus; if you really care for them, wouldn't you want to give them Jesus? Conversely, this is also not a watering down of anything;

it's an embrace of the natural growth of healthy relationships in order for people to develop healthy relationships with Jesus. There are many strategies here, and if you are really trying to introduce a friend to Jesus, you'll know the situation better than I. There is no single way to do this, in spite of what the fire-and-brimstone types suggest. But friendship is a fantastic first step because, once again, we often accept Jesus as a friend before a Savior.

If there are thorns, help the friend clear the thorns. Chances are, if they're not clearing thorns already in themselves, they still have to work through some things personally. At that point, you just need to be a good friend as someone finds their way to a more emotionally and mentally healthy place. Life situations can provide rocky ground. Trauma and personal struggles throw up thorns, and just throwing Jesus at them, expecting all that to burn away, is naïve. Be a friend before you push Jesus. That's a good rule of thumb of which J. C. would approve, I think.

Friendship is presence, presence is friendship. Half of the missionary adventure is just presence: we have to be present and accompany our fellow human beings as human beings before we introduce the Jesus whose reputation goes before him. Imagine Jesus himself walking into the room. You may be at a comfort level with Jesus to feel totally okay with him seeing you crying. Don't expect others to automatically feel the same way. Friendship first: friends help friends with their mental health and point them in the direction of some help. We can't just say, don't be sad, don't suffer . . . *because Jesus!* That isn't creating anything lasting or transformative. That often won't even cause conversion in real-life situations with real-life problems at work. Once again, witness according to love for God and others, and say it with me: *consent*. You need to create a friendship strong enough to find a place of explicit consent to bring Jesus into the picture. Jesus doesn't go where he's not welcome. He respects each and every one of us too much for that. The most effective, lasting conversion will come from a place of self-esteem and consent.

Self-esteem or self-love is worth going into deeper here. Saint Cyril of Jerusalem spoke of our doing God's will in a very interesting way. When he was writing in the fourth century, the teachings of Jesus were interspersed in the legal deliberations of the Roman Empire, and the mechanics of grace, forgiveness, and whatnot were of paramount importance in the legal life of that society. The Roman emperors, after the legalization of Christianity, thought themselves arbiters of religious law as much as the bishop of Rome was, if not greater. The religious obsessives of our day would still recognize this world. Cyril says:[2]

> For though remission of sins is given equally to all, the communion of the Holy Ghost is bestowed in proportion to each man's faith.... You are running for yourself, see to your own interest.

The canny observation of Cyril is lacking among us followers of Christ nowadays. We know God forgives all equally and by Jesus invites everyone to the party accordingly, but then we forget truly entering into the work of the Holy Spirit is yet another act of our own free will.

Bringing Jesus to others can't be pressurized to the point you feel like you need to save souls with every interaction. That can be a route for discouragement, cynicism, losing faith, and religious trauma, at worst. You do you, but the more weight we put on our own shoulders, the more we tend to topple over. As Cyril says: "See your own interest." The reciprocity of your own relationship with Jesus is implied therein. Where are you at interest-wise in this?

In other words, you are doing this as yourself; what is your degree of interest in truly being in communion with the Holy Spirit in order to do these works? We make a choice every day. The Holy Spirit comes through us in our missionary work as far as we have allowed it to and as far as we reach out to go along with it. Access your own inner dynamics before you decide how you'll try to bring Jesus into the lives of friends. A change is a change. More personally, change, if it will be effective in our lives, including conversion to Christ, must come from a positive place within—fertile soil, if you will. In my millennial lingo, personal change comes from a place of self-love.

All effective change that moves others and ourselves, the truly personally transformative stuff, has to come from some place of self-love. No meaningful change arises from a self-hate. We miss this in our efforts to give Christ to others as much as we miss it with ourselves. Nobody ever got closer to Christ through absolute self-hatred. Those who think it does work that way mistake self-hatred for redemptive suffering. Jesus doesn't demand hatred in anyway. That may come across a tad confusing, given most of this book has been selflessness this and self-gift that. Now I'm trying to tell you to love yourself?

This is zero-sum thinking, that we have to hate ourselves to sacrifice ourselves in self-gift. Both *a* and *b* can be true. We can give of ourselves

---

2. Cyril of Jerusalem, "Catechetical Lecture 1," §5.

while also loving ourselves. The idea we cannot do both is something born of the evil one. Dividing us within, pitting our individuality against our self-gift, is classic Satan stuff. In chapter 3, we laid out how sin is just separation from God and others. In chapter 4, we briefly discussed truth and mercy as a way some, even within the faith itself, divide up factions. That dividing can be thought of as a sin itself: seeking to arrange everyone, opposed to one another, on a conservative to liberal spectrum. The devil divides. This perceived friction between self-love and self-gift is the work of the devil. How better could the evil one drive us away from God and each other than to say our giving of self requires us to hate ourselves? Is there a more divisive stumbling block then the notion the transformative change of Jesus Christ is violence against our own personalities, ourselves and others, and things about ourselves we love?

I don't throw around the devil lightly. I have so rarely done so through the course of this book because one might be tempted to think invoking the name of non-God supernatural entities is fundamentally superstitious and counterproductive to actually . . . you know . . . catching feelings for Jesus. But I do it here because in spite of our natural sinfulness that separates us from God, some things are evils that are even more primordial and beyond us. We crave unity. We as human beings crave each other and the ultimate unifier in God. Therefore, the devil is the perverter of these things, dividing us even within ourselves, between our desire to give of ourselves and our desire to preserve and aggrandize ourselves. Division is of the devil; unity is of God.

We talked very briefly about heaven, hell, and purgatory in the last chapter. For fear of sounding too fire-and-brimstone, I'll keep it brief again here. Nobody is in any of these three places unless they want to be there and are prepared to be there. Purgatory must be a grossly overpopulated place because very, extremely few people have no good will in their souls. Especially after death, one must realize there is nothing worthwhile in evil, which is, after all, just the deprivation of some good. I imagine purgatory is populated by the countless billions working their way into heaven. We talked about how "working your way to heaven" doesn't mean Jesus's sacrifice for us wasn't enough. Heaven is just such a profound place of intimacy with God that you have to prepare for something like that, the "purification," in the words of 1 Cor 3:11–15. Hell, then, has to be such a lonely, barren place, lit only by the resentment for God and others that guides anyone there. It's not a place to which God condemns anyone; those who are there are there only because they don't want to be with him. There is no relationship with God there, just the lack of one that its inhabitants never wanted.

God's grace is the defining force of Christian thought. Consider this, then, when you see those who go on yelling rants upon those they think are sinners in the name of Jesus: are they transforming anyone to the unifying Jesus or even informing them of anything meaningful about who he is? They envision hell as a vacuum cleaner, sucking those not bolted to Christ into pits of despair. They imagine hell as the place where God finally tortures those who evaded him. This is not the God Christians actually worship. Jesus wants us to be with him, so if there is any vacuum cleaner in the next life, you better believe it's heaven, not hell! This belief in sin as the defining force in Christian thought is junk theology when religious people do it and naked misinterpretation of who God is when nonreligious people do it. This view of all-consuming sin is in itself a rupture from the true gospel of Jesus Christ. That framework is designed to create in-groups and out-groups—sacred saints and sinful villains. It's counterproductive to Christ at best, actively destructive at worse. It gives rise to so many evils that corrupt the Christian world, which we'll discuss in the next chapter.

This is something we can't forget when we attempt to answer Jesus's Great Commission in Matthew 28:16–20. We can't look at the holy Jesus Christ with whom we've fallen in love and insist on the purification only God can do. We can't build a system of exclusion and distinction according to perceived sinfulness and holiness. Yes, we want others to be ready to ascend into the New Life of Jesus on that metaphorical hilltop, if you will, but sincere conversion is a consent relationship. Consent means not withholding any information while also allowing a choice free of troubling insistence. Conversion that lasts is rooted in full consent. Conversion to Christ comes from the same inner place from which all effective change comes, a place of self-improvement or, more ideally, a place of self-love.

Yeah, some people will speak of Jesus as having broken into their lives and shaken them out of a sleep. Particularly self-aware conversion can involve converts feeling a strong sense of conviction, as if they have been sentenced for their crimes or, conversely, released from imprisonment. But even where Jesus appears to forcefully awaken us, he does so respecting our consent at every turn. All sins of missionaries arise from an erosion or outright violation of consent. In those sins, they divert from Jesus and commit spiritual and material atrocities.

If we are to make God's will our own will, we must truly imitate Jesus. We have to imitate not just the truth that provides us a fortress of prayer and strength but the mercy that goes out and eats with sinners and outcasts. "So that his will may be my will" is difficult not simply because it's a surrender to the doings of a being beyond our reach or understanding; it's tough because it requires us to do things right here in our time and place that are difficult to imagine ourselves doing. The devil will be there attempting to divide us even within ourselves, but God is always within earshot. No matter how unthinkable the task may be, we have to resist the temptation of Jonah to run the other way. Truly encountering others in all their being, not just the parts with which we are comfortable, is the underlying orientation of giving Jesus Christ to others. In a way, we are participating in God's creation itself, some practical theosis, I suppose. Though God is the great originator of all things, we might participate in his creation by taking something he gives us and using it to do his will. In a sentimental way, it's like a child asking their parent for the supplies to make a gift for them. God knows us and where we're going with this. He wants us to use our free will for him, and he will certainly provide the supplies to do so if we provide our own will to do so.

Take it a step further. If we participate in God's creative work by using our free will to go about showing Jesus Christ to others, then a vast world of possibilities is opened up. The tendency among religious zealots to create parallel societies, walled enclaves for Jesus to be properly followed, is frighteningly un-Christlike. When the first abbeys and cloisters, the prayerful communities of St. Benedict were established, they were not separate from society, as if to protect the goods of Jesus Christ from the world. They were forces of prayer for the world and almost always producers, to this very day, of some material goods for the world around them, from beer and bread to books and education. Frankly, in the pre-Reformation church, many of the impactful reform movements originated in the monasteries and religious communities. I don't even need to go pre-Reformation: Martin Luther was an Augustinian monk! To establish isolated communities of some puritanism, on the other hand, is contrary to the gospel Jesus Christ actually preached. To be blunt, Jesus didn't die so his followers could flee from the world. He came into the world to save it, not to take away those who would follow him from it. He came to build a church, not an ark.

There is a power to seeing the connecting pieces to the gospel in the world. The Second Vatican Council in the Catholic Church had a whole pastoral constitution dedicated to this newly reconsidered mission: *Gaudium et Spes* (*Joy and Hope*). More than just the conversion of individuals, society and human systems on a broader scale need to be transformed in light of the dignity and grace of Jesus Christ. Don't mistake this for simply another missionary call to pull the world out of its sin to Jesus. Rather, think about what it really means to live imitating Jesus in the real world. Our relationship with Jesus Christ can transform not just how we interact with the world around us but the world itself. We are not just to save the people in the world through Jesus Christ but to save the world by Jesus as well. This is not done through a puritanical, proselytizing aggression, and certainly not by way of throwing up isolationist walls around the gospel, but through the way of the humble Jesus inviting everyone who would come to his table, so to speak. Moreover, it's a deeper encounter of God and others I don't think we followers of Jesus have really fully conceived of yet: building a world of compassion for all.

Jesus washed feet and said the first will be last. Sure, he called out sin, but there is a social dimension to that, beyond individual piety. Jesus got mad and flipped the tables in the temple as a witness to one of society's most stubborn sins: the pursuit of selfish gain, particularly flagrant in that example by way of these sellers setting up as distractions right outside the place of worship. Indeed Jesus was telling us a universal justice for all is part of his gospel message.

On a bigger scale, Jesus knew some human institutions were irredeemable. Some tables one ought not try to sit at as Jesus prepares to flip. And beyond the missionary call of the Great Commission, there is simply the call to active discernment, the process of discovering what are God's doings in the world and how to help with those. We'll talk about the will of God in the reality around us more in the next chapter, but for now, consider how Pope Francis talks about discernment: "Ideas are debated, but reality is discerned."[3] There is a space between the ideas we fashion for the world and the world as it actually is. If we are to bring Jesus's gospel message across this gap, we have to be healers to the world as it actually is.

The Greek verb often translated as "repent" in English in the New Testament is a tad misleading. The Greek is *metanoiete* or actually two words in a clearer form, *meta* and *nous*, meaning "beyond" and "mind or spirit," respectively. Repent in English has this moralizing, insular

---

3. Francis, *Let Us Dream*, 54.

usage, while the Greek from which it's translated really could be better understood as "have a change of mind." Jesus is, more than simply asking us to reject sin and come to him, asking us to change our ways of seeing the world around us. He wants us to change our perceptions and all the things we think we know for the higher purpose of his revolutionary will. Jesus is calling us to a mind transformation, if you will. This is how Second Man becomes more than just being good to others; this is how New Life in Christ is really a new frame of reference for everything. This is where the revolution is. So how does discernment come into this?

Discernment: Suggestion, Not Imposition

Discernment is a deeper thinking. It's the deeper debate, the change of mind, if you will. It goes beyond mere debate into the realm of how wills interact with one another. We often don't consider different ideas this way. The ideas that fly around at any given time in history are debated and often fought over. Along these lines, there is a crucial difference between ideology and theology. God doesn't really exist in the world of ideology. Ideology is often a framework we design for ourselves to rationalize actions we already want to take. God, by his very nature, draws us out of that. He doesn't traffic in the divisive work of rival partisans. Remember, God is the voice of unity, not division. God is love.

The debating of ideas rarely rises to a place of perceiving the will of God because discernment requires us to go a whole metaphysical level deeper. Making God's will our own requires a discernment of the deeper doings of Jesus in the world around us. One might ask, how is discerning the will of God any more complex than how we debate right and wrong ethically or the relative efficacy of this or that line of argument or action? Reductionism. We reduce ideas into black-and-white to avoid the hard work of discerning what the more complete, effective truth might be. This is true in everything over which we regularly debate. Ideological debate exists in the realm of definitive principles, so it naturally reduces more complex, nuanced realities into simple controllable ones. God cannot be contained; therefore, discerning his will takes on a deeper searching and cooperation.

When we seek the one, black-and-white answer to a prompt, we tend to reduce more splendid things into rigid mindsets that are simply not the life-giving work of Jesus Christ or even effective within the reality of things, for that matter. We love ideologies these days more than we like each other or any shared identities we may have as peoples. We prefer that reductionist certainty. Ideology is dangerous when it lacks humanity. Fundamentalism is just the most obvious religious example of this. The reduction of truth to something containable, to be fought over or defended—this is outside the will of God for the basic reason that it has closed itself off to further revelation, as if God gave fundamentalism the last word. We do this in every facet of human experience these days, and it's destructive. We'll sometimes sacrifice lifelong relationships at the altar of an ideology we hold dearer than the people in our lives.

How is discernment so much better? Discernment is the will of God active through the contexts and situations of time and place, considered and focused through the lens of the Jesus we know in faith through personal experience. Let's break that down a bit. For starters—and this is really important—discernment doesn't require we ever impose Jesus on others to make the world a better place. We can discern a better world before we even evangelize Jesus to it.

To be clear here, I'm not talking about the dogmatic truths of belief when I speak of discernment this way. Yes, as we discussed in chapter 2, discernment is prefaced by the things that are rocks, immovable truths of faith in Jesus Christ. You have to sincerely get to know the one whose will you want to be yours before the deeper work of discernment is possible. Jesus Christ manifested himself to us, subjected himself to a full humanity, in order that we might experience true divinity. This is the key to discernment. Jesus revealed to us the certainty of his truth. This is the spawn point of religious dogma, yes, but also the inflection point of humility. That is, when the one eternal God reveals his true self to us, we preserve the truth of course, but we must also not close ourselves off around it. The deposit of faith isn't a treasure to be buried. We are not guards at a museum; we are tending to a garden. Gardeners prefer you don't blow up their garden or seal their plants in glass boxes in which they'll die. In the secular world, this is true as well. If we imagine our identity (in the form of anything from political group, people, or nationality) as a museum of truths to be protected, we kill the very things we love. If we're gardeners of these things we love, we develop them further and seek a peaceful world that doesn't harm our plants.

In other words, even when it comes to how we identify in various ways, truth cannot be locked in a box. When it comes to discernment, we have to remain open to how the encounter of Christ continues on forever. Our conversion is always in progress. That's discernment. That openness to which Jesus prompts us, the same openness that welcomed sinners and outcasts, is how we encounter the cutting edge of what is true and beautiful—what is the will of God in our time and place. Once more: the reality discerned, more than an idea simply debated. We find God's will as a nourishing *suggestion*, not an *imposition* for a certain program of life.

I'm going to really upset the completionists and the anxious among us right now: discernment is the work of unfinished thoughts. Pope Francis describes his reading of Romano Guardini's book *The Lord* and lays out some compelling parameters for discernment:[4]

> With Guardini I learned not to demand absolute certainties in everything, which is a sign of an anxious spirit . . . using instead a kind of thinking that allows you to navigate conflicts without being trapped in them.

Again, the operative mode of discernment is openness. Francis goes as far as to say he has an allergy to moralism because if you're not open to the sometimes-subversive guidance of a God beyond all our understanding, the being of which no greater being can be thought, you cut yourself off from Jesus Christ. Discernment is the Christian art of facing the seemingly contradictory truths of the world around you and being possessed by the truth of Jesus Christ rather than seeking to possess it yourself. We look into the world and find where God is at work. We read the signs of the times. As Francis goes onto say: "The voice of God never imposes but proposes, whereas the enemy is strident, insistent and even monotonous."[5]

This conception of discernment has caused critics of Pope Francis, post-Vatican II Catholicism, and the whole imagining of the Church in the world explicit in *Gaudium et Spes*, as I mentioned earlier, to accuse them of a relativism that erodes away the truth of the Gospel and uses mercy as a pretext to the destruction of genuine Christian faith. To put it in a more Protestant lens: newer interpretations of Christian faith in action always threaten those who benefit from an enclosed Christian faith that is more easily controlled by clerics. But this discernment is of Christ. We must not simply return to a reflexive thumping of the Bible and/or Christian tradition as if to keep conversion to Christ clean and controlled. Nobody controls Christ, not even Christians.

---

4. Francis, *Let Us Dream*, 55–56.
5. Francis, *Let Us Dream*, 61.

We have to unleash Jesus through our witness, not reduce him to our own fan fictions. If this conception of discernment is frightening, we have to remember Jesus gave it to us: "The Holy Spirit will guide you into all truth" (John 16:13). Jesus didn't say "I've given you all truth." He gave us the Advocate to help us find all truth. In the Catholic sense, Francis reminds us: "True religion is not a freezer, and doctrine is not static but grows and develops, like a tree that remains the same but grows bigger and bears ever more fruit."[6] We have to go beyond regurgitation of religious truths or even acts of mercy "so that his will may be my will." We have to be patient in allowing the Holy Spirit to guide us and then give to others Jesus as wisely and intuitively as we can before allowing them the space to catch feelings for Jesus.

It's "caught, not taught," folks. And change is explicit in *metaneite*, the verb form of repentance to which Jesus calls us. Changing our minds is the call of Jesus Christ. In a post-truth world, we risk confusing this for a dictatorship of polarization. We might be tempted to think we need to pick a side when, in fact, that charism of Jesus Christ is all-inclusive. Nobody is to be excluded from the community of those who love Jesus; hence, we must consider how we might change and, in that change, become a better imitation of Jesus. We cannot flee subversive realities, we cannot flee worldly changes and trends. Jesus does not call us to flee from the difficulties but go right into them and onto our own crosses of self-giving.

Christian preachers of all stripes love to talk about the "signs of the times" I briefly mentioned a couple paragraphs ago. When we contemplate the signs of the times as Christians, it's not to be what we ought to avoid in a sinful world as much as it is the prompt to consider how humanity at large "hungers and thirsts for righteousness" (Matt 5:6) in these specific times in which we live. Point out hungers to be fed, not sins to be punished. All people of good will hunger and thirst for God at all times and places historically because they have souls that yearn for the infinite and final satisfaction of God. There are opportunities for Jesus to come into the picture in all ages, all places of human life, if only we can be witnesses to his love in those ages and places.

To use the signs of the times to paint fascinating pictures of the end of the world is not so much a witness to Jesus Christ as it is a bastardization of what is a much more powerful message. We cannot look for the end of days as if we don't have to work to bring Jesus Christ to the

---

6. Francis, *Let Us Dream*, 57.

So That His Will May Be My Will

world in which we live today. The desire to write end-times narratives that ought to scare those who don't know Jesus into finding him might work time to time but it's the blunt-force trauma catching of Christ that may not work at all after the headache has subsided. Those who believe because of fear of damnation are hostages, not converts.

There were a number of times in the development of my faith I was blindsided by Jesus in ways that seem quaint in retrospect. In middle school, I thought I needed to be an adamant defender of creationism to be a good Christian. I delivered a packet of papers from a creationist website to my eighth-grade science teacher as if I were rehearsing a scene from *God's Not Dead* or something. I now realize there's no need to defend creationism, and *God's Not Dead* is a terrible movie. Cringey in retrospect, but edifying in that it was a child's attempt at doing what God wanted. There was a summer when I was around the same age where my mother was listening to the audiobooks for the popular *Left Behind* series detailing the very theologically convoluted and narratively compelling story of contemporary evangelicalism's "rapture theology" and surrounding theology of the end times. At the time, I had no concept of my own Catholic faith preaching a very different understanding of the end of the world, so when my mother said she didn't think this is how it would actually go down, I was shook to my young core. My mother said Jesus would just come back on "some Tuesday." I don't know if my mom realized what a concisely brilliant summation of Catholic end times theology (eschatology) she had given. That statement was the beginning of me diving into my Catholic faith in a deeper way than I ever had before.

I tell you those stories because we view conversion to Christ and discernment and all these fundamental Christian truths we are to pass on as static up-down votes we make privately for ourselves sometime after our age of reason. It may be because we're afraid of rejection or something when we try to consolidate it all into an ornament in our lives or, as I have here in this book, a collection of personal religious realizations with a snappy title like "God's Canon in My Life." Jesus Christ is dynamic! God cannot be summarized or contained. Jesus Christ's will for us, even for cradle Christians born into this, is dynamic and powerful in the active process of change, not averse to it. I'm still being converted every day. The first day we find Jesus often embodies our "conversion story," but if our finding Jesus has a hard end date, we're not growing in Christ but shrinking into sin. At the very least, we begin to domesticate Jesus when we refuse discernment and don't allow ourselves to be challenged at all by what God might be telling us.

One of the things outwardly religious people always get asked is how do you know what God wants? I'm annoying because I always respond to this question with prayer, which then prompts a follow-up question: how does one hear anything in prayer? My answers vary on this quite a bit more, but this discussion of discernment is always at the root of it. Don't come with your answers already figured out. We let God into our lives the same way we let new people into our lives: an open heart and an open mind. A dear friend of mine confided to me after some therapy that they were going to identify as queer. They weren't ready to tell family. It's humbling to this day to realize they felt comfortable telling me not just out of the trust of a good friendship but the knowledge that my religion didn't make me toxic. Rather, my belief in Jesus Christ is what opened my heart and mind for exactly this kind of reciprocity.

Let's circle back around to the loving reciprocity of Jesus Christ. Just as faith without works is dead, so is conversion without transformation. I've thrown around transformation a lot in this book. I probably will pitch it at you a few more times. If we have advanced to a point where we sincerely say "so that his will may be my will," are we ready to pour ourselves out? Jesus removes all barriers for us, but once again, this is a consent structure here. On a deeper mental level, we have to remove the final blocks to what may, in our unconscious minds, separate us from God. These are the subtle mindsets that may cause us issues. There is a deep transformation that happens when we introspect at this level.

This is where we look to another saint: St. John of the Cross. Yeah, he's the same guy I brought up way back in chapter 2, describing the structure of the soul. John of the Cross was a reformer despised by his own religious brothers because he challenged them to make their conversion to Christ real in the latent structures of how they conducted their religious order. The latent structures of his Carmelite order had grown weary and strayed from the true gospel message of Jesus in various forms of sixteenth-century corruption. John's solution was a purgative way. He and other Doctors of the Church, as we say in the Catholic faith, perfected two "Dark Night" ways of mental/spiritual retreat and refocus. And when that phrase inevitably makes you think of Batman, try to imagine low-key, detective Batman because we're talking thoughtful retreats where we investigate ourselves here.

When we talk about retreats and any kind of fasting, really, it is important to understand it is not a denial of the goods of the natural world or even human experience. This is the way the spiritually attentive stop themselves from worshipping or being led astray by any temporal thing—anything less than God. These exercises are not a rejection of anything except idolatry, an effort to refocus on our spiritual center, Jesus Christ. Think of them as a retreat that way—a healthy way to get back to basics while also expanding your possibilities for the present and future. Self-care inevitably requires us to deny ourselves some things. There is the Dark Night of the Spirit and the Dark Night of the Senses. Each of these ways allows us to look at a different set of spiritual dead ends and set them aside intentionally once we realize they are only petty substitutes for God.

With the spirit retreat, we are fasting from the things we make up within ourselves to be little idols. In the Spanish in which St. John of the Cross was writing, "mind images" would be a closer translation. Let go of the different mental and intellectual misconceptions that may be incorrectly driving your relationship with God. Think of the misconceptions we've gone over as an example—Jesus as a taskmaster or Jesus as our neat little ornament. The things you know aren't accurate portrayals of Jesus you need to intentionally dispatch of.

With the senses retreat, we find something more akin to the religious season of Lent. Here, we might literally fast as we let go of the tangible substitutes for God. Think of the four substitutes for God we talked about with the Beatitudes way back in chapter 2: wealth, pleasure, power, and honor. A very visceral, tangible experience probably comes to mind thinking about those four things: the sound of paper fluttering, sexual ecstasy, commanding others in a business or government, and a medal being placed around your neck. Let go of these tangible substitutes for God. Some of us here in the consumerist world live for the thrill of Christmas and its wide range of traditions and celebrations. Some years, it does feel like a cult of Santa Claus is unfolding around me as the jolliness of Yuletide drives people to a compulsory worship of the feelings it all brings on. We have to be careful not to worship feelings.

The earlier disclaimer bears repeating. Those visceral, tangible experiences aren't fundamentally bad. I watch the Olympics excitedly every two years; I certainly wouldn't want to discourage anyone from pursuing the honors of athletic excellence. However, if one cannot properly order oneself as to not worship such experiences, then they can readily become rather toxic preoccupations. These preoccupations can become our own little gods. Luckily, today, we have more and more stories of Olympians who understand the cost to their mental health when their dreams turned to toxic preoccupation. It's key to realize all good things in life are here for us to enjoy—not worship. That distinction saves lives and, for our purposes, directs us back toward God.

If we can come back to these two kinds of retreats, Dark Nights in the writings of St. John of the Cross, we can regularly remove from ourselves the more stubborn forces that keep us from doing God's will. This is one way we can remove from ourselves the distractions that send us astray and subvert our witness. A lot of false teaching and misguided thinking can be avoided by way of asserting the kind of humility that comes with these Dark Nights. How many destructive cult leaders were simply captured by a fixation on honor or power? We need humility as our first line of defense against toxic and outright false religion.

More than that, this is an excellent time to recall Jesus's example as an antidote for burnout. We mentioned earlier how good religious folks often seem to pour themselves out to the point of personal desolation. They appear overly pious not just because Christian holiness often allows us to be more attuned to our shortcomings but also because they are burnt out in a way that some of us have regrettably made into a sign of Christlikeness. Burnout does not equal redemptive suffering. You look at any given passage in the Gospels, and you will find Jesus doing something for someone, whether that be healing or teaching or any number of things, and then withdrawing regularly for some retreat and refocusing. He'd withdraw across the Jordan, up into the hills, or into a secluded place. Yes, he did this to pray, but in doing so, he was renewing himself. He spent a not insignificant chunk of his ministry rejuvenating. He does not call us to burnout of any kind! When we consider where Jesus is actually guiding us, we have to resist the temptation to imagine him simply using us for an end. He loves us uniquely. Nobody is simply a tool in God's plan; we're all beloved beyond burnout.

For those of us who imagine the strong, supernatural Jesus more often than not, it's weird to consider Jesus resting; but he did. Sometimes, God calls us out of the fray to recuperate and be with him in prayer. Sometimes, God simply tells us to take a breather. Once you've really gotten into a synced relationship with Jesus, he'll start pointing you in the direction of your favorite leisure-time activities even. I'm not kidding. We have so stigmatized any force telling us how to live our lives that we can't imagine God giving us some off time that we'll actually enjoy or by which we'll flourish more for having in our lives. All measures of human flourishing involve beautiful, useless things—that is, useless for some profitable, productive end. Useless isn't a bad thing, because nothing oriented toward a healthy relationship with God and others is sinful or truly useless. Sometimes we need to take stock of our own house. Jesus doesn't want us to neglect our own sanity, because he knows we're human: he's been there. He knows what it's like. He knows we aren't perfect and does not overwhelm us.

When we work hard to make God's will our own, when we provide the best witness to Jesus we can, when we learn to discern Jesus's voice over that of the deceiver, when we retreat and relax as needed, when we go 110%, we may still be ultimately frustrated. We can be the best missionaries individually and still consistently combat perceptions of who Jesus is based on how his churches behave. The mystical body of Christ aches for its hands and feet to bring Jesus to everyone possible, but that same body is often hurt by pains within itself. We have to talk about this Jesus fan club we're in: it doesn't have the best reputation.

That's where we're going next chapter. Before we go there, let's take that necessary retreat into prayer for that vital rejuvenation. This prayer exercise is going to seem a bit less of a retreat than you may have expected. Intercessory prayer is the kind you do for others. In a way, all prayer involves us asking God to help with this or that. But when we consider intercessions, they're normally followed with "on behalf of." Consider who in your life or your broader world needs some help with something, anything. Hold on to those intercessions.

Now find a peaceful place and some silence. Close your eyes and relax. If you manage not to fall asleep, relax all your muscles by groups and then finally that big one in your skull: relax your brain and all its continuous thoughts. If you're having trouble paring down all the things rushing through your head, it sometimes helps me to keep coming back to a little script. I like the simplicity of the Jesus Prayer. This prayer orients us to God the way we should be oriented toward God in a short formula:

> Lord Jesus Christ, Son of God, have mercy on me, a sinner.

Keep coming back to your script until there is some level of peacefulness in your mind. If peacefulness in your mind is something uniquely hard to accomplish for you, as many of us struggle with such ailments, don't worry: Jesus can sit there with you too. Go there with Jesus. Imagine being with him in a place that centers you. If it's helpful to imagine Jesus as woman or in some way different than a popular interpretation, think of him that way. Build the retreat place that is unique to your personality. It can be a real place, an imagined place, anywhere that some love can be felt. Jesus is there with you.

Now recall those intercessions. Those people who you know need peace, love, or some other good that Jesus ought to provide them. Pray with Jesus for those in need in your life, as well as the needy beyond your corner of the world. Note Jesus's sacred heart, burning with redemptive, reciprocal love for all those you mentioned. Notice it burns for you as well. Allow Jesus to draw you in in an embrace. Both of you linger on the needs of your intercessions, perhaps even emotionally. When the time is right, thank Jesus for listening and being with you in these intercessions. Hear him as he says: "I am with you always."

Chapter Six

Co-workers with Christ

LIFE IS CHANGE. JESUS wants us to work in the change, not refuse it all as unholy erosion. Jesus Christ is our permanent, the person through whom our faith refreshes us always. Jesus also happened to give us the church for living together in him; he means for us to live the gospel together with others. This call to community is inseparable from Christianity. That call Jesus gives us to live together in faith, encouraging one another and building the kingdom of God, has resulted in numerous Christian communities that are vastly internally diverse. The various denominations and sects within Christianity look very different, the more you look.

Within the Christian world, it seems like all churches have fallen somewhere along this spectrum of truth and mercy, as if the two are opposite poles. Some churches waste little time in integrating every popular belief of the world around them into their theology. These churches are often indistinguishable from the broader communities within which they live, for better or for worse. Others are so rigidly traditional or obsessed with their own view of things that various bigotries seem to find a home and rationale for guarding the door.

For the sake of this chapter flowing well for as many readers as possible, allow me to throw around that word *church* with some variations. I am going to jump in between the Catholic/Orthodox concept of church and the Protestant version as much as I can, in the name of inclusion. I'm going to try to balance Catholic examples with Protestant ones where I can. I prefer the Catholic version of Christianity because I think it's the fullest realization of Jesus's whole message, but I'm not going to judge you for whoever you decide mediates your relationship with him. What all Jesus-believers can agree on is a certain basic conception of how any truly Christian church should operate. "Wherever two or three gathers in my name, there I am with them" (Matt 18:20). That is, Jesus is present for those who call on him. This can be a challenging truth in itself, considering what some Christian churches claim to believe.

Another thing I think on which we Christians can all agree: Jesus redeems us. In the community of believers, we ought to forgive like he taught us to—endlessly. In that same chapter in Matthew's Gospel, Jesus gives us a blueprint for rectifying community disputes: forgiveness through one, then two or three, then the whole community, then by Jesus himself. How we as a community of believers in Jesus carry ourselves matters. It matters so much for how Jesus might be found among those who claim to follow him. In other words, we have to imitate Jesus as much as possible, as to allow others to find him through us.

We have to engage with each other on some level of Christian community life. In the famous words of John Donne, quoted in Thomas Merton's book title: "No man is an island." We need each other, and this is only truer when it comes to practicing the faith. It's quite a discrediting image when others look at communities of believers only to see squabbling and condemning. Moreover, it's an even greater indictment when "all are welcome" is a false promise and we instead use the God who is love to exclude and wound others.

The way Christians conceive of communities of Jesus Christ's followers tells you a lot about where the state of Christianity is at any given point. Christianity was once an illegal religion practiced in people's homes in secret. It was later the practice of emperors and monarchs. It had traveled full circle to state religion before it's first five centuries had passed. Scandal and fundamentalism overwhelmed a faith that simply became the impetus of power, fought over like just another throne. Another five centuries would pass before the systemic reform needed to survive it through the Middle Ages was finally enacted. Another five centuries later, and it became so atrophied for its privilege that reform broke out as if a revolution in the form of the Protestant Reformation. By the end of the twentieth century, the Christian faith still occupied a place of privilege in many cultures, often to its detriment there, as scandal and fundamentalism beset its missionary abilities again. Either way, the long history of what it means to be church in this faith has always shaped how we imitate Jesus and how possible it is even to evangelize the faith to our own time and place. Yes, we're going to dabble in an accounting of history, but more on that later.

If Jesus Christ is the mystical body of the whole church of his followers, then you'd think those truly committed to him within that community would seek to follow him and do his work along with him at every turn. Any community of Jesus Christ is a human institution smudged by sin and imperfection, no matter how perfect the gospel contained within it is, but too often we use that as an excuse. The broader context of organized church is too often allowed to atrophy because we either believe we can't do anything to actually change it, or we sincerely believe we've come to fully understand the gospel and don't need to translate it to our specific time and place in history. Some of us see this state of affairs and choose the spirituality over religiosity route, refusing to be a part of any church or becoming only a casual member at best.

We Christians can't separate our relationship with Jesus from the broader community of believers. When we decide the other followers of Christ are of no importance to us, we fracture that mystical body of Christ. We shrink from full embrace of the calling of the gospel. Moreover, as Christians, wherever we fail to include as many of our fellow people at the table as possible, Christians or not, we are missing the full power of Jesus Christ. When it comes to fully embracing Jesus's gospel, excluding others from our own journey is just as problematic as excluding others from our church communities. Inner freedom and outer freedom are inseparable in Christian thought. We need each other, and part of being Christian is living that reality. All of us as Christians need to work together as co-workers in Christ. Before we get into the broader dynamics of communities of believers in Jesus, let's talk about what exactly I mean by co-workers in Christ.

God Works through Everyday Things Too

This final rung of God's Canon in My Life is the most recent. After I had been a youth minister, gotten married, gone to grad school, and entered into what might be called properly "adult life" (if such a thing exists), I found myself going back to what I meant by New Life in Christ years earlier. I found myself wondering if I weren't going to work for the Church in the direct sense, what would my life's work be? How would I know I was living the gospel in secularized society? Surely, good followers of Jesus work in the secular world, no problem there, but how would that look in my life?

These questions were answered by a handful of things all revolving around this core idea that no matter what we're doing with our employment, our personal lives, our public lives, our relationships, and all the trappings of our lived experience, we are to live according to Jesus Christ as if he were our co-worker in all those things. This is the New Life in Christ of chapter 2 but made active and effective through us on a day-to-day basis. This is the awakening part of the faith, where you finally smash the idea that Jesus is a private devotion. No, Jesus is pertinent in all of life's activities, even if you're not explicitly preaching him in each one. Not everything needs to be candles and testimonies to be of Jesus.

The autumn before COVID-19 first really hit the United States, I was closing in on my last semester of grad school. I had to write a master's project in my field of study, public administration. I had an idea that lent itself to the research requirements I would have to do and also was in my advisor's realm of expertise. It felt a little too good to be true. How could a good idea come to me that easily? It was even something about which I had a healthy curiosity! I wondered if I needed to sit on it for a few weeks or months before the project really needed to get started in the New Year. This was a time I was also finding myself praying more regularly, a habit I had always struggled to maintain. It was in that spiritual space I felt the nudge.

We all sense various nudges as we go through life. In the economy of mental nudges, this one was inspirational in terms of what interested me about my degree program, but it was also this very down-to-earth idea I could actually see myself doing. So I did it: I proposed the idea to my advisor months ahead of time. That October, I was also in the early phases of applying for a post-graduate fellowship that would have taken me to Albany, New York, to work in the executive branch of state government, a budding dream of mine. This was a bit of a motivational perfect storm for me: driven by prayer and infatuation for a potential dream job in Albany, I forged ahead with the master's project idea and a prayerful reexamining of what New Life in Christ really meant in my adult life. All those aforementioned questions still lingered, coming up in prayer on a day-to-day basis, while all these things were happening.

My advisor loved the project idea, and we got working on it the very next week. It was a dive into how truly inclusive and democratic the engagement strategies of elected officials and civil servants were in practice. I won't bore you with the details and jargon. In terms of my properly adult life, this was the clearest sign yet that God was showing me the way forward. I was having a spiritual awakening. My spiritual contemplation always returned to this idea of process. Engaging the process. Sometimes, there is no spiritualizing what God is telling you. Sometimes, working with him is a practical endeavor more than anything else. If you see God working through some seemingly a-religious process, go engage that process. You don't need to cake it in religious terms if you don't have them at your fingertips; just follow God's nudges.

If you want to talk about how a-religious things, things that would not even appear vaguely spiritual on the surface can influence your relationship with God, here is a funny example. That phrase, "engage the process," probably arose in my head because the Buffalo Bills were having their first great season since my infancy while all this was happening. Yes, the National Football League team of American football was what probably gave me the words for this mindset. In that context, "trust the process" was a proverbial directive of the coaching staff of a team that hadn't seen any success in a generation. After a few years of drumbeating, that message was turning results. So, uh . . . yeah, the Bills being good for once in my life helped me find the words for a spiritual development! How about that for God's work in everyday things? I did not expect football to come up on three separate occasions in this book but here we are.

By Christmas 2019, I was already in the research phase of that master's project and ahead of schedule in a way I wouldn't realize was so important until a few months later. In early March 2020, I'd be in what would turn out to be my last interview for that fellowship in Albany. The panel heard my excited responses and hopeful words concerning who I am and what doing this fellowship would look like for me. In the last week before COVID hit, I found out I was rejected; I wasn't going to Albany as I had hoped for months at that point. I hadn't felt so disappointed in myself and my place in life since some of my bigger flubs as a youth minister. That rejection was easily a Top Five saddest moment for me. But as that saying goes, which you've certainly seen on a piece of driftwood in a novelties store: when God closes a door, he opens a window.

My master's project was through the research phase now, and as everything shut down and social distancing was imposed, the promptness of having begun it months earlier probably saved the project. That gentle mental nudge five months earlier was decisively helpful. While I wouldn't go to Albany or a sweet research conference in Anaheim that spring, I had a new spiritual outlook and a nearly completed project my advisor said he could seriously see getting published. My project would get published eventually, and months later this "engaging the process" of secularized life with the vigor of spiritual action would give genesis to the very book you're reading right now.

This is a long personal anecdote to say that an active faith can express itself through secularized life in myriad ways just as much as one's more private spiritual life. We can make a difference with Jesus in our lives before we ever do any evangelizing. If we're prepared to do our various jobs and duties in life with the Jesus who goes with us always as our co-worker, there is no work that cannot be holy. If we engage the various processes of life with Jesus at our side, all of life's deeds become imbued with deeper purpose and strength.

Through those transformative yet tumultuous months, I found out New Life in Christ could be more than a set of spiritual guideposts. I could live that New Life in Christ actively through otherwise nonreligious means to make good things in the world God could use in other ways. Just because I wasn't working directly in the church anymore didn't mean that Jesus Christ had to be an ornament more than an active agent in my life. If I engaged the process of the life right here in front of me, with a grateful heart, committed to the divine justice of progress and whatever God's will could be in this time and place in life, I could be Christ's co-worker, in the words of 1 Corinthians 3:9.

In all life's different parts, particularly in our modern world with all its alienating work structures and mores, we tend to section apart every different work and its sets of relationships. Where we can invite Jesus into all sections of our lives, there are opportunities to be co-workers with Christ. Oftentimes, if we do embrace working with Jesus in all these different areas, we find our lives feeling more whole and together instead of just different activities in the same person. This isn't simply the power of feels, bringing Jesus into this or that part of life with a mere emotional intuition. This is a connection to the power of Jesus's divine love in all works.

How can we become co-workers with Christ in this life? Don't overthink it. In the earliest days of the Christian faith, right after the ascension and Pentecost, the apostles haven't even left Jerusalem yet on missionary adventures. This is when the apostle Peter delivers the most powerful line for all of us mere humans who want to be co-workers with Christ: "Silver or gold I do not have, but what I do have I give you: . . . [pause for dramatic effect] in the name of Jesus Christ of Nazareth, walk" (Acts 3:6). Sometimes, we lose sight of the simplicity of doing God's will for high moral principles and heroic virtue. Those are well and good, but Peter didn't invoke anyone but Jesus and his own relative material poverty before healing someone who had been unable to walk since birth. There is so much power in simply knowing Jesus and channeling his strength and conversion through our own relative empathy and belief that Jesus can do the work we can't. All believers are just vulnerable, suffering flesh and bones who happen to have the faith in the one they're talking about. Just start from where you are. Work with Jesus where you are. Work where you are with belief.

Sometimes, dread and other frightful facts of life, internal or external, will slow us down in our mission. But we get up and walk. What we do have, we give in self-gift. With Jesus Christ as our reason, we are rallied to the task. Consider the acknowledgement of weakness by Peter, a noted denier of Jesus, and yet Peter engages the process and gets it done in a miraculous way as a result of faith and the power of Jesus Christ working through him. We are weak, but Jesus Christ is our strength. And not just the divine power of Jesus. Peter uses the title "of Nazareth" here. Jesus of Nazareth is often the academic, nonreligious title given to Jesus the historical figure. It's almost as if we're also being reminded of Jesus's humanity, suffering our lived experience with us, as another motivating force driving us on. Co-workers as it were, together in the trenches doing the work.

Forgive the corniness here: God calls us to believe in ourselves. Just like all meaningful personal change arrives from someplace of self-love, so too does our co-working with God arise from an inner place where we believe in ourselves, at least some fraction of the degree to which God believes in us. This is where we truly enter into an active faith, an active divine life in Christ. Where faith informs confidence, God's work begins in those who know him. And we will not do God's work, we will not be his co-workers in spite of our flaws but because of our flaws. They don't just show us where we have yet to grow; they show us where we can be humble and empathize in ways we might not see from our natural footing in defensive self-interest.

I'm a big St. Peter stan but let's give St. Paul his fair shake. In talking about infighting in early Christian communities, he points out the various messengers through which Jesus comes to us aren't worth fighting over; they're all servants of the same Christ. "For we are co-workers in God's service" (1 Cor 3:9). At this point in the journey, our flaws, our sins, embodied in our differences and imperfections, actually become opportunities to collaborate with God. Just as co-workers correspond on problems they face (in an effective workplace), so we actively work with God through our problems within and in front of us. When we believe in ourselves and collaborate with God, we can enter into his acts of creation in the world around us, maybe even ascend to some level of that theosis we talked about earlier! As co-workers with Christ, we really do the will of God day to day in ways that we cannot forecast before we work with God on them.

The Unitarian minister, author, and nineteenth-century American political commentator Edward Everett Hale had a reflection on this that sticks with me: "I am only one, but I am one. I cannot do everything, but I can do something. And because I cannot do everything, I will not refuse to do the something that I can do."[1] That is what pulls us onto this level of Christian life: the need to make a difference, the need to do something. Whatever that work may be, engage in it actively, and by God, you will be a co-worker in Jesus's work. Even if you are not to be one of God's great Doctors of the Church, you have a part to play as his co-worker, even in some small sense, in your time and place.

That reminds me. This is our framework for understanding Christian church communities. Let's start right here with that discussion, time and place.

Our Time and Place

Our time and place. Therein lies the providential work of right here and now. If our divine life in Christ is to be active and powerfully alive, it is not a private affair. Engaging the processes of life, being active co-workers of Christ, does not exist exclusively on the plane of prayer and private devotion. It cannot. But you may be surprised to find out that this may not mean what you think it means. I don't think our time and place calls us to beat Bibles as much as plant seeds we can nurture only so much. The time and place, the right here and now of being co-workers with Christ, is not a culture war. It is not the clash of civilizations. It is not, as we discussed earlier, the enclave thinking of our good Christian world set apart from the secular, sinful society with which we dare not contaminate

---

1. As cited by Grover, *Book of Good Cheer*, 28.

ourselves. Jesus Christ did not flee from the world; he invited it to eat a meal with him.

When it comes to being co-workers with Christ, I do need to say something about our here and now that is said far too little by those of us who call ourselves Christians: our witness is broken. Christianity, or at least how it is given to the world today, is completely, painfully, and obviously broken. The church is increasingly irrelevant in many quarters of society. The mystical body of Christ is hurting in poverty, hunger, and homelessness. We don't practice what we preach. Christianity is in crisis. It's more than just a crisis of how we're perceived by the culture at large; it's a crisis of how we see ourselves and what we think is actually helpful in saving souls. Of course, Christianity is such a giant collection of internally diverse groups. Some of us value different elements of the gospel more than others, and interpretation does vary quite a bit from denomination to denomination. But all else being equal, we're doing Jesus quite a disservice with how we behave as church in many ways.

I've gone into great depth on theology and beliefs so far in this book. Before this book is concluded, we need to dive into the praxis of actively living with Jesus. Praxis is a much broader academic term, but in this context, think of it this way: the actual practices of our faith in Jesus in the world. This is the practical expressions of how we are church inwardly as congregations and outwardly as witness to the world around us. Perhaps the gap between our beliefs and our practices is one of our biggest problems as Christians in our time and place today. Our belief in the gospel of Jesus Christ is often betrayed by our praxis in the world. If you've really encountered Jesus and the power of his gospel, you've likely been moved by a monumental love story. The whole crisis of Christianity today could be traced to this dissonance between the love we receive and the lack of love we often give. Too often, we don't carry the love that converted us in a sincere, compelling way. Too often, we make love into hate.

The most relevant Catholic example right now is the sex abuse crisis, which has undermined human dignity, consent, and therefore our whole witness to the gospel of Jesus Christ. The response to this crisis has been spotty at best. A collective recentering on Jesus could have helped prevent the myriad abuses, but instead, we often put our heads in the sand. Too many of us in the Catholic Church have reacted with a clericalism, as if to cling to institutional authority at the expense of what Jesus would actually have us do. Clericalism (an overly reverent respect for clergy), by the way, is a uniquely religious sin we'll talk about later, which is also visited upon Protestants in the form of wildly wealthy preachers who feel no sense of social responsibility (and preach the false gospel of prosperity), if not the same outright sexual abuses. When I talk about Protestant examples of the crisis of Christianity in the world today, the consent structures are different, but the systemic sins are the same. Christianity across the board faces internal issues that undermine our ability to evangelize Jesus externally. That practically goes without saying, twenty years on from the Spotlight investigations by the *Boston Globe*, which cracked open the clergy abuse crisis in North America.[2]

Speaking of things that go almost without saying: the transmission of the faith generation to generation suffers as a result of this large-scale crisis. All other things being equal, one may find Jesus through family rituals and the folk-religiosity of the communities in which they find themselves. This chain of faith transmission is the bluntest and least elegant way we find Jesus, but to the degree it's worked for generations, it at least helped people feel like they belonged somewhere. The breakup of these cycles of transmission has reasons deeper than the purview of this book, but the crisis within Christianity itself is one of them. The contemporary uninitiated searcher who might find Jesus is rightfully put off by Christian communities in much of the world once at the faith's epicenter, for the simple reason that the gospel message doesn't seem evident in his church.

In some places in the post-industrial West, we're in a situation where we're two generations deep into a nonreligious trend that many people my age take for granted. We've only known a world that is becoming less and less religious; so we think, as a reflexive observation, that's just how things go. To be real here, of course, the most Christian periods in history weren't necessarily better or even more apparently Christian. There are deep contradictions in every age. But secularization is the standard in much of the world today in a way that has never been seen before. And let me be clear here as someone writing a book about Jesus: this state of affairs was something Christianity in the developed world did to itself, via hypocrisy and toxic crisis after brutally toxic crisis. Some of us prefer to blame disbelief on cultural issues and this or that trend in social or political life. This is a red herring for people who don't want to face the reality of the crisis, in my opinion. Where Jesus's gospel goes, revolution follows. There are many places where the power brokers in Christian faith don't

---

2. See, for example, https://www.bostonglobe.com/news/special-reports/2002/01/06/church-allowed-abuse-priest-for-years/cSHfGkTIrAT25qKGvBuDNM/story.html.

want the revolution part, so they very much benefit from the decline in their own beliefs.

Younger generations (really, a majority of those under sixty, if we're being sincere here) are disassociating from the denomination into which they were born, not because the faith wasn't transmitted well but because we've stopped tolerating hypocritical teachers who don't practice in the streets what they preach in the pulpits. This book is called *How to Catch Feelings for Jesus* in part because a lot of these folks about whom we're always panicking for their not coming to church aren't necessarily abandoning Jesus as much as they're abandoning the organized religion built around him. In that, it's hard to blame them. In the Catholic world, there are distinct conservative and progressive camps, from seminaries to advocacy groups, that distract from the real first concerns of the Church today regarding the sex abuse crisis and hierarchical corruption. In the Protestant world, the contemporary Evangelical movement has not only eroded away most traditional consent structures that would hold it accountable for wild theologies and bigoted practices, but it's also become enabler to a vast multitude of darker evils, from purity culture and violent individualism to a global resurgence of authoritarianism and Christian nationalism. We've got a lot to talk about.

To get back to the praxis of the faith more specifically, if I am going to talk about these trends of our time and place, I have to disclose my own biases therein, to help you see where my accounting fails. I've got three disclosures before we really dive headlong into this. First, I, Andrew Uttaro, am a Catholic, straight, white man who grew up in the northeast United States in the early twenty-first century. My perspectives therein will be evident here. Naturally, we are products of our environments, and what I say here is reflective of the societal and cultural reality of my time and place. I am trying to make this book as accessible as possible but—confession—I am speaking about what I know. I know some voices who deserve to be amplified in all this, and I will do my best; but some stories I am just not the best person for. I'm checking my privilege here and decentering myself with a big helping of humility. I am just another sinful, imperfect human like you, and I don't have all the answers either. I don't pretend to be above reproach in the slightest, and I'm already preparing for how this book may prompt many future confessions. I wouldn't be saying Christianity is in crisis unless I felt a conviction to draw attention to it. *Mea culpa.*

Second disclosure: much of what we're about to talk about is practical, not doctrinal. In other words, the way Christianity applies itself, more than the substance of the faith itself—the praxis, rather than the preaching, if you will. I probably don't need to say to you that shouting at someone that they're going to hell isn't what Jesus would have recommended, but stating the obvious is a worthy academic exercise in these times. A lot of the history, contemporary issues, and religious politics, for lack of a better term, that I'm going to talk about in this chapter are in service of contextualizing practical methods for how the church can better evangelize Jesus Christ to others. Moreover, there is a lot of historical and contemporary context for this crisis of Christianity that it seems like religious folks lack even more than nonreligious people. There should be a constant conversion as individuals as well as a community when we talk about how faith in Jesus Christ should exist in the world. This is to say, there is an honesty missing when we can't even speak of ourselves and our faith within a full accounting of facts. As Pope Benedict XVI said: "A freedom from which the truth has been removed is a lie."[3]

Final disclosure: this is going to get a little political. When I say *politics*, what I mean is the uncapitalized, lower-case form of that word, not any specific agenda or political outlook, though such things are never really removed from any facet of our lives. Every institution, community, group of individuals has a bit of politicking involved. Wherever decisions are made, resources are allocated, or messaging debated, there is an element of politics happening there. Even Christian churches that have very distributed, egalitarian power structures have politics unfolding within them. Part of what makes Christian thought poisonous to broad swaths of contemporary listeners is not really anything about Jesus Christ's message as much as it is about how churches exist politically. How religious institutions express temporal power has a huge impact on where the gospel might be received and just the general feelings toward the faith.

Where do we start? Naturally, historical context comes first, but let's think about how we got here. In chapter 3, we defined some things and spoke a lot about how misconceptions shape how Jesus—the revelation of him and his gospel message—affect how we may encounter him. We prayed, asking, what draws me to or interests me about Jesus? What repels or scares me from Jesus? Has something made it difficult for me to encounter Jesus that may not be Jesus? How far am I willing to

---

3. Benedict, *Christology and Anthropology*, 95.

go to follow Jesus? What might he be trying to tell me? Why does Jesus Christ matter to me at all? Keep these questions in mind, even as we go into a history lesson.

Now we will consider these questions on not just the individual level, but the level on which enthusiastic co-workers in Christ yearn to answer them—on a global, interpersonal, and societally powerful level. Jesus Christ in the world: not just one's personal practice but how our beloved Savior interacts with the proverbial nowadays. This is where disagreement among the faithful arises, and the mystical body of Christ is fractured in many places. This is where we have to find some kind of general terms of engagement across Christian faith to move forward in a constructive way that reforms the toxicity out of our faith and builds a church in which all feel welcome. Jesus would have his church no other way.

A Brief History of Christianity in the World

As Christians, some of our disagreements are valid and important, others are not. I'd venture to say most of our disagreements do not rise to something that would really upset Jesus. At least not to the extent that we shouldn't be able to come together to repair the wounds of the past. As someone who dedicated a significant part of his education to studying the theological side of this, I find the doctrinal reasons schisms happen very interesting. In a discussion of the contemporary crisis in Christianity, I'd be remiss not to at least attempt a cursory overview for contextual purposes. If we want to bring believers together in the name of Jesus's gospel, we have to know what we're talking about. It's hard to be cursory on a topic this vast, but here I go.

For the sake of brevity, I won't be getting into all the splits and schisms and the theological, political, and other reasons that led to them. These many distinctions more often than not make clear how many ways, often unhelpfully so, we divide ourselves. Yes, organized religion deserves the critical eye of all other organizations that claim the authority to dictate our lives. But beyond the sinfulness of Christian churches as human institutions, there is another discussion to be had about the movement of history. For the first millennium of Christianity, there were vanishingly few schisms, in spite of the faith dealing with myriad heresies. Now that's a word loaded with cynicism and opinion, is it not? For the sake of this discussion, heresy is different from schism in terms of impact. Heresies are when the shared center for theological authority properly deals with a misunderstanding before it festers into a schism. Widespread schism was largely avoided for care of what Jesus's gospel actually was.

That said, even in the first millennium, we have at least three major schisms, though the total number of truly separate churches remained within a range you could count with just the digits on your hands and feet. Illiteracy and travel time certainly contributed to this state of affairs, but we'll circle back around to that. Let's zoom back out to the broader world, as that's probably more helpful in understanding our current state of affairs in the faith. Contextualizing Christian communities in nonreligious terms is important to understanding where they are now.

We have to contextualize for time and place when it comes to the schisms in our faith. This is not the same as moralizing obviously wrong things that occurred hundreds of years ago. If people in a different age looked at the gospel seriously, they would not do the evil things they did. To contextualize is simply to understand history in motion. In the case of the Reformation, the rulers of Europe used splitting from the pope as an opportunity to raise funds by plundering Church property and setting themselves apart from political foes. The piety of the beliefs of the Reformers themselves aside, we have to acknowledge politics affects the continuance of the faith in church form, because politics is in every social part of life. In a Europe where the bishops were effectively barons of their localities, the Reformation made practical sense for those monarchs. Even in the emerging nation-states where Catholicism was upheld as state religion, like France and Spain, in the centuries that followed, there was considerable control exercised over the Church in their lands, with rulers appointing their own bishops and seizing property. The acute political reasons for the Great Schism of 1054, the Protestant Reformation, and many of the more partisan stances of the Catholic Church, for that matter, were of a different consent structure that viewed the gospel of Jesus Christ as a commodity to be administered to obedient subjects—not a free gift to all. Our understanding of sacred consent has developed considerably over the centuries, across the denominational board. That's why we need to contextualize our history.

For the centuries before the Protestant Reformation, the whole diversity of Christian groups was only a few dozen or so, if only because travel was slow and basic literacy was almost nonexistent, outside the monied classes. The accessibility of any higher learning, never mind just religious learning, was extremely limited. I mention those very practical realities because it's true in religion and life in general that lack of education and illiteracy are conditions that slow progress. In modern times, the democratization of information with the internet age has sped up general progress so fast that many of the more rhetorical ways we access Jesus and his gospel are antiquated within a generation. If nothing else, information must always be met with information before evangelization comes into the discussion at all. The first demand of consent is always education. We need factual information to decide anything rightfully. To counteract my apparent Catholic bias so far in this section, allow me to offer up our big historical failing on the information point first.

The Catholic Church refused the idea of translating the Bible and the Mass out of Latin and into all the native tongues of believers for five centuries *after* the advent of the printing press, for reasons that were half fear of misinterpretation as literacy rates went up and half fear of more fractures in the Christian body and therefore less power over the Christian world. That is, some pious concerns were wrapped in layers of less admirable power politics. Many sixteenth-century monarchs conducted splits with the Church as a means of greater national autonomy and property control. As we dive into the history of this, let's accept that some splits are more theological, some are for naked political expediency. It's case by case.

When we ask how Jesus relates to the world and why he should matter to the world at all, we have to acknowledge and work with such historical and anthropological realities. Religion is used for power, and like we discussed in chapter 3, religion is always culturally embedded in the time and place where it is lived. We embody our own religiosity, and nobody is ever truly free of their cultural genesis. We will always deal with the cultural indicators that were given to us with the faith we receive. Similarly, we will always have to parse through the culture apparent in any religiosity we are trying to access. This is not a debatable truth; it's just reality. But how do we work within that reality and beyond it? We have to be honest, acknowledge it, and do good in spite of the negative effects of cultural embeddedness. Always acknowledge the reality; never craft your own just to make your case better. That's an extremely important distinction to make nowadays. We need to work with the same facts.

That said, the often-ignored reality of human history is that we always hold apparently contradictory truths simultaneously. Good can come from bad places, and certainly bad things can come from good intentions. In other words, something can be problematic for reasons *a* and *b* and still be relevant and important for reason *c*. This is true in every part of our lives, particularly our political lives; but when it comes to religion, we readily craft these contradictions into reasons for disbelief. Christianity's long history of anti-Semitism is a great example of this. It's a deeply problematic truth that Christian teachings were used to justify atrocities against Jewish people for centuries, but that doesn't need to be a reason for disbelief if you understand the true gospel message was always wronged by that tendency. Many far less nefarious things we think about the faith are like this as well.

Before we go on with the history lesson, let's define some terms: legal secularism, secularized culture, and Christendom. These are really three ways of talking about the same thing—how religious society is and how religious it should be. Those in religious positions of power (and, really, just anyone inclined to moralize and make religion into merely a code to obeyed) will often talk about secularism gripping the outside world. This is an expression of enclave thinking, yes, but it also misunderstands the state of modern secular public life. The world today, at large, is not secular in the sense that religion is removed from it; rather, there is a growing secularized culture across many parts of world. This is a subtle distinction that makes a world of difference. Enforced *legal secularism* is religion's exclusion from public life; a *secularized culture*, on the other hand, normally sees religion remaining in public life, as long as it's kept within the rules by which everyone else abides. If you can't tell if what you're seeing is legal secularism or just a secularized culture, then it's almost certainly just a secularized culture, and you're probably being the drama in the equation.

Excluding some religious exclusion laws in scattered places across the world and nationalist policies of less democratic places like Vladimir Putin's Russia, there is nowhere in the post-Christian West where a secularist regime in the strict sense really exists. Communism is another story, but let's not get on a tangent within a tangent here. There are very few places where culture permits, and government enforces, policies of excluding religion and religious practice from the public square. To the degree religious people feel unwelcomed in expressing themselves publicly, that is a cultural trend that gets more toward how we're perceived. We can complain about how we're perceived all day long, but ultimately, that's more our responsibility to address—not the collection of norms, legal and otherwise, we envision as society.

A secularized culture is one that has, in the political modernism of the last two hundred years, moved past the need for religious authority to legitimize secular authority. Moreover, the conceptual framework of modern democracy enforces no state-sanctioned religion set above the rest in most places in the West, as a way to construct truly powerful, multifaceted nation-states. The more different people can be a part of your nation, the stronger your nation can be (fascism is obviously a rejection of this idea, but we'll come back to that), in the modern understanding of what makes a healthy society. This arrangement leads to less armed conflict and higher frequencies of safe societies with a lot of genuine human flourishing. Generally secularized culture in multicultural nation-states is a stabilizing influence in the world in the broad sense. Sure, it's not helpful for latent cultural transmission of religious beliefs in terms of raw general instances of encountering religious signs, but I think that's too subtle an issue to get too worked up about while still following the example of Jesus Christ.

The peace and stability of a secularized culture is good by the fundamental tenets of the gospel of Jesus Christ. The Protestant world first became somewhat comfortable with this reality particularly after the American Revolution, where such a conception of the political order proved advantageous for the new, emerging nation-state—though there remain various Protestant groups who don't like this arrangement up through the present day (see the frighteningly real 2006 documentary *Jesus Camp*).[4] Contemporary Christian fundamentalists often reject secularized culture in pursuit of a certain kind of isolationism and Christian nationalism, but I'll circle back around to that. Most of the mainline Protestant world has long accepted this state of affairs and begun working in it in a positive way. Secularized culture is not controversial for most Christians in America nowadays. You can probably feel the *but* coming.

As with most things post-Reformation, the Catholic world took a bit longer to wrap their heads around the goodness of the post-Enlightenment nation-state. This has historical reasons: the French Revolution was a bloody conflict that saw the Church repressed and the mass murder of myriad clerics and laypeople alike. In a nation that had been reliably Catholic for centuries, the revolutionaries instituted Enlightenment-inspired state religion—like, I'm talking, devotion designed around the worshipping of humanity itself. Napoleon considered himself a deity in the mold of rulers of ancient Rome, Greece, and Egypt. It followed then that even popes and priests must bow to him. Even after Napoleon was deposed,

---

4. Grady and Ewing, *Jesus Camp*.

his legacy for France and the broader Western world is still not as cut and dry as some later dictators'. For lack of a better way to put this, Napoleon brought about some reforms along the lines of education and civil service that are hard to condemn even now, two hundred plus years later.

There is a reason—well, numerous reasons, actually—historians speak of the French Revolution and its long-term repercussions with such awe. The Congress of Vienna in 1815 sought to stop future people's revolutions like the one Napoleon came to lead, by instituting policies that entrenched political and cultural conservatism and a general reverence for monarchy and the systems of old. This extended to all sectors, from literature to art, from politics to religion. For a religion as entrenched in Europe as Catholicism, all these events were directly affected by the Church and the Church by them. In a lot of ways, excluding the globalization and anti-war institutions set up post-World War II, we are still living with the cultural and political reverberations of events throughout the 1800s. As the cultural and political conservatism of 1815 would be overturned by an increasingly reasonable progressivism within a generation, the same could not be said for Catholicism.

In the Catholic Church, overreaction to revolutionary liberalism prevailed. A failure of imagination arose within theology trying to conceive of the Holy Spirit working in a world that didn't proclaim a loving God at the center of its very organization anymore. The ultramontanism of this period saw local religious authorities set aside, as people looked to the Vatican in Rome for all the answers. France was the bellwether of Catholics realizing they couldn't have state-enforced religion reliably anymore, so they thought the centralized authority of the pope would be their way through the chaos of those decades. A paradigm shift had occurred, and for a long time the Church looked for ways to condemn the modern world and fortify itself against it.

Modernism or the modernist crisis, with everything from Enlightenment philosophy to the Industrial Revolution, led Catholic leadership to decry many things we take for granted today. It was certainly a time of existential searching for Catholicism. The Catholic Church needed time to process the rapid change of the world on its own terms. In 1870, it began doing that at the First Vatican Council. Rapid political change came knocking in the form of Italian revolutionaries sacking Rome, and so the Council was cut short. Almost a century later, the Church would rediscover how best to preach the gospel in the modern world with the Second Vatican Council in the early 1960s. This was also when the Catholic Bible and Catholic liturgy were finally translated into all the world's languages. Finally, the Church made official what had been developing for at least three hundred years prior: a modern world in which Jesus and his gospel would have to be related to in a new way. The old way they were abandoning was *Christendom*.

Before defining Christendom, let me provide the more Protestant perspective of this era over which we've been going. The post-revolutionary 1800s saw a yearning for tradition alongside a rethinking of what exactly that meant. This century saw two Great Awakenings marked by a newfound preaching fervor among ministers in North America. Mormonism and many of the more uniquely North American sects of Christianity arose in this time. Later in the century, the first theological expressions of modern biblical inerrancy and Christian fundamentalism like rapture theology arrived, with which we're still struggling. Back in Europe, the likes of Otto von Bismarck unified Germany in part by way of a shared understanding of the importance of Lutheranism in the people's history. Nationalism in the 1800s supercharged religious bigotry as a way of national identity, leading to an otherizing of minorities at a new, horrifying scale. As is often the case historically, it was Jewish populations who suffered greatly for this trend. With a new wave of colonialism and pseudoscientific developments like social Darwinism in the second half of the century, the toxic form of Christianity that so readily otherizes those deemed outsiders as inferior was exported across the world.

How might we further contextualize our understanding of Christianity historically? In spite of differences within Christianity, there is a broad, normative, now outmoded understanding of the faith that used to be the only way we thought about our faith in the political context: Christendom. If you've encountered Christianity in North America in the twenty-first century, you've probably encountered this archaic way of viewing Christianity in the broader world. It's a holdover from centuries long ago, but old habits die hard.

Christendom is a term with a double meaning. On one hand, it just means the Christian world, spoken of as one collective whole. Beyond this epistemological definition, there lies the more problematic conception of Christendom. In the earlier image, Christendom is the belief that Christian teaching should have a place of privilege in the structures of government. Historically speaking, the first millennia of Christianity saw big-name saints believing that the whole world could be converted to Christ and live under a political state subservient to the religion. Saints like Augustine, Jerome, Ambrose, Gregory the Great, John Chrysostom, and many others saw this as a wonderful possibility they worked toward. The political rulers of the time fancied themselves religious rulers all the same and would go as far as calling doctrinal councils. They lived in a world long before the modern nation-state when the most powerful political force in Europe after the fall of the Western Roman Empire was the Catholic Church.

In fact, the Church in the Middle Ages was really the only way toward education, social mobility, or any kind of attainment beyond mere survival, if you weren't born into royalty. Literacy was low, and the vast majority of people lived in generational feudal states. In that world, there was a logic to this thinking that could not see the sociopolitical revolutions that would occur a thousand years on. As you might be guessing, this thinking is part of what led to the Crusades, the Inquisitions, and other events in Church history that are flatly abhorrent to our modern sensibilities around human freedom and self-determination, never mind the aforementioned sacred consent. Indeed, it's a very different consent structure that envisions religious conquest as a worthy goal. In that, I suppose consent very hardly comes into the Christendom worldview. It's a whole different conception of how this works.

I'm not writing any part of this book, including this historical piece here, trying to convince any Christian in 1550 CE of anything. Looking at Western political history, it was somewhat inevitable the temporal powers of Christendom would decline or at least change. Change is inevitable, and the political change of these centuries affected religion because religion was the dominant political force at the time. All parts of human life are interconnected, and once again we remind ourselves religion is always culturally embedded.

For fear of my book about spirituality turning into a rambling discussion of history, let's focus on the content of the religion itself historically. This is where Christendom has had its most distinctive negative effects in the second millennium. The temporal/political nature of disputes within Christianity in the second millennia contextualizes a lot of the seemingly late-to-the-party stances of the Church in later centuries. After at least two hundred years of complacent power in Europe, the Reformation and the Council of Trent thereafter caused the Catholic Church to become something of a cult of severity. Trent made the bishops far less politically powerful, but the spirituality of the faith was still to suffer for its continued prominence in all facets of society. Though there are certainly great spiritual revolutionaries even within the Catholic Counter-Reformation, something is lost in the rigorous approach that came to dominate the Catholic worldview in the seventeenth century onward. This is why Protestantism and Catholicism, on the whole, generally look so different from practice to theology and everything in between. Like two rival nation-states in an arms race, the two defined every subtlety of praxis and theology in defiance of the other. For four centuries, they bound up their identities in not being the other.

In these centuries, we see Protestants developing a theology of personal relationship that was, coming from a Catholic here, ahead of its time. On the other hand, you had Catholics pushing all their chips in on an overly rigorous sacramental approach to spirituality and a political worldview that saw ourselves as the true arbiters of all things Christendom. Institutionally speaking, the modern papacy arises as the result of political conditions changing beyond its control. The popes of the 1800s were big skeptics of democracy, not because they thought individual freedom and self-determination are wrong; those things just happened to be directly threatening their worldly power at the time. The Catholic reckoning with democracy and freedom of religion would come in breadcrumbs until its full realization at the Second Vatican Council. The finer principle of national self-determination was something actively threatening the Vatican's very existence, as Italian revolutionaries dreamed of marching up the steps of St. Peter's Basilica. Contextualizing history, particularly religious history, shows you how different the gospel of Christ can be from those actually preaching it. We're always victims of our time and place in the grand sweep of history.

Long before the dream of Italian unification was afoot, Pope Pius VI was carried off by Napoleon, where he died in exile. At the time, he was nicknamed "The Last Pope," as if to say, if popes have no political autonomy, now they really have no spiritual authority either. It goes to show you how ingrained Christendom was. The seven popes who immediately succeeded him were fearful of secular power because it threatened them not just in their temporal power but in the authority they had over their own clergy. This rethinking of the Church's place in the political order brings about the modern papacy. I'm not saying the Church is always the good guy historically—hell, no—but temporal reality always impacts how the faith is practiced.

If we avoid using history as an excuse for evil, we can learn from it. Half of the study of religion is understanding how the world reacts back toward it. As you consider the worthiness of any Christian community, you may have to realize history informs social reality. Culture flows in a linear way from past to present to future. This is true in the politics of religion as well. Sometimes, religion motivates politics; sometimes, politics motivates religion. My fellow Americans know this dynamic all too well. Let's start talking about some more recent Christian history.

Christendom persevered in the centuries after the Reformation, as political leaders continued to seek moral legitimacy from religious leaders—except now those religious leaders were often under their implicit or explicit control as a national church or in legal concordats. Fascist regimes in more recent centuries often identify the religions embedded in their societies as part of a protected way of life to be preserved and defended from some out-group trying to destroy it. Fascism is fundamentally a perversion of Christianity, because it depends upon exclusion and purity in a way Jesus Christ never did. If history is in fact a channel of God's grace, it's worth recalling the instances Christianity did learn from history in a time-efficient way.

I sense the need for a sidebar: how is Christianity not, by definition, a force for conformity and exclusion in the world? The short answer is Jesus, but the longer answer is that functional Christian churches are responsive to their time and place in history even if they are late in getting there. The Catholic Church made a concerted effort after the Second World War to make it clear Christianity isn't just a religious fascism, for, among other reasons, the fact that from its earliest days, it embraced a diverse integration of anyone who would come to believe Jesus into the community—the conversion of Jews as well as gentiles being a big example. A beautiful integration is possible in the words of Jesus, where Jesus reaches out to the cultural minorities of his day in spite of what the cultural background of his disciples might say. All that can be included into the mystical body of Christ ought to be. That is, true Christian faith is always an embrace of diversity, like Jesus welcomed all into his flock.

Vatican II codified these truths, as it occurred in the aftermath of the Second World War and the Holocaust. The Church knew it had failed to do enough about that genocide. It had provided so many historical prefigurements in its own past. Explicit condemnations of anti-Semitism were finally written and religious liberty explicitly endorsed, among other declarations that the gospel would have had the Church practice centuries earlier. Protestants concurrently sought to abandon their longstanding systems of anti-Semitism at this time. This had a mind-opening effect across many Christian circles, just as the world at large was changing. What some in religious studies consider the Fourth Great Awakening exploded in the Protestant world during this same time span. Many of the movements for racial equality in the 60s and 70s took from broader religious movements of the time.

There is a wide array of ways religion interacts with the political order and culture more broadly. Once again, remember, I am writing this from my own time and place in history while also trying to look to how God works in all contexts. When we sincerely seek to be co-workers with Christ, we need to look at these broader political and historical trends happening all around us—reading the signs of the times, if you will. I shudder to imagine trying to be a good Catholic in 1870, 1525, or 1013, but that's what believers in those eras had to figure out. There are certainly many things now our descendants will look back on as betrayals of the gospel, a century down the line. That's how the flow of time works: we come to know the gospel better once we are able to see the broader picture, and unfortunately, it's difficult to look at events in context when they are upon you in the present. Let's get into the time and place with which I am best acquainted: twenty-first century America.

History as an Epicenter of God's Grace

Christianity in America is one of those uniquely layered experiences. On one hand, the history of the faith in this country is surprisingly diverse, while on the other hand, there is a consistent theme of reductive theology that runs throughout that same history. Those of us prone to deconstruct our various Christian sects here need to remember that the U.S. has always been the laboratory for evermore exotic, weird, and sometimes horrific variations of Christianity. While you generally get only one Great Awakening a century, that ethos continues to this day. Something about Christianity in America exudes a certain entitlement to interpreting Jesus however one wants here. I'm not trying to paint a negative picture, but when we talk about this religion in America, the background is that this place is perhaps second only to Reformation-era Germany in terms of experimenting with what the gospel really means.

In the American context, you will hear it proclaimed frequently that the United States is a "Christian nation," bound by a Judeo-Christian moral code. In the twentieth century, the Cold War ideological struggle led American politicians to add "under God" to many things here, including our money. Opponents of this thinking will point to the separation of church and state as a founding principle of America. Their criticism is that a truly pluralistic, free society requires a separation from the institutional and moralistic force of organized religion. The most honest truth is that both of these notions are composed of a handful of convenient oversights.

The former is a longing for Christendom that comes to mean Christian nationalism in our American context—thinking that there is anything relevant about the religiosity of the founding fathers of this country. The latter is an allergy to moralism that escalates to the point of artificially excluding any moral thinking from public thought. With the former, we're talking about a dangerous precursor to fascism that should be roundly avoided. With the latter, we're talking about trying to control each other's consciences in a way that is not sustainable. To be clear: keeping government free of institutional meddling by religious institutions is a good thing. This separation is perfectly necessary and fine as long as it isn't fearful of anyone motivated by faith acting according to the convictions therein. We have to avoid regimes of legal secularization that end up being forces for otherizing masked as tolerance.

What would this book be worth if it doesn't motivate you to act with Christ's mercy in the realm of political action? Elected officials are there to represent a group of people who also have convictions. Diversity of opinion is good in a truly pluralistic democracy. As American society becomes more diverse in its voices, this will be very rejuvenating as Americans of other faiths also bring their worldview to bear in their governing. It's not a problem if we can all flavor the system together with healthy doses of our own beliefs. Even nonreligious people have values in the way they govern. To make a distinction between religious and nonreligious convictions always ends up being a distinction without a difference.

Historically speaking, the founding fathers established separation of church and state not because they felt strongly about free religious practice. They wrote an arbitrary deism into the founding documents that referenced God but never got so specific about it as to impose a certain dogma or denomination. They did this because the religious makeup of the thirteen colonies and then the early republic was diverse enough that they couldn't pick which one they wanted to set apart. And by diverse, I mean in terms of just the five or six sects of breakaway Protestant Christianity. It was more of a fifty shades of WASP situation at that point. Looking back on the authorities of the world in which the founders lived, it was standard to establish some religion. For them, it would have been an open question whether the state needed to be protected from the church or the church needed to be protected from the state. Remember, the early United States was composed of many people who were often members of churches that existed in North America because they were unwelcomed in England. But let's also address the other side of coin here, which is more frequently attempted here in America, in my lifetime, at least: America as a distinctly Christian nation.

Contrary to what Christians in America may think today, the founding fathers had a conception of God that was very different from our modern perspective. For the founders, the God of Christianity was an impersonal, unrelatable type: he was the "clockmaker" God who is at best a distant supreme being à la the aforementioned Jeffersonian Bible. Even if they had written the Christian God into the founding documents, he wouldn't have been the same guy you think you're talking about today.

It's important we abandon the "one nation under God" thinking because it leads to Christian nationalism when unchecked—the aforementioned insidious perversion of the faith that sees the U.S. Constitution just as divinely inspired as the Bible. We also shouldn't look to the founding fathers as our only source on how America should be operating, because . . . well, you know, where this is going: they also didn't mind slavery and they didn't enfranchise women, natives, or just non-landowning people, for that matter. They intentionally wrote many means of exclusion into those founding documents. Try to decenter your own perspective when considering why you believe America needs to be a certain way. The more you study the history of this nation, the more you can see its evolution through history was its strength—its ability to change and integrate new people, truths, and conceptions of itself.

How Christianity exists in America is more a cultural question than a governmental question. Religion is always culturally embedded, almost always deeper than the political order is. Church and state are both spoken of specifically in America's founding documents because the founders, for as flawed as they were, knew both institutions would always exist in their new country. They knew we'd struggle with this friction between the two great authorities affecting any person's daily life. Nowadays, we recognize both sides of this church and state coin because we understand neither should dominate the other if we're to have a truly inclusive, multicultural society.

This is all to say, this is a more complicated question than either "don't be religious in public" or "submit all law to God" extreme. Both of those approaches don't work anymore, if they ever did, and shouldn't be tried. Once again, we live in a secularized culture that functions well enough for the religious and nonreligious alike, if we can each respectively repress that sinful human desire to dominate others. Freedom and domination are two principles that really don't get along. Recent history in this country seems to think the latter is the only way. At the very least, Jesus calls us to a consensual society that airs on the side of freedom, not oppression and domination.

So let's get consent back into this then. Just like a sincere relationship with Jesus is rooted in a consent that doesn't diminish either person, so too are modern nation-states supposed to be free societies formed by the consent of the governed. The social contract that holds democratic government together is rooted in the same principle that . . . well, allows you to freely catch feelings for Jesus! I guess in this instance, it's meant to compel patriotism. I guess it all comes together! In good Christianity and good democracy, consent is a key. Understanding the relationships in play are key in both cases, just as the act of will to be a part of either one is key; the true version of both these things requires a yes to truly live within it. Moreover, when we consider the necessity of an excellent freedom, a freedom bound to consent and the goal of a harmonious pluralistic society, we assent to something that is anything but aimless or oppressive. In the words of Pope John Paul II: "Freedom consists not in doing what we like, but in having the right to do what we ought."[5]

In America right now, we are struggling with deeper levels of cultural and political nuance on the whole. We are engrossed in destructive, unwinnable culture wars that have jumped the shark to the degree they aren't really in the realm of government anymore. In the fully modern context, legal secularism can lead to religious persecution, as we can see with authoritarian regimes across the world; *but* that persecution doesn't exist anywhere that the democratic principles of a free republic are strong, fascism is banished, and we can all accept that not everyone around us needs to believe the same things in order to live together in peace. A secularized culture is not devoid of God or any religious influence. Far from it. It's flatly stupid to try to tell people not to acknowledge

---

5. John Paul II, "Homily of His Holiness," §7.

their values in the way they live in the world. A truly free America that lives up to its vision demands such tolerance and inclusion.

Nonetheless, Christendom still tries to subvert this order, led by those thirsty for power. Christian nationalism reaches for that domineering perversion of the gospel that knows conformity, not consent.

We worship a crucified Christ. We worship a God who subjected himself to human existence to sacrifice himself for love for us. He was executed with an instrument of state torture willingly. He did not himself become or elevate a sociopolitical leader to impose some universal law of culture and legal order. Yes, I say that as a Catholic who submits to the pope. Not the same thing. Jesus himself worked outside the political order of his time and preached a just submission to it when possible. Being second to God and others in today's world doesn't require rejecting fundamental doctrines of Christian faith in order to fit into the modern societal order. It does require us to have a more practical approach to how we present Jesus Christ. We have to remember Jesus uses our time and place and puts us where we are for a reason. Consider that reality for a moment: there is some good for you to do where and when you find yourself. That can be a helpful lens to consider how you might be a co-worker with Christ in your own time and place.

History is an epicenter of God's grace all its own—and indeed, some of God's most powerful graces and transformative works come to us as a result of historical and contemporary struggles. Where the political order goes beyond a secularized culture into real legal secularism, there is the possibility of religious persecution; but if there's not, don't try to find a way to feel persecuted. Christians in the United States of America are not persecuted in any meaningful way. On the contrary, we have a certain level of privilege. How many explicitly atheist politicians or public figures can you think of in this country? Maybe one or two, but you'd be hard pressed to count all the people who would identify as some kind of Christian. We as Christians should certainly be able to exercise the restraint to live peaceably with those who disagree with us. To fail in this generalized tolerance is to sin against basic tenets of Jesus's teaching. To use Jesus to justify intolerance is a special kind of sin that spits in the face of the Son of God himself.

God works through history, and political leaders exist in their current form as an expression of the permissive will of God. I don't mean this in a divine-right kind of way, that was always a mere power grab, rather nobody comes to power without God allowing it to happen in an amoral way. Not everything politicians do is ordained by God, and oftentimes none of it is. Power corrupts, and absolute power corrupts absolutely, as the old adage goes. Ironically, this is the same reason I prefer nationalist symbols stay out of my places of worship, but that's another discussion for another day.

It is safe to say if a political leader claims to be a religious leader, they are a fascist; and if a religious leader claims to be a political leader, they are probably starting a cult. In the modern political order, God doesn't need to be the central focus of public life. God works through circumstances of society in ways we can't pretend to understand. In fact, I venture to guess free, pluralistic societies better produce the conditions for the sincerest conversions. To those who preach against secularism, there is a refusal to acknowledge God working in ways they don't understand. The existence of a secularized culture has to be an affront to God if they don't control it, their thinking goes. To the religious leaders who have carried favor in the halls of power, they are jealously afraid of losing it. For the privileged, equality is indeed oppression.

This vilification of secularism in the broad sense denotes a yearning for the lost dream of Christendom that God has shown through the progression of history is not where followers of Jesus Christ need to be looking right now. It is an idolatry of power that gives rise to sin personally and then institutionally. We shouldn't yearn for our civic leaders to embrace some religious dogma as a platform. That's not what power needs to look like in a functional democracy. The real power of faith in Jesus Christ will not be the fascistic bravado of a demagogue like Donald Trump. People who yearn for angry rebukes of those with whom they disagree are departing from Christ's charism on a very basic level. Contemporary political populism often leaves its adherents indebted to an isolating, morally corrosive dogma stripped of their individual agency beyond the rigid platform. That's not Christian at all, and it tends to infect others like a disease, even if they don't subscribe to the same worldview. One might even call that approach the call of false prophets, if you want to sound really biblical about it. Since I said that name, I guess I should confess that, yes, I think who you vote for and what political principles you believe in have moral ramifications and divine ramifications.

Christendom, if we're going to diagnosis it spiritually, might be called spiritual worldliness. That is the reduction of religious devotion to an instrument of power and control. On a spiritual level, it is really one of the worst social sins we can commit as Christian people. It is a gun of otherizing to use our belief not for the propagation of the gospel and helping the poor but for condemnation and our own self-exaltation. Those are direct contraries to who Jesus was and what he taught. Our self-righteousness is not the goal of devotion and relationship with Jesus Christ. Such an aim is ultimately a domestication of Jesus and an effort to possess the unfathomable God. Therein lies the keystone of the crisis of Christianity today: possessiveness.

Possessiveness and the Crisis of Christianity Today

Before we diagnose the crisis of Christianity today, we have to understand its causes. Christendom is only a toxic expression—a symptom, if you will—of the deeper illness among Christians nowadays. I don't pretend to have all the answers, but one wouldn't be too hard pressed to see the problems. Though new conversions and retention are often parsed out into different issues, the failure to nourish the seeds of the gospel evident in both trends speaks first to an overly simplistic assessment of what to do with our thirst for God. Once we catch feelings for Jesus, those feelings are often taken advantage of for ends that don't ultimately bring us back around to the true Jesus.

When we are really head-over-heels in love with Jesus and aspire to discipleship in his example, we risk becoming narrow-minded crusaders. Immature faith in Jesus, new faith in Jesus, can often cause us to not know what to do with ourselves. We might turn to our more basic, belligerent tendencies as sinful human beings to project our love for what we've found. This enthusiasm needs to be offered up to Jesus and purified by the gospel, because it might lead us to toxic Christendom. Christendom always diminishes the gospel. A culture war narrows our vision of what might be the movements of the grand scheme of God's plan in our time and place in history for fights about menial trappings of societal privilege or vain devices of power. Think about the travesty it is that some people sincerely desire after Jesus and are then told they need to exclude whole groups of people from their lives, as if Jesus calls us to isolate ourselves. It makes my skin crawl, honestly.

Some people see converts as merely new fighters in the culture wars. Culture wars are foolishness. Temporal, worldly power brings on stasis and corruption. If you engage in a deeper dive into Christian history than the lesson you endured earlier in this chapter, you'll discover that when

Christian churches have expansive temporal, worldly power, they're generally worse for it. There is a marked difference in the early church between how it existed before legalization and how it did afterwards. The corruption begins immediately, and it's something we must be weary of in every time. That historic reality should not prompt an aspiration to being persecuted but rather an invitation to meekness in the face of worldly power. A lot of the crisis of Christianity today can be traced to these kinds of pseudo-religious cultural battles that don't help us embody Christ to anyone as much as make new enemies.

Let's ground this practically again. What does this have to do with being co-workers with Christ? We as Christians have to be a light to the world in a lived sense. We cannot simply preach a moralistic excellence that never goes beyond itself into the broader cultural context. Are we a light at all if we're indistinguishable from the darkness? Is excluding a wide range of groups from ethnic, racial, and sexual minorities anything more than darkness with a religious flavor? Such bigotries undermine our witness, explicit or implicit. On a very basic level, the imagined, prototypical convert-in-waiting who is a truly worldly, self-obsessed individual needs to be able to see Jesus Christ as an improvement over their situation. He is, but he will not be able to reach anyone if his mystical body on earth in the church—the Christian faith, more broadly—is no more than another moralizing bludgeon for exceptionally critical hypocrites hiding behind the guise of organized religion. I'm not pitching a new marketing scheme for the faith either, because I really think Jesus's intent from the beginning was always to be as inclusive as divinely possible. At least, here in my homeland, it seems like inclusivity is hardly a priority.

I understand the Christian faith in its Christ-correct form is one "set apart" from the world in Jesus's holiness and divine life for us, but we have overstated this to a grievous degree. To some Christian preachers, pretty much everything outside of the church building is just oozing with sin. That's a problematic way for us to look at a world in which we're trying to evangelize Jesus. It's part of a mindset that feeds the aggressively hell-focused, yearning-for-the-end-times toxicity of many Christian groups here in America. In that thinking, why would anyone work too hard to make the world a better place, if it's all abhorrent and to be avoided? Again, immature faith in Jesus will be swayed by these kinds of appeals. It's when we mature in our faith, when we hear Jesus's call to justice, we realize such preaching leads us to otherize anyone outside the purview of that preaching in a way that is simply not of Jesus.

Anyone who believes they have something sacred will experience what I call "wall instinct." It's that primordial drive to protect the sacred over sharing it. It goes right back to our survival instincts' protecting sources of nourishment. This is not Jesus's calling. Jesus was not a segregationist in any usage of that term. "The world" from which he calls us out is his language for self-absorbed existence, a sinful state natural to all humanity post-original sin. When you understand that, it erases the need for theological or behavioral purity tests for entry into a community of Jesus followers. Nonetheless, the possessiveness implicit in these immature Christian worldviews remains.

Moreover, when you wall in the Christian message, the message mutates, like every teaching that is isolated and hidden. Those trapped within the walls who have no power in the dynamic suffer the most and become resentful at best or destructive at worse. The power brokers within the walls eventually buy their own hype and become completely toxic. This is the frequent outcome of nascent cults. We must be Christians in engaging the world as it is. Wherever there is any selflessness, any generosity, any good will, Christians must be there. We Christians must be Jesus to the world in a way the world might actually recognize. We have to live in the world as it is, not as we wish it were. We have to be Christians willing to be tested. And we have to express real love, Christ's love, the kind that is free from possessiveness toward the gospel itself or the people we hope to evangelize.

When we are armed with Christ's love, free from possessiveness, that's when we are able to be co-workers with Christ in our time and place more readily. That's when we are able to make sense of even the most nonreligious realities of our world through Jesus, not by judging the world's moral fiber. Possessiveness among Christians really colors our view of the gospel message because it's us trying to control Jesus. We want to craft the message the way we want it to come across politically or historically in order to get our desired outcome. In that, we violate the consent of the ones we evangelize by holding back the full story, and in a way, we violate Christ's consent, turning him into our puppet. Possessiveness within the cultural framework of our Christian institutions is destroying us, our witness, and, yes, the myriad helpless victims who are objectified by it.

Christian religious institutions—and allow me to be frank, the Catholic Church—are facing the biggest crisis for the faithful since the Protestant Reformation. The child sex abuse crisis so weakens the authority of the Church as to point out how Christendom has corrupted it. The dignity of so many has been violated and ignored by a hierarchical order that valued its civic power over the gospel message. Immeasurable evil has been done by the Church and those who serve it often with little to no accountability. And as these sins were uncovered on an increasingly mass scale, the leadership of the Catholic Church—here in the United States, at least—resorted to political alignments that would allow them to be a force in culture wars. When the Catholic Church in America should have entered into a prolonged state of contrition, the hierarchy largely chose clericalism and culture wars over the process of healing.

If your credibility to preach the gospel message has been so thoroughly undermined, then you might find yourself reduced to a moralizing body with purely superficial importance. The American Catholic Church is in desperate straits of its own doing. It is my conviction that to be faithful to it as it is presently conducting itself—and always, for that matter—means criticizing it in good faith, avidly. This willingness to criticize churches cannot be viewed as breaking rank, as if the culture wars must be our priority. The willingness to criticize churches and the power structures within them is profoundly Christlike. We're talking about the guy who flipped tables at the temple and gave the Pharisees a piece of his mind, after all.

Now let me fulfill the promise at the beginning of this chapter with the Protestant side of this. The crisis of Christianity today is a bit more cultural on the Protestant side. For a little over three generations now, the Evangelical movement in America has evolved from a genuine revival movement into an increasingly belligerent cultural insurgency. Organizationally, most Evangelical churches aim to be everything the mainline Protestant churches here in America aren't. They rejected the idea of church membership altogether and unmoored themselves from any overarching religious authority that might regulate how crazy the theology and politics of their congregations might get. Their evolution over the decades has capitalized on the growing weaknesses of the mainline Protestants on whom they preyed. In the 1990s, when culture war issues à la abortion, gay marriage, and whatnot became explicitly connected to "how Christian you are" here in America, the mainline Protestant denominations were really hurt by it. Possessiveness of what it means to be Christian turned off many and has annihilated whole denominations in a demographic crunch.

The Presbyterian, Episcopalian, and Baptist denominations, previously the big three of American Christianity, saw a generation up and leave, not wanting to be part of a possessive, judgmental culture. Now, by simple lack of membership replacement (i.e., the older generation dying off, to be blunt about it) that generation and their children have no connection to any church. Some mainline Protestant churches will simply shrink into oblivion in the next three to four decades. Most American Protestants who still want to be a part of something will be stuck between the rigid hierarchical churches of high liturgy (i.e,. Lutheranism, the Orthodox Church, and Catholicism) and the evermore radicalizing Evangelical movement. Fifty years from now, all Christianity might be broadly categorized into churches with heavily centralized authority and churches with heavily decentralized authority. The post-Christian world will more and more have only a few centers of Christian togetherness.

Post-Christian: what do I mean by that? In North America, Europe, and much of the industrialized West, we have entered into a post-Christian era. This is not to say Christianity can't exist in it or even grow in it. What it does mean is that the former hotbeds of Christianity are moving to a position of being predominantly non-Christian or straight up non-religious. For many religiously unattached people in the post-Christian world, their idea of Christianity is the Christendom we've laid out here. That's a negative image before you even add in the child sex abuse crisis and other institutional crises. The unattached may have some experiences with Christian faith that were positive, but the power-hungry Christendom of past ages undermines the credibility of those of us who would like to show them how to catch feelings for Jesus. A demographic crunch born of many Christians drawing lines in the sand of culture wars has led to an impasse in the evangelizing mission that the culture warriors have no hope of overcoming.

The toxic possessiveness that seems synonymous with Christian faith in our culture has brought about the undoing of the Christian witness—the fear of saying that truth is disappearing more and more with each passing year. Unattached people, or "nones," as sociologists talk about them, are the fastest growing group in recent studies. These aren't necessarily atheists or agnostics—that's a more specific group. These folks shrug their shoulders at the question of religious affiliation. Nothing in particular is their answer. This is in part because it's simply more socially acceptable to identify that way than it was even twenty years ago. It's also preferable to identifying with any religion as to take on their historical, theological, and social baggage, if you will. We've already gone over a lot of things with which one wouldn't want to be associated, eh?

Now if that idea upsets you, that's fine; you might just feel strongly about Jesus and others coming to know him. But if that's how you really feel, then don't make the insane, possessive rhetorical step that says Christianity is dying. That's a fatalistic viewpoint that just doesn't want to face change. What has happened over the last seventy years here in the United States is not the death of our Christianity. Secularization has unfolded, certainly, but nothing really approaching the "death of Christianity," whatever that would look like. Toxic Christianity is dying here in the United States. The kind of Christian faith that hurts readily and gives Jesus only to an increasingly scarce self-righteous bunch—that way of living Christianity is dying, but that's not the gospel message anyway, so I am not mourning it.

If you feel that Christianity is dying in America, a country that is more influenced politically and culturally by Christian moralism than perhaps anywhere else in the world right now, than I think you need to reevaluate some things about your own worldview. If simple numbers on a graph or cultural privileges are paramount for you, you might not be talking about the same faith I am. If the toxic version of Jesus Christ's gospel is what you're actually trying to protect, bring that to Jesus for some discernment. That's a dead-end street.

Ornamental Christianity is also dying. Earlier in this book, we talked about how we are often tempted to keep Jesus at arms' length. On a personal level, it's a natural reaction to change; we seek to preserve ourselves, so we avoid transformations unknown. On an individual level, this is procrastination or resignation to a more sheltered existence. On an organizational, societal level, this is nothing short of destructive. As cultural change shook American life in the 1960s and 1970s, it wasn't fundamentally a rebellion against organized Christianity as much as it was a rebellion against the weak, toxic, ornamental faith that lends itself only to moralizing rigidity and bigoted exclusion. Feminism, racial and economic liberation, and general openness to diversity are not enemies of Christianity any more than they are enemies to Christ. Fearing the liberation of those long oppressed is not of Christ at all. Fear, as it almost always is, comes from the deceiver who only looks for our further disintegration and erosion of the gospel message. Ornamental faith always values the stasis of its trappings, repressing the revolutionary Jesus no matter from where he appears.

The Christian people, clergy and lay, who marched in protests and were activists on the front lines of those mid-century movements knew the beacon of justice explicit in the gospel and acted upon it. They were ahead of their time, and it took the consent structures of organized Christianity a generation to catch up. By then, the walls of moral rigidity had already been assembled around the old ornaments. The forces of organized Christendom in America have aligned themselves in an anti-progressive cultural stance because they desperately want to hold onto places of power that are rapidly slipping through their fingers. When change comes knocking, those in power will resist, appropriate it to dull the rough edges, or both. That reaction exists in the halls of religious power as well. To fear liberation is to fear the gospel of Jesus Christ. Then, like today, we have to actively discern the work of Jesus Christ, resist the rigidity that tempts us for Christendom's sake, and become co-workers with Christ in tangible ways, even beyond religious contexts. You have to be willing to risk seeing Jesus in the secular world.

If you want to be helpful going forward, you have to reacquaint yourself with a living Jesus who is at work in our time and place in history. That is the timeless liberator Jesus who never sided with the rich and powerful. The most effective Christians in the post-Christian world are those who don't need to feel persecuted by every slight. Protecting religious freedom is one thing; a persecution complex is another altogether. Accountability, if nothing else, validates our witness within the post-Christian context. If you insist you have to be a cut above the rest, with a certain kind of cultural immunity and introversion to protect your beliefs, you have already lost track of the true Jesus.

This post-Christian state of affairs is, in a way, a reset of our evangelizing Jesus to the world. We shouldn't walk into any contemporary context and just assume everyone in the room knows this Jesus guy. Though it's not a true blank slate, it's an opportunity to recast the gospel for ears that have never *really* known it. It also provides a new challenge that those in the pre-Christian world didn't have to consider: how to disabuse others of misunderstandings about Jesus without coming across patronizing or needlessly preachy.

In both the Protestant and Catholic worlds, the possessiveness that violates the missionary consent, the moralizing bigotry of walled enclave-building preachers dreaming of Christendom, and the vilifying of the unbeliever will only further destroy our church communities and scare off potential converts. Change comes for all of us. The winds of change blow the sails of all boats. If you think you can just not put your sails out, you're just sitting there waiting to sink. You're taking the first step toward fading away into history. We have to set sail in the winds of change, not be content with merely floating. We have to turn back to Jesus sincerely if we're ever to really address the crisis of Christianity today, if we'll ever repair our witness in a meaningful way.

So where do we start? How do we bring Jesus to a world fully engrossed in its autonomy, imbued with an aimless freedom that knows only false interpretations of Jesus? How do we effectively inform the world of Jesus Christ and then transform it as God would have us? How can we be co-workers with Christ in this context of our current time and place in history if our churches are so weighed down by the erosion of possessiveness and moralizing bigotry? How do we meet the crisis of Christianity today?

The power of Christianity for a post-Christian world will be our love. Sometimes, that will simply be our acceptance of the unknown. Where other forms of knowledge fail to satisfy the human soul, churches may still be a place of consolation. No verdict or diagnosis, no matter how accurate, can prepare a scared soul for what lies ahead. We should not look at this like an unhappy last resort but as God providing the opportunity for revival. The challenges that face society at large today are not solved overnight. Our shared natural environment is in peril. Our sense of global community and dialogue seems to be eroding away into ever smaller groups, in spite of how interconnected we actually are. The poor are getting poorer, and the rich are getting richer. Systems of bigotry and oppression aren't going down without a fight. There is no shortage of need in the world, and we are called to be part of the solutions.

The patience and faithfulness of the gentle Jesus has the power to shepherd scared souls through the turbulent times between broader resolutions. Moreover, in a world increasingly defined by cynicism and nihilism, it is the Jesus of true Christian faith, the one who made love and service to the needy a core virtue, who can help us embrace hope as more than just a quaint luxury for the naïve. We will have to show up in our actions more than our words, going back into the trenches of service as a church of the poor. We will have to be sincere, loving co-workers with Christ. A humble church is the point. It is when we are most depleted in worldly power and impoverished in morale that we are closest to Jesus Christ. If Christian faith is ever going to be endeared to the general public again, it will not be taught; it will be caught, in proximity to the helping hands and feet of Jesus Christ's followers.

We as Christians have to be perceived as trustworthy and truthful. Transparency is the only option, and the fact we have to clarify that is a little window into how needing we are of a new approach. Perhaps it strikes you as un-Christian to be concerned with how non-Christians perceive you. Sure, we have to hold fast to Christ, but make no mistake: the more you don't care how you're perceived as a Christian, the more you refuse to see Jesus in others, and the more you build those fickle, un-Christian enclaves. That is, the more you become comfortable with building walls, the more you take pride in not caring about the world outside your church, the more the missionary zeal of Christ's faith leaves you. The more this occurs, the more your faith lacks works and then love; and if your faith lacks works for the love that prompts those works, your faith is dead. At that point, we're not followers of Jesus Christ anymore; we're just an insular fan club that wouldn't recognized our Savior if he were there sitting with us.

We need to build Christian communities that are accessible, churches that are universal.

What Is a Universal Church?

The church needs to be universal. That is, everyone, no matter their race, age, sex, sexual orientation, or any other differentiating factor, needs to be able to see themselves at home in our faith. Our churches need to be theologically and practically, as a matter of community elements, welcoming to all. Jesus was welcoming to all, and so we need to be. Everyone—and I mean *everyone*—needs to be able to articulate the church as a place they can feel at home. At a very basic level, this means not looking at the flock, the people in the pews who are with you, as mere collections of identities or even receptacles of beliefs. Every person must be viewed with the dignity of the image of God: an unrepeatable creation of the being who is love and salvation provided freely, in starkly blunt terms.

We're not selling salvation here. We're not even inviting people to a collection of lifestyle choices as much as a relationship with Jesus. Why should we not make Jesus as accessible as possible, then? Repeat it with me: if the only reason you're in church is because you're afraid of going to hell, that isn't a home; that's a hostage situation. I've already said it, but it's worth repeating: fire and brimstone isn't an effective way to evangelize people for Christ anymore. That is an emotional colonization that is toxic and unhealthy from square one.

The Church has to be a welcoming home for all, first and foremost. This is what us Catholics mean when we call our Church universal. I know, take a moment to have a chuckle at that assertion, if not a complete spit take. The Catholic Church struggles nowadays to come across as a welcoming home for all. That sign of the true church is one with which it's always struggled. By that, I mean Catholicism is definitely more well known for who it excludes than anything else it has to say. We're not nearly welcoming enough in our theology or our practice, though I hope and pray we're moving in that direction. When we turn to Jesus sincerely in the challenges of our own time and place, we find ourselves rediscovering the power of his message as it truly is—truth and mercy, with a special attentiveness for practicing what you're preaching and making Jesus felt in a real, if only sacramental, way.

If we are to be true co-workers with Christ, pursuing that theosis of being a part of his work for real, we have to ask ourselves what the obstacles are to truly becoming the universal church in which all can come to know Jesus Christ. How can we build an institution that people want to be part of? How do we chose action over reaction? How do we craft our praxis of the gospel into something that both makes sense and is true to who Jesus Christ is?

Jesus said: "Love one another as I have loved you" (John 15:12, 13:34). Everywhere I've seen a beautiful Christian community, it's been so beautiful because it practiced social love, not just devotion to a rarified image of Jesus. Jesus commanded us to love, not just as a matter of individual virtue but as a social call. It's a social love that is self-giving in the model of Jesus. If there will ever be a Catholic revival in the post-Christian world, it will not be by the coercive machinery of the hierarchy and its secular allies, which has committed so many social sins of abuse and bigotry. No, the revival starts where a critical mass voluntarily embraces the faith and lives holy lives in this example of the social love of the gospel in their communities. This is the most basic way we fail to be a universal church nowadays. Once more, Jesus calls us to an even more radical vision of his love lived out: "Love your enemies" (Matt 5:44). Is there any greater calling to communal love in all history?

So if this is the radical calling of Jesus Christ, then what stops us from building such a church? Beyond historical context, it's worth revisiting the primary source that all Christians observe. Anyone who's been unexpectedly hit with a stream of numbers and colon-verse numbers knows the Bible is used as shorthand to justify a whole lot of things. So let's start with the book. Yeah, that book. We already had a basic overview of the Bible in chapter 2, but a thorough sidebar of its social dimension opens up our eyes to how even the unifying text of Christian faith calls us to revolutionary social love. Let's talk about building a more welcoming, universal church via the things that unite all Christians.

Why and how is the Bible used to exclude and otherize people so much in Christian churches? Contemporary biblical fundamentalism holds that the Bible needs to be read wholly literally, as if it is without error or any antiquated logic or consent structures. This is sometimes called the Bible's "plain sense reading," and to be fair to Protestants, this is a somewhat out-of-control modern reinterpretation of what Martin Luther originally called *sola scriptura*. *Sola scriptura* means the Bible alone, and even though Luther pioneered this theology, he probably would not agree with biblical fundamentalists of contemporary Evangelical Christianity. The bible is the inspired word of God to all Christians, but the extent to which that makes it flawless is a real flash point among different Christian groups, particularly in the Protestant world. While the forces that undermine truly gospel-like church communities in the Catholic world often come back around to clericalism and other hierarchical failings, many toxic Protestant churches often become that way due to a particular reading of the Bible. For many such denominations, the only authoritative source is the Bible.

This idea, ingrained in so much of modern fundamentalism, is really a whole new beast evolved beyond that centuries-old theology of Luther. Nowadays, biblical passages like Matt 19:5, Gen 3, or 1 Tim 2:12 are used to make women into second-class citizens in various ways: bound to subservience to husbands, ridiculed for the sin of Eve, and unable to preach in the stead of a man. I bring up those specific examples because nobody who seriously participates in the modern world considers women to be inferior by nature unless they're into some really toxic shit. If the Bible is your exclusive, only source of Christian teaching, and you insist it has to be read literally without any historical or critical context, then you create a regressive form of the faith. This is like finding a tire and using it by running on top of it. You'll get somewhere, I suppose, but you'll hurt yourself in the process (probably others as well) and miss out on the far more effective usage of tires: automobiles.

To get Catholic again for a minute, *Dei Verbum*, the Vatican II constitution that dealt with the Bible, specifically said that the Bible needs to be read in historical context.[6] This has big implications, because it is our embrace of the reality that the Bible has all the errors any document written by humans will have, no matter how much it is the inspired word of God. The writers of the Bible—and, yes, Jesus himself—didn't question the existence of slavery or the oppression of women in their time. The books written by Paul, for example, feature him frequently using the image of being a "slave to Christ." Later translations used servant there instead, because they wanted to censor the unsightly historical context of that word. Nonetheless, the use of slavery in the Bible was used to justify the sinful institution in more recent centuries. Women were similarly made second-class citizens by way of Eve's sin and interpretations of the Bible unmoored from the development of theology beyond the historical biases to which the authors were originally blindly indifferent. Like we said way back in chapter 2, the message of the Bible and the content of the Bible are very different things. If you refuse that reality at the altar of absolute biblical inerrancy, you corrupt the very thing you claim to be faithfully preserving. This then becomes corrosive to church communities, when one discovers they are not believing in a strictly biblical Christianity as much as a very specific interpretation of it moored to the biases of the preachers at hand.

The common retort to such a criticism is that building our faith around anything other than the Bible and this "plain sense reading" of it is the work of humanity corrupting the good news by changing it. The gospel of Jesus Christ does not change, but its time and place implementation does develop. The structure and deposit of the faith itself are unchanging, but how the faith is dressed up and expressed in the context of our time and place has to be renewed. Even within the Bible, you can see the revelation of God's will develop through time. For example, the idea that the sins of the father are visited upon the son and following generations changes from the books of Exodus and Numbers to the books of Deuteronomy and Ezekiel; even within the Old Testament, some doctrines develop and evolve! Like we said at the beginning of this chapter, change is something within which Jesus wants us to work, not resist at all costs.

We don't need to give into this fiction that the Bible is plainly comprehensible to all people at all times. It needs interpretation and

---

6. Second Vatican Council, *Dei Verbum*.

contextualization because Jesus knew, as his Gospel message would be written down and canonized, that it would be open to myriad misinterpretation and perversion. The apostle Peter even acknowledges this in 2 Pet 3:16 when he says, "[Paul's] letters contain some things that are hard to understand, which ignorant and unstable people distort, as they do the other Scriptures, to their own destruction." It then follows that Jesus would give us a definitive interpretation, if not something imbued directly by him with the authority to provide such definitive interpretations once he left. But I've already expressed my belief in Catholicism's keys enough. If you want more on that, check out the Council of Rome in AD 382.

This is all to say, the truth of the gospel of Jesus Christ is powerful for all our Christian living and teaching, but when you read it, you have to be aware of the contextual frameworks in play and how things have developed over the centuries. Jesus didn't stop teaching when the last apostles died. You don't even need to be Catholic to acknowledge that Jesus is alive in the world today, doing work with and without us. Oceans of ink have been spilled on the Bible and who has the right to interpret what is and isn't God's will through it. I said many intra-Christian disputes do not rise to the level of offending Jesus, not because I don't think the core tenets of the faith are important, but because if we were really listening to the Holy Spirit, we'd resolve them without schism. Perhaps that sounds naïve, but God is love, and if religion in his name bars love between people, it's not of him. That is true of how we interpret his word too. If we use it to wound others, we're doing it wrong.

The more research you do into ecumenism, the more you intentionally look for Jesus in the efforts toward Christian unity, the more you realize some of our most insistent and lasting differences are rooted in solvable theological disputes that got buried underneath a mountain of otherizing and the atrocities that flow from such selfish triumphalism. Moreover, every era of Christian history has its one sacred idol. The thing that is chosen over Jesus in order to be the tip of the arrow in a divide. Right now, we're living in the Bible-idolizing period. The current waves of deconstruction sweeping biblical fundamentalist sects are the first closing act in this era of idolatry. All of this is to say, if we're driving further away from other Christians as a result of our interpretation of Jesus message, we're doing it wrong—even if we think what we're doing is Bible-based. Love Jesus and others, and you're on the way. Pursue ecumenism, the reunion of Christian believers.

Evangelizing Jesus to the world in our time and place is often discussed as physically bringing people back to church. That's an admirable goal we should reach for, but it's really a half answer, if you ask me. To many younger people, and the religiously unattached in general, such a goal can actually be unhelpful. For those who never went to church, it is awkward to enter that space, unless you're going there for yourself. I have been railing on about the religious dimension of consent throughout this book for a reason. It's got to be their choice without anything but Jesus compelling them.

This doesn't just mean telling people what goes on inside a church during a service if they're not asking; this means making our churches into communities people want to be a part of anyway—communities in which anyone could see themselves at home. Oftentimes, I find the more appealing element is community life—the extracurriculars of parish life, if you will—that may be the first point of contact for the uninitiated. That's really the disposition of any authentically Christian community: outstretched arms that welcome everyone, regardless of anything, because that is how Jesus welcomed people in—without reservation or judgment. Let's repeat it: *everyone* needs to be able to see themselves at home in the church.

We can't massage this calling into a controllable version that doesn't compel us to conversion within ourselves. If you feel the reservations or prejudices welling up inside of you when certain people walk in the door—congratulations, you have something to confess to Jesus and pray for healing about! Anywhere Jesus is held up as the central organizing force needs to be a safe space. I use those last two words together very intentionally. "Safe space" is what Jesus was creating when he brought all society's rejects together in his ministry. Don't talk down to others just because you don't understand their lives and their struggles. Judgment-free zones are what allow for our most sincere spiritual nourishment.

When you judge somebody before they've even found their pew, you've already begun the process of trying to kill the seeds of Christ's New Life in them. You are already committing a more damnable sin than any mere outward identity of the people walking in the door. The call to free Christian communities of judgment is clear in Paul's Letter to the Romans. This is the early Christian church in the most diverse, metropolitan city in the ancient world, Rome. Paul tells them explicitly "Let's not judge one another anymore" (Rom 14:13–23). When we exclude anyone from the body of Christ for any reason, we are wounding people. We are not doing Jesus's work if we are actively hurting people with our distorted version of his message. We cannot and we must not put conditions on the unconditional love of God.

How to Build an Actually Universal Church

I don't really think we know how many ways we are driving people away. How many former believers are exhausted with the simple, austere moralism of Christian congregations? How many people have been traumatized by someone claiming God's authority declaring them sinful, disordered, or damnable? How many spiritual wounds have been delivered in the name of Jesus? Before any physical violence always comes the spiritual violence of otherizing and condemnation. A universal church is impossible if this is acceptable behavior for followers of Jesus Christ.

There's baggage here to be addressed. Speaking as a millennial, my generation grew up with a certain siege viewpoint as a Christian. People my age have only ever known Christianity in crisis, the church in scandal, so holding onto it will feel edgy or truly scary at times. Even in a small town like the one in which I grew up, those who might identify as Christian don't often go any deeper than that because of all the ugly baggage they'd have to take on. Therefore, if a church is to be truly universal, it starts within. Our church communities have to be welcoming enough to overcome the baggage hanging overhead, if you will—the baggage of the Christendom preoccupied with the past, yes, but also the baggage of the flatly moralizing perversion of Jesus's gospel message of our present time and place. We have to be able to see that our creeds and liturgies are not cudgels for mere private comfort or swords for spiritual violence. They are places to encounter the true Jesus.

We have to really catch an internal faith first that feeds us. That internal faith is born of sincerely unselfish people honestly living the sacramental realities of Jesus Christ in their lives. "Caught, not taught" is such a powerful catechetical saying because that's what happens inside functional Christian churches. Jesus is caught like a new friendship and nourished into a lifelong relationship. That's something you have to catch, which is not helped by isolation or triumphalism.

Being from a small town, I always got a kick out of the thinking rural communities are somehow "God's country," simply by the seeming lack of open dissent in those places. That's more the result of a lack of diversity than a lack of people dissenting on the common religious tradition in that particular area. It's clear to me the consent structures that lead to healthy relationships with Jesus and healthy church communities as a result can be just as broken (if not more broken, considering how unopposed cultural beliefs naturally mutate and degenerate the gospel, if it's not renewed by diverse interpretations) where it seems like they have more sway among the populace. We'll put on elaborate acts of personal and public piety in an effort to mask the failure of our isolated belief. It's just different kinds of religious baggage to be overcome on the two sides of the urban-rural divide.

Baggage exists everywhere, just like you're not magically a better person for living near people with different perspectives. And when I say baggage here, I am referring to those sins that are somehow more common among the religious: racism, sexism, homophobia, and transphobia. Religiosity often brings our deeper-set bigotries out, under the cover of piety. When this pattern goes unchecked for a while, you'll get people running to religion as if it were shelter for their bias and racial animus. At that point, you'll begin to see the wide-eyed theological gymnastics that go beyond domesticating Jesus into the territory of weaponizing the gospel.

We can't mistake the baggage for the treasure of our beliefs. Just because this is the way things have always been doesn't mean that's how they always should be. This is true with our church communities. Yes, the deposit of faith, the who of Jesus Christ, and the dynamics of his gospel message have to be preserved. But too many people think they have to hold onto every toxic cultural morsel of what was passed down to them. That is simply not the case when it comes to Jesus Christ. He uprooted the toxic beliefs and practices where he could, because he knew they were obstacles to a sincere relationship with God. Toxic Christianity is dying, and we cannot go down with that ship. If you establish a sincerely lived, unselfish community of believers who refuse to domesticate Jesus, weaponize him, or subscribe to myriad different toxic interpretations of his Gospel—well, now you're ready to truly start looking outward.

Take it a step further and imagine you're lesbian, gay, bisexual, transgender, or even just questioning your sexual orientation. Some of you reading this book don't have to imagine this in the theoretical; it is your life. Imagine you are trying to worship Jesus Christ and those around you are constantly pushing you away because so much social teaching in American forms of Christianity has been reduced to sexual morality. So much practical theology in contemporary Christianity is a pass-fail test along lines of how well you adhere to teachings on sex. We reduce the LGBTQ population to sex acts as to otherize them and put them outside the reach of Jesus's all-encompassing love.

As Catholics, we often fall back on the phraseology of "disordered affections" in the catechism, forgetting the other parts of that same passage that teach about how non-heteronormative relationships have just as much potential for good and holiness within them. We focus on the sinfulness with our LGBTQ brothers and sisters because we ourselves have not developed properly ordered affections in our relationships and sexual lives. We fail to welcome this community because we don't want to see them as equal human beings; that would require us to look at how we've sinned in areas where we insist they exclusively are the sinners. For them to profess these beliefs in spite of all they've been through makes us feel less, so we all too often decide we have to knock them down a peg. Nothing is less Christian than this tendency.

We're all sinners, and Jesus built his church for sinners on the back of a guy who sinned to his face repeatedly. However, when we talk about our brothers and sisters of communities like LGBTQ, the repetition of the reality we're all sinners is not necessarily what's needed. This is a check-your-privilege thing. As a straight Christian, I've not had to deal with being told my very identity is sinful all the time. For our LGBTQ brothers and sisters, it is far more healing and welcoming to speak of the church community as what Jesus promises we can become in it: co-heirs to the kingdom of heaven. Little things go a long way for groups who are consistently otherized by Christian churches. If we hope to be a universal church, these are not supplementary bonus options for really forward-thinking communities. No, these kinds of considerations are essential to living out the gospel sincerely.

If you are lesbian, gay, bisexual, transgender, or not heteronormative in any way and remain in a community of other Christians, I applaud you. Your decision to not leave the faith is a profound witness to the power of Jesus Christ. To you, I say it's not just the true gospel of Jesus Christ that proves your goodness, it's the catechism of the Catholic Church and canon law. It's just the parts of those books the moralizing power brokers of our day like to ignore. Our Christian churches need to reevaluate our pastoral, practical priorities. We have to reconsider our approach. When whole communities readily feel excluded, implicitly or very explicitly, in many cases, we haven't built the universal church to which Jesus calls us.

I'd also go as far to say there is a sacramental holiness to the LGBTQ experience of coming out of the closet to loved ones. It's a Christlike act loaded with fear and a very sacrificial risk to your social belonging if you don't know how it's going to turn out. It's really a form of redemptive suffering. The coming out of those who identify that way are witnessing to Jesus in a uniquely powerful way, but that story and theology are not mine to write.

What needs to be said here is something for which Pope Francis found particularly incisive words: reality is more important than ideas. The excellent freedom I wrote so much about in chapter 3, that freedom with justice in mind, is the age-old Christian principle that finds new meaning in our time and place. We deny the gospel when we preach only the parts of it that don't change our world. Conversely, we impose Jesus as a mere idea when we ignore the contextual significance of the realities around us. Our world right here and now, as it is, can be transformed for the good of everyone, Christian or not, by the gospel of Jesus Christ. To save the world the way to which Jesus calls us, we must know it at the secular level.

That's why Christianity cannot become an enclave religion. That's why we have to stop pretending that if our faith is not held up in a place of privilege, it must be protected behind walls. That's why we must allow Jesus to guide change through us, not imprison him in fundamentalism. That's why Jesus cannot be domesticated and perverted into the moral backing for oppressors. Being a co-worker with Christ is not a matter of imposing ideas but seeing his work already in action in the reality around you and then going there to the work.

When we refuse to preach and live out the fullness of Jesus Christ's message to all facets of reality, not just the ones with which we're culturally comfortable, we begin to abandon the work of true faith and justice in general, for that matter. The gospel message doesn't live in a vacuum outside of the linear progression of reality. Reality contains so much suffering, particularly for out-groups downtrodden by ideas that don't consider reality in their theology. The dictatorship of ideas over reality is really the core of the crisis in Christianity in which many churches in the post-Christian West find themselves. Our faith has become completely disembodied from the reality it exists in. We find ourselves in love with Jesus, and instead of unleashing it on the world, we imprison it as our commodity, believing that if we build some fan fiction about why it's not working in the world today, we'll exonerate ourselves of responsibility for the Great Commission. Insisting upon this moral principle or that behavioral norm is simply another domestication, commodification, or weaponization of Jesus. Decades now of doing that has made Christian faith, and therefore the living of it in public life, a seemingly intractable affair, unless you resign yourself to the enclave.

Waving off that problem to blame the inverse, a crisis of moral relativism in our society, is to treat cultural relativism as if it is not the symptom of human beings designed to yearn for God in the first place (I see you bringing up Benedict XVI, and I promise you he would similarly demand a theology of church that acknowledges and works within reality before idealized austerity). Ideas over reality always turn Christian faith into an enclave religion, moving it toward becoming another mere tool of division, welcoming the deceiver to the doors of the sanctuary. This is how you can have atrocious churches like the Westboro Baptist Church express such pernicious hate. The examples of this today are almost countless. But what then of my alternative? What makes us genuine co-workers with Christ in these times?

That portion of chapter 3 where I posited the contemporary Black Lives Matter movement is an expression of the Christian calling to justice is relevant here in the context of church organization. Structures of racism within Christian churches have to be thrown off explicitly. There are clerics and laypeople alike in Christian circles today who decry "wokeism" as a vile sin akin to racism itself. To clear up the philosophical side of things: there is no hardened academic connection between critical race theory (CRT) and the anti-religious Enlightenment figures to whom "anti-woke" Christians feel the need to connect activists. It is not Christian at all to assert that the anti-racist efforts and the legitimate philosophical underpinnings that center the black experience historically are somehow in conflict with Jesus. If genuine Christian reconciliation requires penance for past sins between peoples, then what you might call "collective guilt" may come into play. This is to be our doorway to reconciliation for past and present wrongs, not a weight upon our national and ethnic identities, as if we must be shackled in the proverbial stockades of shame. There is an invitation to build a more just world there.

CRT and restorative justice theory in general are not nefarious. They're simply challenging to dominant groups. White fragility, a tendency to feel wronged by any collective guilt from the past, is deepening a divide between white Christianity and black Christianity. That's a huge problem. This expresses itself in so many white Christian leaders in this country tap dancing around anything that might decenter the white experience of things. Dictatorial ideas in the form of narratives of heritage and a specific kind of present shared experience can be a powerful trap of division for Christians. The U.S. Catholic Bishops Conference, for example, makes token efforts to address racial inequality, refusing to critically discuss issues at the institutional level—never mind speak to a need for liberating change or abolition of police and prison systems that have consistently, from their creation, furthered white supremacy and undermined the common good in this country.

A basic understanding of critical race theory is absent or openly decried. CRT is not a threat to the family. CRT is not anti-Christian or even counter to the gospel message in any meaningful way. This is Jesus calling us to greater conversion to him through racial critique. It is a call to be that universal Christian church in which everyone can find a home. Just as Jesus calls us to love others as ourselves, we have to decenter ourselves in the ways we think about ideas and reality. Reality informs us that life has spiritually relevant social ramifications for simply being black in our American cultural context. God is always close to the dispossessed, and if we are to be co-workers with Christ, we must be as well. Bigotry cannot exist in any church that claims to be of Jesus Christ. Jesus demands no bigotry can guide us, as we will be judged as we judge others (Matt 7:2).

Excellent freedom is God calling us not only to justice, and progress as a result, but to the gentle healing and conversion of a human family that is deeply distrustful, in spite of being more connected than ever before. Just as the genuine voice of God expresses itself in proposition, not imposition, so should our witness as a whole Christian community be of united grace, not standoffish zeal. Respect the yes of Mary, the consent of conversion, and build the shared table. This is not to say we shouldn't denounce the sin when we encounter it but on a person-to-person level that's more complicated than proselytizing.

When we express and act upon the kind of excellent freedom to which Jesus Christ calls us, the kind that seeks justice and therefore brings progress to church and culture alike, we break free of these toxic, moralizing idolatries destroying the very Christianity we think we're preaching. Unfortunately, in my experience, the toxic faith of those who think Jesus's love extends only to those who are sufficiently subservient to a narrow set of moral teachings is commonplace. This worldview ultimately ignores practical realities of life, which prevents out-groups from living up to its superfluous standards. Reality is more important than ideas. Yet, as Christian churches, we often don't act that way. For Protestants, the source of this disconnect is often rooted in a more fundamentalist view of Scripture. For Catholics, it's often the way we envision authority and how believers should relate to said authority. Let's dive a bit deeper into this widespread Christian disconnect between theological ideas and the reality in which the gospel actually exists.

I'd contend clericalism is on a par with all the other bigoted *isms* and phobias—racism, sexism, homophobia, and transphobia—in that those who believe the clergy are above reproach in any way seek an elevated class of moral superiority. Clericalism might be thought of as an overly exalted view of priests, bishops, and other clerics. Supremacy as an idea is simply the other side of the coin of bigotry. Jesus can work within most institutions for the good, but it is so easy to lose sight of him when one thinks too highly of oneself. For laypeople who struggle with scrupulosity in their faith, clericalism just distances them from potential help. You can almost hear the rant about the Pharisees coming on here, eh? I'll spare you the obvious biblical comparison and point to the Jesus who flipped tables.

The angry, table-flipping Jesus story pops up in both Matthew 21 and Mark 11. Stories and teachings that appear in multiple Gospels are often the very important ones. Jesus knew why those vendors were in the outer court of the temple. They had practical purposes for worshippers there selling the necessities of the temple. So why did God in the flesh get angry, then? He was mad at them because they epitomized the institutional rot that distracts and excludes people from right relationship with each other and right worship of God. He says: "My house will be called a house of prayer for all nations . . . but you have made it a den of robbers!" (Matt 21:13). Jesus was quoting Scripture there, specifically Jer 7:11 or Isa 56:7. We can recontextualize this, given how the people of Israel of that time felt they had exclusive access to God and realize Jesus really wanted all out-groups who were put down and excluded in society instead to be welcomed to him. At the Council of Jerusalem in AD 49, his apostles would declare gentiles didn't need to become Jews before becoming Christian, calling back to that important episode at the temple. This has massive implications for contemporary Christianity, particularly here in a country that has prefaced so much of its national identity on believing itself the righteous actor in all matters.

Jesus is flipping the tables of institutional oppression. He was upsetting the clerics of his time who started seriously plotting his arrest and execution that day. Consider the question at stake in that event in our own context. What tables need to be flipped in the time and place in which God has put me? What institutions plot the suffering of those whom they should be serving? How many of those tables of institutional sin are right here within my own church? What is the right way to flip them?

Contemporary clericalism assumes moral clarity rests only with those who pretend they have no doubt and can therefore control or exclude others. Clericalism seeks to exclude and raise up a moral certainty that is not only not true faith but also an authoritarian tendency. It's a form of Christendom. For Christianity as a whole, but especially Catholicism, there is a need to consciously avoid authoritarian tendencies in order to adhere to the gospel of Jesus Christ. As clergy became scarcer in recent decades here, more and more laypeople became a part of running official church ministries and operations, which often exacerbated the clericalism problem. We have to work for unity in spite of these tendencies that seem to be the entry point for a lot of the evils tearing churches apart. In many parishes, I've seen rebellions against pastors originating from a sense of powerlessness against an autocrat. There are exceptionally easy ways to avoid that kind of dynamic.

This is the entry point into the faith for the sin of all the toxic, bigoted *isms* and phobias I mentioned earlier. Clericalism is authoritarianism's religious cousin. Clericalism is an appeal to ordained authority at a time it's profoundly unhelpful to make such appeals. As you read this, you may be put off by the idea that any clergy has the authority to exclude anyone after the tragedy of the sex abuse crisis or the indigenous residential schools. You'd be right before those crises even entered the discussion. Clericalism reinforces the dictatorship of ideas over the reality in which we need to evangelize the gospel of Jesus Christ. The crises of modern Christianity are the result of us Christians not only building walls against reality but insisting the eternal ideas of our deposit of faith don't need to be translated for the world. Many clerics and laypeople in the Christian world today espouse some kind of clericalism as an answer to this existential crisis in the religion, as congregations hemorrhage worshipers in huge numbers. Exalting clerics doesn't ground the faith in the lives of the aimless. A good, holy priest can be a great example of faith but rarely does that example smack of exaltation or supremacy. This kind of Christian faith does not and will not survive in the modern world because it denies reality and definitively fails to evangelize therein. True social love is lost on us these days.

I really believe we Christians must make a concerted effort to hold our preachers and clerics to a higher standard more anchored firmly amongst their flocks. The unity of Christians, and therefore our witness to Jesus, is at stake whenever a collared co-worker with Christ calls another co-worker with Christ a mocking name. Theological and practical disagreements aside, we should not be calling each other heretics or demons and writing up fantasies about schism and division. Disunity is not of Jesus; yearning for it is a distinct sign of the voice of the deceiver. Tell me zeal for the gospel is motivating your monologue all you want; we can have edifying discussions without fracturing the mystical body of Christ. It hurts our witness too.

We have to be dramatically more critical, because when our debates overflow out of our religious echo chambers into the general public, real harm is done to the perception of Jesus among those we need to reach. Condemnation and excommunication are not smart tools of the church in this third millennium of Christianity; but if they are to be used, they need to be used not just on genuine heresy but on those who openly and maliciously fracture the body of Christ for their own purposes. The people who claim to have the authority need to be addressed with the critical eye with which such authority comes in any other arena of society. Who are most openly co-workers with Christ? Preachers, ministers, and priests. All these authorities need to share accountability when they hurt their flocks, while also humbly accepting the right kind of external accountability. Accountability is so easily forgotten when one sets oneself on a personal mission to share Jesus. The deceiver's voice has a special sound in the minister's ear: "You've given your all to this cause. You deserve to be absolved of this without consequence." For Catholicism and Christianity's other more rigidly hierarchical denominations, we ought to better use that rigidity for accountability.

Anyone who wears that distinctive collar needs to be reprimanded far more readily for all kinds of abuse. I understand the clergy has a consent structure all its own, but what is the use of hierarchical authority if it cannot protect against evil done in the name of the gospels? I am asking that question in a totally non-rhetorical way. Though the Catholic Church has done more to combat the child sex abuse crisis than is often reported and Pope Francis's papacy has been marked by myriad financial and organizational reforms, I think the question runs deeper than headline-grabbing institutional abuses. This is a matter of divine mercy.

We need ministers in the church who are first and foremost merciful, like God has been merciful to us by Jesus.

If you refuse the common good for the sake of your own stance, you're missing the point of Jesus's message, which gives to one another according to what is needed. Selfish bad-faith resistance to the common good is never needed from Christ's followers. That includes both members of the clergy and laypeople. People who do not even attempt good-faith encounters with the world as it is actively undermine the gospel message.

To those excluded from full participation in Christian life, you need to know your lived experience of Jesus Christ is a righteous dissent. In the Catholic context with which I am most familiar, there is a theological dissent rooted in practical reality. This exists among the laity and reflects a dissent among the clergy. Dissent is important in Christian thought, particularly when it comes from the margins, where those made into out-groups by moralizing clerics and laypeople who see only trenches of the culture wars in which to fight, yearn and thirst for Jesus. When you speak up in good faith, even within the context of Christian faith, Jesus will go with you in the work of restorative justice and progress toward a more universal church in which you can find a home. Just like we speak up for secular issues that matter to people, so too we must speak up for theological issues that matter to people in how the church conducts itself. Don't balk from the idea this kind of dissent doesn't lead to reform in the church. That's what the Second Vatican Council was, and that's what the next council will be brought on by: a thirst for Jesus not yet fully quenched by the theology and praxis of the Catholic Church. This is often the way co-workers with Christ move toward an actually universal church.

A Mercy-First Church for an Ideology-First World

This all sounds very theoretical, so let me put it a different way: I have many friends of no faith at all. They know I love Jesus as a core trait of who I am, but they also know it's the source of my better tendencies, not a force adding toxic sludge to their lives. From there, it's the old religion-and-politics-at-the-dinner-table gambit—or just the dinner table gambit, if you're trying to save on syllables. You let them initiate a conversation and go from there with their preconceptions and needs at the front of mind—friendship first, as we went over last chapter. Our missionary credibility comes not from our insistence on moralism; it comes from our accountability, trustworthiness, and mercifulness. Remember that the truest relationships with Jesus are rooted in consent as the minimum standard on which you build friendship.

If we don't respect the free will of a nonbeliever, than why should they expect our God to? Our approach has to engage the world as it is with a Jesus who embraced the world as it is. It's not one or the other. The authentic Jesus didn't just sacrifice himself in total self-gift; he also ate with the sinners. Truth and mercy. We have to remind ourselves God doesn't impose himself on us, violating our consent; he proposes himself to us. We must abandon aimless culture wars that impose Jesus. The true way his gospel endears itself to us is encounter on a human level that can lead to the proposal of Jesus in our lives on a practical level.

Consider the finale of my father's favorite TV show and 1990s classic, *Seinfeld*.[7] The group of morally ambiguous (hedonistic, if you like), self-obsessed friends find themselves on trial for their past sins, particularly the main character, Jerry Seinfeld. The Good Samaritan Law that got them in this predicament is a visitation of legislating morality, a fictionalized example of similar holdovers of the toxic Christendom many Americans still hold onto as some kind of constitutional legacy. Putting aside the discussion of Christendom and religion in the public square that we've already gone over quite a bit, the ridiculous situation in this series finale also points out how you can't effectively thrust institutional or practical morality upon anyone who does not want it. The premise of the trial and ultimate result are stupid on stupid.

Consent is the foundation of any healthy relationship with Jesus. Even before meaningful devotion or sincere faith is formed, a free choice has to be made. I would extend this repudiation of compulsory morality to us members of Christian churches the whole world round. Living with Jesus, being converted to his way in our lives more and more as we grow closer, finding our cruciform identity, is a journey that requires free consent on the personal level at every stage of the journey. Why should we try to circumvent that consent on the interpersonal, institutional, and clerical levels? It is the bare minimum of mercy to respect consent first.

To be clear, I'm not advocating for a bland third way that ultimately stands for nothing. We have to affirm core beliefs in Jesus Christ and his gospel, but that includes the things with which you may not be comfortable yet culturally, like Jesus's ardent and rather clear criticism for the monied owning class. There are myriad groups that we religious folks have been

---

7. See David, *Seinfeld*.

complicit, if not driving, in otherizing and marginalizing to the point of violence. Solidarity and confraternity with all people, even those who don't believe, is the only way forward. Practically, this means fighting homophobia, anti-Semitism, and all bigotry that dehumanizes others. We are to do this not because we don't believe in Jesus Christ's teachings on various moral issues but because it is exactly what Jesus Christ calls us to. This is a big part of what makes a church community: they'll know we are Christians by our love.[8] That's not just a fun hymn; it's a manifesto.

Recall our reflections on discernment from the last chapter. We have to weigh the call of the gospel to love one another against all manners of the realities of the world in our time and place. We have to resist the "voice of the deceiver"—that selfish urge to fortify ourselves and tune out a broader, more complex world, because that is precisely the opposite of Jesus's message and his example. We have to refuse to ignore the needs of the time and place we find ourselves in. For us Catholics here in the US, we have been so unwilling to face the truth of history that includes colonial abuse and slavery of which, yes, our institutional Church was supportive at one time. Jesus was on the side of the outcast victim, and so must we be to truly be his hands and feet in the world today as his co-workers.

Silence in the face of dignity disrespected is sin and consent for unjust systems. Silence is indeed violence when you have the power to do something about it. Those of us willing to respect religious authority have to venture out of our comfort zones on this. That's the kicker here: sometimes, we have to use the discernment we talked about last chapter to do what is right and be present and active where we're needed before the magisterium (the teaching authority of the Church) catches up. For a movement like Black Lives Matter, this shouldn't be hard, considering what a basic good acknowledging human dignity is. Religion is always culturally embedded. Sometimes religion blinds us culturally, sometimes culture blinds us religiously. There are things our churches won't say or do on what is ultimately cultural, not religious, grounds. American bishops, for example, are too culturally predisposed to respecting law enforcement to forcefully call out police abuses in recent years. Jesus knew these cultural blind spots happen as part of human nature and established an institutional church nonetheless. God put that fight-the-power instinct in us because he knew our institutions would fail and fall short often. Don't check that fight-the-power instinct at the door when it comes to

---

8. See Scholtes, "They'll Know We Are Christians," for the hymn that includes this line.

accountability and the content of our working with Christ. Disrupt systems of unjust power, call out systemic oppression, and fight for the least of these. We have to live Jesus's gospel in our present time and place in ways our culture blinds us religiously.

If you think its crass and un-Christian to go do the right thing before the official teachings of your Church catch up, I have a saint to introduce you to! St. Bartolomé de las Casas (1484–1566) was a Spanish bishop in Mexico at a time when the country was called New Spain. He lived in a time everyone, religious or not, thought it was no big deal to enslave the native populations, believing they were less than human. Casas believed Jesus would respect the human dignity of the natives, and he was right. He was made officially right by the authority of the Church in 1537 when Pope Paul III's encyclical *Sublimis Deus* said no people should be denied the dignity that is merited by us all being made in the image of God (the *imago Dei*). Saints are not made just by praying in chapels; they're also made by fighting for dignity in the outside world.

Saint Augustine once wrote the church was "ever ancient, ever new."[9] Latin would have dominated his intellectual life, and the language later attributed to him about these matters was *ecclesia semper reformanda* (the church must always be reformed). In our time and space in history that seems like a novel idea against the backdrops of institutions so identified with unchanging rhetoric. But this is the calling of any church that seriously claims the Holy Spirit guides it. Few things are more clearly guaranteed to all by God than the endless march of change. Co-workers with Christ work with the change.

Moreover, the most effective, edifying developments in the history of the church always arise from those not trying to change the church as if submitting it to an external principle but by way of walking together with the church, as hard as that may be, as to demonstrate with our own works what more Jesus is calling his church to. It's "thinking with the church," if you will. If you can suffer getting on the same wavelength as the magisterium, while retaining the critical fight-the-power eye that Bartolomé de las Casas had, you can be a part of the rejuvenation of church communities. Revival is coming, and it's the timeless revolution of Jesus Christ. This may perk up the ears of some longtime Christians wondering how faithful obedience can coexist with fight-the-power. The answer is mercy. We've talked about that a lot on the personal level, but how does that play

---

9. Augustine, *Confessions*, bk. 10, p. 236.

out at the scale of meaningful systemic change in churches that pride themselves on continuity?

Mercy is how God responds to evil and violence. Jesus demonstrated this himself with his passion and death. To all the forces of evil and violence, he responded with mercy and sacrifice, to the point of praying on the cross as he died: "Father, forgive them, for they do not know what they are doing" (Luke 23:24). In more recent history, this can be seen in the post-World War II Catholic Church. The Second Vatican Council was brought about by Pope St. John XXIII in the context of a continent and world very recently ravaged by war. That call of the Holy Spirit that opened the doors of the Church to let in the fresh air, as Pope John said, arose from a sense of "How are we going to do better?" They saw a world devastated by conflict that they felt they could have done more to stop. They understood a new imagining of how Jesus's gospel would meet the modern world was needed, to restore the dignity of all those trampled under the boot of tyranny and now alienated in its aftermath.

Our new approach, similarly, is a mercy-first mindset that works both ways—toward how we as church, we as Christians, conceive of ourselves and the meaning of our theology; and toward a world that needs mercy way more than it needs more ideology, judgment, and condemnation. To take our Christian beliefs seriously means to take action. We have to be co-workers with Christ if we are ever to be mature Christians, because to be Christian and do anything less is to simply be in a fan club. To the ones we might point toward Jesus, we violate their consent by some omission when we both pretend that their own lived experience doesn't matter in the message or that the divine ultimately breaks into our reality to never challenge us to a more excellent freedom that liberates ourselves and others. In other words, nobody akin to Jesus will evangelize salvation by a divine entity that does not care for the land, lodging, and labor of the people they're evangelizing. The dignity of the human person goes beyond the social issues on which you feel more comfortable taking a stance, to the full embrace of the human family Jesus died to relate to once again. We must have a love for humanity rooted in God's image in all of them—loving all others, regardless of any background or trait. This means caring about the material needs of others. The receivers of Jesus's message must know the churches reaching out to them are not just bringers of the gospel, but also sustenance, material safety, dignified living, and all the means deserving of God's own image. That is the theopoetics of the incarnation of Jesus Christ.

Historically, Christian churches have always understood, by way of the corporal and spiritual works of mercy, among many other gospel teachings, that this care for the whole person is essential to our calling as Christians to spread the good news. The alternative is nothing short of utter irrelevance and anachronism. Equality and self-determination are principles to which those who are very basically morally literate all subscribe now, across the educated world. That is something we should meet where it is, not from atop our high horse that says something is altogether evil if it does not submit itself to Jesus. That's not how Jesus would have us be church to the world as it exists today.

This is another way we domesticate Jesus: reducing him to an oversimplified moral standard to be asserted bullheadedly. It's the difference between crossing a river and crossing an ocean. We Christians are often crossing the rivers of straw man arguments nowadays, while the ones we need to reach are deconstructing historical and literary contexts we look past for the language that makes us sound smart. We've put a straw man—reductionist thinking about every contemporary objection—in the place of every contemporary belief, while most serious thinkers of the world today seek to cross the ocean of generational biases to a new land of true equality and self-realization for all. Godless utopia doesn't exist, but a better society without God can, if we keep focusing on unconvincing triumphalism. Are we going to be the hands and feet of Jesus, or will we disintegrate as insular walled communities?

Generational biases are at work here. If you think that is a time horizon to which you're not prepared to orient yourself, then it's going to be awfully hard for you to co-work with the being of which no greater being can be thought. Jesus works in ways beyond our perspective, even our church perspective. Are you willing to work with him? Allow me to repeat myself: anywhere Jesus is held up as the central organizing force needs to be a safe space for the ongoing conversion of every kind of sinner. We are all sinners, and Jesus Christ founded a church for sinners. Anyone who claims to speak for a church founded in Jesus Christ's name should be mature enough to accept that as more than a theological truth: it is a practical reality. When we fail in this mission, we must love and trust Jesus enough to look inward for what's wrong first. Start with the man in the mirror, as it were. Why is it hard for me to contemplate contemporary impediments to Jesus's Great Commission and work within them?

If we are asked what the problem with the church is, what is the problem with Christianity, we have to respond: me. I, a sinner, am in need of Jesus. We can't just do our best for ourselves and ignore obstacles in others' way. We have to be co-workers with Christ in his work. All the aforementioned conflicts and confusions in the faith that affect the continuation of churches and communities of faith are solved only by those who are truly co-workers with Christ. Those of us who decide consciously to work with the true Jesus who reaches out to all can save the church and the world through it, even by way of what seem like completely a-religious actions. We have to be co-workers with Jesus. We can't bottle him up and domesticate him or weaponize him or any other reduction of the full gospel message Jesus Christ founded the church to project.

A truly Christian church has to be in conversation with the culture in which it lives. Isolation stigmatizes the gospel. Examining our own sinfulness first is the path back to credibility for the church community at large. We are accountable in this mission to each other as communities in Christ. We need to push one another toward a more just, welcoming, and finally Christ-centered church. We need to transform this Christianity in crisis in our time and place today into a church that models the liberated, holy community that has the power not only to take Jesus to the world but to help abolish the ills oppressing all people of good will. The Holy Spirit, our active Advocate, goes with us in this quest for a church centered on Jesus that is accordingly both crucified in its internal crises and resurrected through that same Jesus Christ.

It took until I was older, longer on the way with Jesus to the point of this sixth canon, to really appreciate Mary. Mary represents everyone who carries in their heart hope of salvation, not just of the divine kind but of a better material life along the way. She was a woman powerless and overlooked in her culture, a teenager, and yet sang with confidence in God upon the annunciation. She embodied, in her life and in that sacred yes, that intrepid spirit of going onward into the unknown with only the faith it will all work out for the good. Her yes reminds us that the humblest actions are enormous in how God fills them with grace. All I did was get a project proposal in early and felt grateful it got done before a global pandemic hit. Don't look to the grand strokes of history as the only canvas on which God calls you to work. Often, he gives us those immediately around us as our greatest foci of love.

This chapter on church communities, on being co-workers with Christ, comes last in this book because, just as it did in my own personal experience, the last rung up this canon of God in my life is something of a launching point for the prior five. It's all about encounter. A genuine relationship with Jesus Christ requires encounter on every level. We're second to God and others by way of encountering them. We enter into new, divine, beatitude-driven, and, hopefully, saintly life, by way of a deepening encounter with Jesus. We find gratefulness is our key to happiness, justice our key to progress, when we encounter our own interdependence and need for the true, more excellent freedom. We discover Jesus Christ as our reason when we encounter the true, all-loving Savior within our own context—our own time and place. We then move to unite our will with his will because we believe that encounter with Jesus Christ is transformative and liberating to every soul willing to consent to it. We then hope to achieve some theosis and maybe finally express some unique theopoetics in how we ourselves show Jesus to the world. Encounter finally reaches the springboard when we fully enter into being co-workers with Christ as communities of believers. Yeah, I'm the kind of writer who feels the need to finish with the greatest hits montage.

The aforementioned St. Óscar Romero is attributed with a prayer that has in many ways transcended the divisions within our Christian churches and the broader crisis of Christianity today. This prayer is challenging when you explore it spiritually, and it is very much the perfect way to wrap up this chapter. If you made it here, only a handful of words away from the epilogue, perhaps you've caught feelings for Jesus. Even if you did, the question that might still remain long down the vein of those first two questions we asked in chapter 1 might be simply: what is it all worth? Why is it worth it to know Jesus and live in him? How do my life and love in Jesus Christ finally, definitively, matter at all? Why be a co-worker with Christ if I may never get anything back in the process? No, it's okay. Think about it that way for a moment.

The answer to this question, this prayer by St. Óscar Romero, I found the same way I found the phrasing of that first rung on this canon of God's doings in my life, Second Man—on a service camp. This prayer always hits me differently in every new phase of life. Nowadays, it resonates as I find the ways to work with Jesus in all the seemingly a-religious ways. It was this prayer that grounded me in the mystery of this whole thing: we strive and sometimes succeed at knowing God on a personal level, but we will simply never fully grasp it on this side of death. It was this prayer that acknowledges we are all, if nothing else, prophets of a future not our own:

The kingdom is not only beyond our efforts, it is even beyond our vision.

We accomplish in our lifetime only a tiny fraction of the magnificent enterprise that is God's work. Nothing we do is complete, which is a way of saying that the kingdom always lies beyond us.

No statement says all that could be said.

No prayer fully expresses our faith.

No confession brings perfection.

No pastoral visit brings wholeness.

No program accomplishes the Church's mission.

No set of goals and objectives includes everything.

This is what we are about.

We plant the seeds that one day will grow.

We water seeds already planted, knowing that they hold future promise.

We lay foundations that will need further development.

We provide yeast that produces far beyond our capabilities.

We cannot do everything, and there is a sense of liberation in realizing that.

This enables us to do something, and to do it very well.

It may be incomplete, but it is a beginning, a step along the way, an opportunity for the Lord's grace to enter and do the rest.

We may never see the end results, but that is the difference between the master builder and the worker.

We are workers, not master builders; ministers, not messiahs.

We are prophets of a future not our own.[10]

---

10. Untener, "Prophets of a Future."

Epilogue

I PRAY I HAVE not overstepped my purview. Throughout writing this book, I reminded myself to ground everything in my own ongoing conversion. The parts of this books that seem like thin summaries of more complex topics are in fact just that. I feared I was weighing this down with too many churchy words the whole way through. Then I got worrying I wasn't doing the churchy stuff justice either. Remembering we're all imperfect (sinful) creatures brings on a virtuous humility that helps us not become self-absorbed pretenders. I use the word pretender because that really gets to the heart of it. Christian faith, particularly the Catholic version, is often thought of as obsessed with sin, condemnation, and self-deprecation. It would be borderline impossible to engage with a way of life that really was just lore for self-loathing. I don't think any of us need more self-loathing.

Jesus always loves us more than we hate ourselves. He also loves us more than we could ever love ourselves. Humility is a liberation from the self-absorbed self. The hidden thing by which most of us who claim to know Jesus really are motivated, buried in that apparent stereotypical self-hatred and scrupulosity, is the drive to avoid being a pretender—avoiding a life of inventing little comforts that all add up to nothing. I can accept the fact I'm a sinner, I know I'm not perfect; it feels much worse to be a pretender. It feels much worse to grasp at a way of life that is both broadly true but personally satisfying and feel yourself wander into self-obsession. Religion always attracts those who want to feel superior. It's some kind of divine irony that Christianity in its purest form is designed to spurn those very people: a ready-made sacrament of humility.

Don't get me wrong, we all design a way of life specific unto ourselves. After all, I just spent six chapters describing God's Canon in My Life, as if any part of it is an original thought. It's a lot of inspirations described alongside personal anecdotes. But in all that, I pray I am not a pretender with what I wrote here, imagining myself as some prophet of a new path. I am not. We're all pretenders if we think we're the arbiters of this. Real religious devotion is the meeting of two wills. In chapter 4, I said what my truest hope in these pages is: that you might encounter the true Jesus. That you might rediscover how the true Jesus engages with us, according to our consent and on shared terms in faith. This is a universal journey to and with Jesus we all likewise make personally. I can only hope I provided some meandering programmatic directions to help on that journey. Don't be afraid to listen to the movements of your own soul. Half the battle of any spiritual life really is believing your own story is worth telling and then having faith enough in Jesus to help you tell it.

Credit where credit is due: I got a lot of help writing this. From all the named and unnamed people who provided inspiration and the people who helped me make this book make sense. I couldn't simply ramble on about my own relationship with Jesus without explaining the inspirations and influences that impacted others, who in turn influenced me. We're all interconnected, and most good things are the result of multiple people of good will. The support groups that form us are what allow us to support others. In those self-giving relationships, the beginning of a relationship with Jesus can be found; feelings, at least, can be caught there. Wherever that selfless drive arises, that's the first message from Jesus. That's where we are introduced.

If I seemed like a fool time to time in this book, that's a good thing. We expect too much of ourselves. We expect too much of religious devotion in itself. Everyone wants some privileged information, and some of us call that religion. Something is lost about religious faith when it is just our own preferred mythology; that would be indistinguishable from any other fan club. Religion isn't an exclusive fan club or some superhuman discipline. We expect loving Jesus to grant devotees access to some divine superpowers, and if not, then they must be uncanny idiots. While we can certainly find people of both those categories in Christian circles, I think those two extremes oversimplify what knowing and living with Jesus is. Having feelings for Jesus, as I have clumsily put it throughout this book, is not simply some special recipe to save you from hell like some bankrupt moralizer would have you believe. It's a relationship built on a consent structure, which beckons us outward and onward by the light of the Holy Spirit. It's a matter of overcoming the barriers between our lived experience and Jesus, to whom no barrier is too large to overcome.

I keep coming back to the apostle Peter who became the first among the apostles not because he was a reliable source for faithfulness or even coherent leadership. He frequently failed, and those errors are the springboard for all the good things he and Jesus accomplished together. The more contemporary example that defies the pretenders and moralizers that reduce it all to performance is Dorothy Day. She founded the Catholic Worker Movement and served the working poor throughout her life on top of myriad personal and social struggles along the way. Seeing the needs of her time and place and not accusing the downtrodden of some moral failing, she went straight at their empowerment via the full truth of the gospel in ways others preferred to hide away in favor of a domesticated Jesus and a pretend faith that allowed them to keep their various comforts.

Pretender and moralizer are two roles all too common among those assembled in Christian churches. To avoid these, we have to really dig deeper, deconstruct if necessary, and find Jesus as he really is. Just like with consent, more generally: a desire to have some kind of eternal plan for your postmortem is really the minimum standard for a complete relationship with Jesus. What you really want is enthusiasm, excitement; and then devotion develops when those things mature and are seasoned by time and life's various ups and downs. We feel distant from Jesus only because we don't see him all around us. I'm not just talking about a nice nature walk or the smiling baby handed to you at a family party. I'm talking about the way the world works. Our distance from God doesn't have to be addressed strictly in the parlance of empirical existence or emotional experiences. This is something to be done consciously, with a sober heart not weighed down by bias and fear. What kind of healthy relationship is built on bias and fear? None.

I don't think it ever stops feeling at least a little awkward. Religiosity expresses itself in nonreligious ways. For some, their religiosity is football on Sundays. For some, their religiosity is a fitness ritual. For some, their religiosity is a shared meal on a regular basis. I really believe if Jesus can be introduced to people the right way, there is no time and place in the cosmos he can't be received. Just like so many popular movies and books, universal stories are repeated à la Hamlet and Romeo and Juliet. Jesus is one of those universal stories. The difference, of course, being that he's actually present to us personally and in all our unique times and places in the world, the way no fictional character or real-life celebrity really is. Prince Charming is a literary archetype that exists strictly in that realm, while Jesus, outside of our own projections and psychoses, breaks into our reality, beyond the artifice of history and religion in which we encase him.

Therein lies the treasure of Jesus. He is God, the archetype to end all archetypes, except he does everything he can to be with us. Our response is the question to figure out; whether we respond in Shakespearian prose or local jargon doesn't matter to Jesus. His arms are open, his heart already aflame for you.

Every generation embraces what they find shared joy in. Religion has often provided my generation only with shared trauma. I have lost count of all the stories of religious trauma I have encountered in my years professing Christian faith. I feel somewhat guilty to have experienced the toxic side of my faith only in personal testimonials and academic study. That's my privilege to check. I can only decenter, be second, pray, and do my best. Part of the mission of this book was to find the way to Jesus in spite of all the wrong done in his name and legitimate criticism of the churches and institutions that claim to be his adherents. I really believe deep down that Jesus calls people of each generation, regardless of the overall state of the faith in their time and place. I really believe Jesus and no part of his gospel will ever be obsolete, as long as we let them grow in our unique world context and personal lives. Eating and sleeping habits change, but they never become obsolete parts of life. They are some of my joys of life, to be honest. Jesus is the breath in our lungs and the tastiness of the pasta I eat too fast, giving the breath in my lungs hiccups.

In our time and place, getting to know Jesus does require some deconstruction doesn't it? I see the kids coming after me—the zoomers, if you will—cutting through the culturally embedded faults of older expressions of Christian faith and finding Jesus in ways even we millennials didn't quite reach. I see the first steps toward Jesus where others see erosion of faith, seeds in the ground ready to take root. The seeds just need to be watered. Jesus is relevant in all ages for all people. For every righteous stab at the hypocritical faith passed down to us, there is a new way to look deeper and find something new. Yikes, that last metaphor was a bit much. Don't stab people.

The hope and change Jesus can bring to the world isn't even first in everyone accepting him. I really do believe Jesus can change the world through us, before conversion comes into it at all. The way of discernment Jesus gives us, not keeping our own material things to ourselves; the way the love of Jesus reciprocates and calls us to a change of mind, that call toward gratefulness and justice: these are our ways out of the various dictatorships of ideology that erode bonds of humanity for the sake of purity of thought. We've misinterpreted Jesus, insisted on belief in mere selfish materialism on one end and interpersonal isolationism on the other, and moved away from those universal bonds that can develop our world toward justice. We only move forward together. Jesus's charism, his mother's yes, the earthly father who had no words recorded in the Gospels: they're timeless calls to go outside ourselves, encounter others, and meet up with the God who loves us for no good reason.

Ah, I don't know how to end this. Be good people. Make good choices. And if you find yourself looking to the next horizon beyond that, Jesus is always there with you. I hope I've helped you recognize him, though only you can turn your eyes to him. You were made in love, for love, and to love you shall return.

Bibliography

Anselm. *St. Anselm's Proslogion*. Edited and translated by M. J. Charlesworth. Oxford, UK: Clarendon, 1965.
Augustine. *The City of God*. Translated by Marcus Dods. From *Nicene and Post-Nicene Fathers*, 1st ser., 2. Edited by Philip Schaff. Buffalo, NY: Christian Literature, 1887. Revised and edited for New Advent by Kevin Knight. http://www.newadvent.org/fathers/1201.htm.
———. *The Confessions of St. Augustine*. Translated by F. J. Sheed. New York: Sheed and Ward, 1943.
Barron, Robert. *Catholicism*. Episode 2, "Happy Are We: The Teachings of Jesus." Des Plaines, IL: Word on Fire, 2011.
Benedict XVI, Pope. *Christology and Anthropology*. Vol. 2 of *Joseph Ratzinger in Communio*. Edited by David L. Schindler and Nicholas J. Healy. Grand Rapids: Eerdmans, 2013.
Cyril of Jerusalem. "Catechetical Lecture 1." Translated by Edwin Hamilton Gifford. From *Nicene and Post-Nicene Fathers*, 2nd ser., 7. Edited by Philip Schaff and Henry Wace. Buffalo, NY: Christian Literature, 1894. Revised and edited for New Advent by Kevin Knight. http://www.newadvent.org/fathers/310101.htm.
David, Larry. *Seinfeld*. Season 9, episode 23, "The Finale: Part 1." Aired May 14, 1998 on *NBC*.
De la Cruz, Juan. *The Living Flame of Love*. Edited and translated by E. Allison Peers. Tunbridge Wells, UK: Burns & Oates, 1987.
Francis, Pope, in conversation with Austen Ivereigh. *Let Us Dream: The Path to a Better Future*. New York: Simon & Schuster, 2020.
Gerrard, Matthew, and Robbie Nevil. "Nobody's Perfect." Burbank, CA: Disney, 2007.
Grady, Rachel, and Heidi Ewing, dirs. *Jesus Camp*. New York: Magnolia, 2006.
Grover, Edwin Osgood. *The Book of Good Cheer: A Little Bundle of Cheery Thoughts*. Chicago: Volland, 1909.

Ignatius. "Rules to Put Oneself in Order for the Future as to Eating." Orig. from *The Spiritual Exercises of St. Ignatius of Loyola*. Sacred Texts, 1914. https://www.sacred-texts.com/chr/seil/seil33.htm.

John Paul II, Pope. *Fides et Ratio* [On the Relationship between Faith and Reason]. Encyclical letter. Vatican, Sept. 14, 1998. https://www.vatican.va/content/john-paul-ii/en/encyclicals/documents/hf_jp-ii_enc_14091998_fides-et-ratio.html.

———. "For the Canonization of Edith Stein." Vatican, Oct. 11, 1998. https://www.vatican.va/content/john-paul-ii/en/homilies/1998/documents/hf_jp-ii_hom_11101998_stein.html.

———. "Homily of His Holiness John Paul II." Vatican, Oct. 8, 1995. https://www.vatican.va/content/john-paul-ii/en/homilies/1995/documents/hf_jp-ii_hom_19951008_baltimore.html.

Levy, Daniel. *Schitt's Creek*. Season 1, episode 10, "Honeymoon." Aired March 10, 2015, on *CBC*. https://www.youtube.com/watch?v=gdcmhvLaNUs.

Lisieux, Thérèse de. *Story of a Soul: The Autobiography of St. Thérèse of Lisieux*. 3rd ed. Translated by John Clarke. Washington: ICS, 1996.

Maurin, Peter. "Easy Essays: Blowing the Dynamite." *Catholic Worker* 28 (May 1, 1962) 2, 8.

Merton, Thomas. *No Man Is an Island*. Boston: Shambhala, 2005.

Scholtes, Peter. "They'll Know We Are Christians by Our Love." Hymnary, 1966. https://hymnary.org/text/we_are_one_in_the_spirit.

Second Vatican Council. *Dei Verbum* (*Dogmatic Constitution on Divine Revelation*). https://www.vatican.va/archive/hist_councils/ii_vatican_council/documents/vat-ii_const_19651118_dei-verbum_en.html.

Thurman, Howard. *Jesus and the Disinherited*. Reprint, Boston: Beacon, 1996.

Untener, Kenneth E. "Prophets of a Future Not Our Own." United States Conference of Catholic Bishops, Oct. 25, 1979. https://www.usccb.org/prayer-and-worship/prayers-and-devotions/prayers/prophets-of-a-future-not-our-own.

Vatican News. "Pope Francis: 'A Faith without Doubts Cannot Advance.'" *Vatican News*, Feb. 28, 2021. https://www.vaticannews.va/en/pope/news/2021-02/pope-francis-faith-doubts-book-interview-don-pozza.html.

Index

abuse, 57, 58–59, 185–86, 207–8, 227
accountability, 55, 59, 211, 227
Adam, 72
addiction, 34, 92
Advocate, Holy Spirit as, 41, 90–91
ambassador, Jesus as, 119
Ambrose, Saint, 53
amen, 20
American football, 101–2, 181
American Revolution, 193
angels, 63
anger, 27, 115, 225–26
apostles, 80, 81, 84
Apse of St. Clement Basilica, 138–39
Aquinas. *See* Thomas Aquinas, Saint
archetype, Jesus as, 240
astrology, 6
atheism, 122–23
Augustine, Saint, 113–14, 132, 231
authoritarianism, 226

baggage, 219, 220
Baptist Church, 209
Barron, Robert, 34
Bartholomew, 80
Bartolomé de las Casas, Saint, 231
Beatitudes, 32–34, 35, 110, 173
Beautiful Letdown, The (Switchfoot), 7–8, 20

belief systems, next step within, 5
Benedict XVI (pope), 84, 119, 188, 223
Bible
    Catholic Church viewpoint regarding, 191, 194–95, 216
    contextual frameworks within, 217
    exclusion usage of, 215
    as flawed human document, 45
    as inspired word of God, 45
    interpretation of, 216–17
    plain sense reading of, 43
    prayer with, 145–46
    significance of, 41–42
    structure of, 42, 44
    theological contradictions within, 110
    Thomas Jefferson's version of, 116
    translation of, 43
    understanding of, 45
biblical fundamentalism, 43
bigotry, 224, 225
bisexuality, 66. *See also* LGBTQ+ community
Bismarck, Otto von, 195
Black Lives Matter movement, 94, 96–97, 223, 230
born-again movement, 26
Buffalo Bills, 181
burnout, 174

call to all people, Jesus as, 63–69
Camden, New Jersey, 28, 29
Canada, 57
Capax Dei, 112
capitalism, 96
Catholic Church/Catholicism
    abuse within, 57, 58
    accusations against, 127
    Bible translation viewpoint of, 191, 194–95
    Bible viewpoint of, 216
    communion within, 140–41
    as cult of severity, 196–97
    disordered affections and, 221
    following World War II, 198, 232
    guilt within, 60–61
    history of, 197
    integration by, 62
    Mass of, 125–26
    priesthood within, 40
    revolutionary liberalism and, 194
    Rome and, 132–33
    sex abuse crisis within, 185–86, 207–8, 227
    social teaching within, 35–36
    thinking with the Church, 79
    welcoming atmosphere within, 214
Catholic-Counter Reformation, 197
Catholic guilt, 60–61
Catholic Worker Movement, 239
checking your privilege, 86
Christendom, 195–99, 200, 203, 204–5, 219
Christian fundamentalism, 195
Christianity
    baggage within, 219
    basics of, 62, 157–58
    as call to all people, 63–69
    Christians as obstacles within, 54
    creeds of, 82–83
    crisis of, 185, 205–13
    cultural sins within, 104
    dictatorship of ideas within, 103
    divisions within, 103, 141–42
    as enclave religion, 223
    guilt within, 61
    history of, 178–79, 189–99
    integration by, 62
    as layered experience, 199
    ornamental, 210
    personal decrease within, 149
    phrases within, 101
    piety within, 99–100, 101
    resistance to Jesus within, 103
    sexual morality teachings within, 220–21
    toxic, 210, 220
Christian nationalism, 200, 201
Christians, 54, 145, 207, 208, 213. *See also* Christianity
Christ of the Breadlines, The (Eichenberg), 15, 16
christomorphic destiny, 124, 125, 131
church
    bringing people back to, 218
    choosing, 100
    corruption within, 206
    in cultural conversations, 234
    exclusion within, 218–19
    as human institution, 78–79
    humility of, 212
    as irrelevant, 185
    Jesus as mystical body of, 137–46, 179
    mercy-first, 228–36
    in the Middle Ages, 196
    obstacles to, 214–15
    origin of, 64
    reciprocity within, 139–40
    segregation within, 98
    truth and mercy within, 177
    universal, 213–28
    variations of, 177–78
    weakening authority of, 207–8
    See also community
City of God, The (Augustine), 132
clericalism, 185–86, 225, 226, 227
closed living, 38
Cold War, 199–200
collective guilt, 223
colonialism, 195
commitment, 39
common good concept, 35–36
communion, 140–41
community
    accessibility of, 213
    appeal of, 218
    call to, 177

creating, 94–95
exclusion within, 218–19
growth of, 25
inclusivity within, 94–95
Jesus within, 178
love within, 214
within religion, 9–10
sin and imperfection within, 179
See also church
conformity, 116–17
confraternity, 230
Congress of Vienna, 194
conscience, 46, 56
consent
    within conversion, 164
    defined, 164
    divine yes and, 69–76
    faith and, 76, 77
    as foundation, 229
    free will and, 77
    of friendship, 161
    lack of, 75
    within nation-state government, 202
    as not equal to control, 77
    overview of, 72
    possessiveness as violation of, 211–12
    steps of, 160
    violation of, 164, 207, 211–12
conversational prayer, 106–7. *See also* prayer
conversion
    consent within, 164
    divine mercy within, 25–26
    God's ways within, 29
    gratefulness and, 71, 75
    Holy Spirit's work within, 101
    within New Life cycle, 25–26
    as ongoing, 89
    process of, 71, 100, 168–69
    steps of, 160
    transformation and, 172
corruption, 56, 204
Council of Jerusalem, 225
Council of Trent, 196–97
COVID-19 pandemic, 93–94
co-workers with Jesus
    maturity and, 232
    mission of, 233–34
    within our time and place, 184–89

process of, 182–83, 184
purpose of, 206
Creator, God as, 41
critical race theory (CRT), 223–24
crucifixion of Jesus, 24, 70, 71, 111–12, 142–43, 149, 203
cruciform identity, 125
cultural clout, 56
cultural embeddedness, of religion, 54–62, 103, 104, 201, 230
cultural privilege, 57
cultural trends, gospel purification of, 65
culture, 54–62, 198, 234
culture wars, 202, 205–6, 208
Cyril of Jerusalem, 161–62
Cyrus, Miley, 69

Dark Nights, 172, 174
Darth Vader, 78
Darwinism, 195
Dawkins, Christopher, 122
Day, Dorothy, 36, 239
Dei Verbum, 216
democracy, 197, 200
devotion, 6
dictatorship of ideas, 103
Diego, Juan, 68
dignity, from Jesus, 62
dinner table metaphor, 128, 228
discernment, 88, 166, 167–76, 230–31, 241
disciples, 64, 80, 81
discouragement, 155
disordered affections, 221
dissent, 228
disunity, 227
Divine Mercy, 23
divine yes, 69–76, 234
dog analogy, 72
Donatist heresy, 61
Donne, John, 178
doubts, 37–38, 78, 87

Easter, 24
economy, individualism within, 99
ecumenism, 217
ego of Freudian identity, 17
Eichenberg, Fritz, 15, 16
Einstein, Albert, 118

emotional intelligence, 157
emotional self-awareness, 22
emotions, spiritual power of, 22
empathy, 16
encounter, grace of, 13
end times, 170–71
English Reformation, 127
Enlightenment, 194
Epiphany, 39
Episcopalian Church, 209
equality, 233
escapism, 155
eschatology, 132
essential truths, 100
Evangelical movement, 208
evangelism, 27–28, 218
Eve, 72, 73, 74
everyday life, Jesus within, 179–84
excellent freedom, 93–94, 95, 96, 97, 222, 224
exhaustion, 153
existential destiny, Jesus as, 123–30
existential self, 121
exploitation and, 96

faith
  adventure within, 78
  of the apostles, 84
  characteristics of, 76
  consent and, 76, 77
  defined, 30
  devotion as by-product of, 6
  doubt and, 37–38, 78, 87
  effects of, 29
  enthusiasm for, 205
  as everywhere, 83
  feelings and, 31–32
  fiction *versus*, 77
  generational transmission of, 186
  immature, 205, 206
  as informed consent, 76
  internal, 219
  as lived experience, 79–80
  misconceptions regarding, 76–86
  overview of, 76–77
  praxis of, 187
  reality disembodiment of, 222
  reason and, 82–83, 84, 119, 129

  religious institutions and, 79
  in science, 83
  sharing of, 27–28
  toxic, 224
  trust choice within, 85–86
  as wounding for others, 53
Faith and Reason (Fides et Ratio) (John Paul II), 84
fascism, 198
fasting, 173
fear, 210
feelings, 31–32, 48–49
Figure of Christ (Hofmann), 125
First Vatican Council, 194
football, American, 101–2
forbidden tree, 72
forgiveness, 74, 141
founding fathers, 200–201
Fourth Great Awakening, 199
fragility, 95
France, 193–94
Francis (pope), 37, 78, 102, 103, 155, 166, 169, 170, 222
Francis of Assisi, 131
Franco, Francisco, 57
freedom
  aimless, 96, 97
  excellent, 93–94, 95, 96, 97, 222, 224
  inner, 25, 92, 93
  justice and, 222
  modern conception of, 92
  outer, 25, 92–93
  saints and, 93
free will, 11–12, 63–64, 72, 77, 165
French Revolution, 193–94
Freudian identity, 17
friendship, 85, 154, 158, 160–61
fundamentalism, 195

gardening, 158–67, 168
garden of Eden, 72
garden of Gethsemane, 136–37
Gaudium et Spes (Joy and Hope), 166, 169
gender nonconformity, 66
generational differences, 75
gentiles, 225
getting behind the waterfall concept, 22
goal of our efforts, Jesus as, 130–37

Index

goals, God's will and, 150–51
God
    as bringer of excellence, 98
    characteristics of, 128
    as clockmaker, 201
    default-version of, 32
    encounter with, 47
    free will and, 11–12
    hearing, 38–46
    as incomprehensible, 119–20
    as love, 41
    love of, 11, 67–68, 237
    mystery of, 41
    names/titles of, 41
    New Testament view of, 42–43
    Old Testament view of, 42–43
    ordered toward, 49
    perfection of, 69
    personal revelation and, 45
    as present human experience, 11
    on relational response axis, 14
    relationship with, 72, 88, 89
    self-giving of, 11
    as Shepherd, 90
    surrender and, 150
    three persons of, 49
    as unifier, 33
    union with, 149
God's Not Dead, 171
Golden Rule, 38
good deeds, ripple effect of, 87
good people, characteristics of, 4
good Samaritan, 146
Good Samaritan Law, 229
Good Shepherd, 89
good works, 35
gospel
    justice within, 211
    mutation of, 207
    revolution following, 102
    spread of, 191
    transformative justice from, 102
    truth of, 217
grace, 31, 156, 164, 199–205
gratefulness
    as act of justice, 90
    characteristics of, 86–87
    as checking your privilege, 86
    contemplation of, 86
    conversion and, 71, 75
    discernment and, 88
    empathy and, 16
    faking it within, 89
    gospel growth within, 97
    motivation of, 86
    of relationships, 87
    ripple effect of, 87
    scolding regarding, 53
    self-awareness of, 54–55
    understanding within, 54
    as uphill, 87
Great Commission, 157
Greatest Commandment, 110–11
Great Schism of 1054, 190
grief, 58
Guardini, Romano, 169
guilt, 46, 60–61

Hale, Edward Everett, 184
happiness, 31–38, 124–25
Harry Potter, 48
healing, 54–62, 157–58
heaven, 131, 163
hell, 132, 163, 164, 213–14
Helper, God the Holy Spirit as, 90–91
heresy, 189–90
higher meaning, searching for, 1–2
history, 178–79, 189–205
Hofmann, Heinrich, 125
holiness, 15, 31–38, 47, 61, 125
Holocaust, 198–99
Holy Spirit
    as Advocate, 41, 90–91
    as church leadership, 78–79
    conversion work of, 101
    creativity activation through, 112
    free will and, 162
    within missionary calling, 162
    as Paraclete, 41, 90–91
    sending of, 90–91
    transformation work of, 101
homophobia, 67–68
homosexuality, 66–67, 220–21. *See also* LGBTQ+ community
honor, 34
hope, 117
horizontal relationships, 14
how-question, 2

human dignity, 36
humanity, 16, 139–40
humility
    benefits of, 29
    of the church, 212
    as liberation from self-absorption, 237
    mental health and, 153
    within New Life map, 30
    purpose of, 134
    requirements of, 38
hunger, for God, 170
Hunger Games, The, 48
hypocrisy, 53, 187

identity, as solidarity lens, 95
ideology, 167–68
id of Freudian identity, 17
Ignatius of Loyola, 128
"I Have a Dream," 97
imago Dei, 112, 231, 232
imitating Jesus, 165–66
impulses, spiritual power of, 22
Indigenous people, 57
individualism, 92, 99
Industrial Revolution, 82, 194
infinity, 48, 118–19
inner freedom, 25, 92, 93
insanity, 118
intercessory prayer, 175, 176. *See also* prayer

James the Lesser, 80
Jefferson, Thomas, 116
Jesus
    accepting, 12
    accessibility of, 213–14
    actively living with, 185
    as ambassador, 119
    anger of, 115, 225–26
    as archetype, 240
    as bridge, 70, 71
    as call to all people, 63–69
    characteristics of, 108, 111, 128
    as the church, 138
    as church leadership, 78–79
    closeness of, 140
    communion with, 64
    cultural portrayals of, 109
    death of, 24
    decisions of, 24
    dignity from, 62
    discernment from, 241
    divinity and humanity of, 11, 109, 124, 127–28, 130
    domestication of, 102, 233
    as embodied with us, 112–13
    encountering, 28
    epiphany of, 39
    example of, 125
    as existential destiny, 123–30
    faithfulness of, 212
    friendships of, 49–50
    friendship with, 22, 115
    in the garden of Gethsemane, 136–37
    as goal of our efforts, 130–37
    as Good Shepherd, 89
    grief of, 58
    as guide, 12
    hope through, 117
    as *imago Dei*, 112
    imitating, 165, 166
    knowing, 110–16
    leading by, 174–75
    as liberator, 62
    as life partner, 151
    lived experience with, 112, 228
    as Lord or lunatic, 73, 85–86
    as love, 64
    mercy from, 23–24
    ministry of, 32–33, 65, 108
    miracles of, 63
    mission of, 62, 64, 91, 125, 217, 229
    as mystical body of the church, 137–46, 179
    of Nazareth, 183
    as nontoxic party animal, 114–15
    as objective meaning, 116–23
    patience of, 212
    peace from, 23
    as perfect, 61
    personal encounter with, 26–27, 98
    personal relationship with, 3
    Pharisees and, 110
    quote of, 54, 87, 113, 214, 232
    reciprocity of, 152
    as redeemer, 178

relationship with, 23, 28, 31, 49–50, 129–30, 143, 154
resistance to, 97, 100
retreat by, 174
sacrifice of, 111–12
self-efficacy through, 111
self-giving by, 10, 25, 31
selflessness and, 10
subversions of, 141
suffering and, 129, 135–36, 140
as teenager, 108–9
as universal story, 239–40
as unknown, 108
values of, 59
viewpoints regarding, 114
as the way, 130
why-question regarding, 3–6, 18–19
worship of, 64
Jesus and the Disinherited (Thurman), 96
Jesus Prayer, 175–76. *See also* prayer
Joan of Arc, 131
John, the apostle, 80
John of the Cross, 48, 172, 173, 174
John Paul II (pope), 84, 202
John XXIII (pope), 232
Jonah, 133–34
Joseph, 74
justice
    demands of, 90
    discernment within, 230–31
    freedom and, 222
    within the gospel, 211
    gospel used against, 100
    gratefulness within, 90
    as key to progress, 59, 86–99
    liberation and, 91–92
    Our Lady of Guadalupe and, 68
    thirst for, 75–76
    transformative, 102

Kaepernick, Colin, 102
Kenyan Catholicism, 60
King, Martin Luther, Jr., 96

Latin American Catholicism, 103
Left Behind series, 171
legal secularism, 192
Let Us Dream (Francis), 155
Levy, Dan, 67

LGBTQ+ community, 67, 220–21, 222
liberation, 91–93, 211
liberator, Jesus as, 62
listening, 104
lived experience, 6, 79–80, 112, 228
Living Flame of Love, The (John of the Cross), 48
Lord, The (Guardini), 169
love
    as Christianity power, 212
    within community, 214
    of God, 11, 67–68, 237
    God as, 41
    holiness within, 15
    for *imago Dei*, 232
    Jesus as, 64
    living by, 159–60
    as primary goal, 42
    reciprocated, 9
loving God and others, 110–11
Luther, Martin, 47, 165, 215

Magi, 38–39
Magnificat canticle, 74
Mark, book of, 44
martyrdom, 80
Mary, mother of Jesus, 73–74, 234
mascots, 17–18
mask-wearing, during COVID-19 pandemic, 93–94
Mass, 125–26
master-apprentice metaphor, 115
mathematics, 121
Maurin, Peter, 102
meaning of life, concepts within, 120–21, 123
mental health, 148–54, 161
mercy
    within the church, 228–36
    of church ministers, 227–28
    confusion regarding, 141–43
    in conversion, 25–26
    defined, 232
    from Jesus, 23–24
    for ourselves, 155–56
    purpose of, 33
    reciprocated love and, 156
    revival and, 231–32
    truth and, 159, 177, 229

Merton, Thomas, 50, 178
Mexico, 231
Middle Ages, 196
millennials, 74–75, 219
mind, 158–67, 170
miracles, 63–64, 68, 82–83
mission/missionary calling
    accountability and, 227
    barriers to, 183
    calling within, 145
    credibility of, 228–29
    gardening within, 158–67
    going to where the need is within, 159
    Holy Spirit within, 162
    tilling within, 160–61
    violation of consent within, 164
    ways of, 158
modernism (modernist crisis), 194–95
monkey mind, 51
moralizers, 239
Mormonism, 195
mystical body of the church, Jesus as, 137–46, 179
myths, in religious context, 6

Napoleon, 193–94, 197
narcissism, 155
nationalism, 195
New Life
    barometer of, 21
    benefits of, 34
    cycle of, 23–26, 37, 100
    defined, 21
    everyday function of, 182
    good works within, 35
    gratefulness as motivator of, 86
    growth of, 86
    happiness within, 34
    healing process within, 55–56
    holiness within, 34
    killing of, 218
    map of, 26–31
    mercy within, 24
    as outwardly effective, 25
    solidarity within, 24
New Testament, overview of, 44
No Man Is an Island (Merton), 50
nones (unattached people), 209

objective meaning, Jesus as, 116–23
objective truth, 121
obligation, 156–57
ocean metaphor, 113–14
Old Testament, overview of, 44
oppression, 59, 96, 225–26
ornamental Christianity, 210. *See also* Christianity
Our Lady of Guadalupe, 68
outer freedom, 25, 92–93

Paraclete, God the Holy Spirit as, 41, 90–91
parallel societies, creation of, 165
party host metaphor, 114–15
Paul, 30–31, 183–84, 216, 218
Paul III (pope), 231
peace, 23
pelagianism, 135
Pentecost, 90–91
performance, within religion, 126
Perks of Being a Wallflower, 48
persecution, 211
personal revelation, 45
pessimism, 155
Peter, 61, 105, 130, 132, 182–83, 217, 239
Pharisees, 110
Philadelphia Eagles, 18
Pius VI (pope), 197
politics, 188, 200, 202, 203, 204
possessiveness, 205–13
post-Christian world, 209
power, 56, 99, 204
prayer
    conversational, 106–7
    defined, 19, 40
    function of, 105–6
    intercessory, 175, 176
    Jesus Prayer, 175–76
    of Óscar Romero, 235–36
    overview of, 51–52
    purpose of, 19
    questions regarding, 172
    rote, 105–6
    with the Scriptures, 145–46
    "Second Man for" prayer, 20
preachers, accountability of, 227
preaching, phrases within, 101

preoccupations, as little gods, 173–74
Presbyterian Church, 209
pretenders, 237–38, 239
priesthood, within Catholicism, 40
progress, justice as key to, 59, 86–99
Protestant Reformation, 46, 190, 196–97
prudence, 93
purgatory, 131–32, 163
puzzle analogy, 153–54

Rahner, Karl, 10
Rand, Ayn, 122, 123
reality, 222, 224–25
reason, 82–83, 84, 119, 129, 134–35
reciprocated love, 9, 152, 156–57
reciprocity, 139–40, 152, 153, 154–58
recommendations, metaphor regarding, 77
reconciliation, 55, 223
redemption, Jesus and, 178
reform, within healing process, 55
Reformers, 44
relational response axis, 14
relationships, 32, 70, 77, 87
religion
   benefits of, 9–10
   community within, 9–10
   as creative works, 79
   cultural embeddedness of, 54–62, 103, 201, 230
   divinity contemplation within, 10
   expectation within, 238
   expressions of, 239
   myths within, 6
   performance within, 126
   purpose of, 1
   relational principle of, 5–6
   selfishness within, 4
   selflessness within, 7
   social ills within, 61
   trauma within, 240
   as useless, 85
   worthiness of, 65
religious institutions
   abuse within, 57
   choosing, 100
   crisis of, 207–8
   deconstructing from, 69
   as power structure, 92–93
   resistance to, 187
   truth factor within, 65
reparation, within healing process, 55
repentance, 166–67
response, humanity within, 134
resting, 155
restorative justice theory, 223–24
retreating, 155, 173
revival, 212, 214, 231–32
righteousness, 110, 111
rock imagery, 114
Rome, 132–33
Romero, Óscar, 38, 235–36
Roosevelt, Theodore, 35
rote prayers, 105–6. *See also* prayer
rules, 32

sacred deconstruction, 27
safe space, 218. *See also* church; community
sailing metaphor, 211–12
saints/sainthood, 93, 124, 125, 127, 131. *See also specific saints*
salvation, 74
Satan, 163, 165, 230
schisms, within Christianity, 189–90
Schitt's Creek, 67
science, 2, 82, 83
scientific method, 82, 83
Second Man
   Beatitudes and, 35
   challenges regarding, 17
   defined, 5
   elevation of, 12
   function of, 15
   gratefulness as motivator of, 86
   overview of, 7–10
   purpose of, 21–22
   risks regarding, 18
   self-control regarding, 22
   self-forgetting nature of, 97
   significance of, 4–5
   as universal human experience, 10
   work regarding, 18
"Second Man for" prayer, 20
Second Vatican Council, 165–66, 194–95, 232
secularism, legal, 192, 204
secularization, 186

secularized culture, 192–93, 202–3
seeds, planting, 160
Seinfeld, 229
self-awareness, 22, 54–55
self-determination, 233
self-efficacy, 111
self-emptying, 157
self-esteem, 161–62
self-giving
    example of, 183
    of God, 11
    of Jesus, 10, 25, 31
    overview of, 7, 12, 19
    transformation to, 12
self-hate, 151, 162
selfishness, 95–96
selflessness, 7, 8, 9, 10
self-love, 161–62, 183
self-worth, 8
Semmelweis, Ignaz, 83
separation of church and state, 200
Sermon on the Mount, 32–33
servant leadership, 154–55
"set apart," 206
sex abuse crisis, 58–59, 185–86, 207–8
sexuality, 67, 220–21
sheep, 89, 90
shepherds, 89
signs of the times, 170–71
silence, as sin, 230
sin
    defined, 69
    denouncing, 224
    freedom from, 92
    origin of, 69–70, 72
    as separation from God, 70, 163
    silence as, 230
    in society, 132
    as "the world," 207
    as universal, 221
    viewpoints regarding, 164
    voice of God within, 64
Skywalker, Luke, 77, 78
slavery, 216
social justice, 100. *See also* justice
social reality, history as informing, 198
social teaching, 35–36
soil, types of, 159, 160

sola scriptura, 215
solidarity, 36, 230
"so that his will may be my will," 150, 152–53, 155, 165
soul, 48–52, 151–54, 158–67
Spain, 57
spiritual objective truth, 121–22
Star Wars, 77, 78
St. Benedict communities, 165
St. Clement Basilica, 138–39
Stein, Edith, 3–4
Sublimis Deus, 231
suffering
    burnout *versus*, 174
    causes of, 117
    function of, 135
    imitation of Jesus within, 128
    Jesus within, 135–36, 140
    misconception regarding, 70–71
    personal experience regarding, 136
    purpose of, 135
    within reality, 222
    unity with Jesus through, 129
    worthwhile, 137
Suhard, Emmanuel, 154–55
Sunday Assembly, 9–10
superego of Freudian identity, 17
supremacy, 225
surrender, 148–49, 150, 152
Switchfoot, 7–8, 20

Tebow, Tim, 101
Teresa of Calcutta (Mother Teresa), Saint, 133
testimony, through personal witness, 159
theology, 112, 149–50
theosis, 151–54
Thérèse of Lisieux, Saint, 49, 131, 133
thinking with the Church concept, 79
Third Man, 8
thirst, for God, 170
Thomas Aquinas, Saint, 125, 129, 130
thorns, clearing, 161
Thurman, Howard, 96
tilling metaphor, 160–61
time and place, Jesus within, 184–89, 211
Touched by an Angel, 63

transformation
    beyond information, 99–107
    by collective liberation, 91
    conversion and, 172
    Holy Spirit's work within, 101
    of the mind, 167
    within New Life cycle, 25–26
    as ongoing, 89
    process of, 100
transformative justice, 102. *See also* justice
transformative relationships, 25
transparency, 213
transsexuality, 66
trauma, 161, 240
Trinity, 49. *See also* God; Holy Spirit; Jesus
true church, marks of, 140–41
trust, faith and, 85–86
truth
    confusion regarding, 141–43
    contradictory, 191–92
    discernment regarding, 168–69
    mercy and, 159, 177, 229
Tyson, Neil deGrasse, 118

United States
    Christianity variations within, 199
    Christian nationalism within, 200, 201
    culture wars within, 202, 208
    founding fathers of, 200–201
    Indigenous people treatment within, 57
    privilege within, 203
    toxic Christianity decline within, 210
universal church, 213–28. *See also* church
universal destination of goods, 37
universe experiencing itself concept, 120
U.S. Catholic Bishops Conference, 224

Vatican II, 198–99, 216
victims, of sex abuse crisis, 58–59
vines, humanity as, 139–40
virtue, 152

wall instinct, 207
whole person, care for, 233
why-question, 2
will, 48
will of God, 167–68, 216
witnessing, 154–58, 170, 209
wokeism, 223
women/womankind, 73–74, 215, 216
World War II, 198–99, 232
worship, 203

zeal, 39–40
zero-sum thinking, 162–63
zoomers, 240
Zwinglian Reformation, 127

www.ingramcontent.com/pod-product-compliance
Lightning Source LLC
Chambersburg PA
CBHW060558230426
43670CB00011B/1875